The Job of the Public Manager

The Job of the Public Manager

John Rehfuss
California State University, Sacramento

The Dorsey Press
Chicago, Illinois 60604

This book is dedicated to my wife, Carol Litchfield Rehfuss, and to our three children, Debbie Fuller, Brent Rehfuss, and Todd Rehfuss.

It is also dedicated to the countless public managers at all levels of government who commit their lives to making government work.

Acquisitions editor: Leo A. W. Wiegman
Project editor: Ethel Shiell
Production manager: Ann Cassady
Cover design: Leon Bolognese & Associates
Compositor: TCSystems
Typeface: 10/12 Palatino
Printer: Arcata Graphics/Kingsport

Library of Congress Cataloging-in-Publication Data

Rehfuss, John.
    The job of the public manager / John Rehfuss.
        p.   cm.
    Includes index.
    ISBN 0-256-05826-1 (pbk.)
    1. Public administration. I. Title.
JF1351.R459 1989
350—dc19   88–7026

Printed in the United States of America

1 2 3 4 5 6 7 8 9 0 K 5 4 3 2 1 0 9 8

Preface

Nobody ever said public managers have an easy job. Their chosen occupation is a tough one—made up of long hours of grinding attention to detail, but relieved occasionally by the elation that comes with a well-done job or a well-managed program. The job demands equal parts of experience, training and education, mental toughness, and good judgment. But that's not all—the manager has two other requirements: First, she must be technologically sophisticated, because modern organizations are complex, and second, she must be able to tolerate ambiguity, because modern organizations operate in uncertain waters.

While managers have difficult jobs, they are not thankless. True, most people take public services for granted. Even so, most top managers get great personal satisfaction out of serving the public. In some cases, highly visible career executives such as city managers get considerable public acclaim. Regardless of public recognition, most good managers have a deep personal commitment to the public service. This accounts for the fact that public business is done in spite of what appears as both a lack of appreciation and an excess of difficulty.

For textbook purposes, the manager's demanding job is divided into three simple parts—simple to explain, but difficult to perform. These jobs are internal or organizational maintenance, organizational representation, and organizational (strategic) planning. Managers don't think of their jobs in these terms; when asked, they answer: "hiring, firing, and seeing that things get done," or "getting people to do what they should be doing without my asking," or "attending too many meetings." Viewed from a distance, however, these managers are maintaining, representing, and planning.

Organizational maintenance is the job of keeping the organization going. It takes most of the manager's time, energy, and concentration. Depending on the organization and the manager's level, all of the manager's time may be spent in organizational maintenance. Indeed, many managers commit so much time to their daily routines that responsibilities for representation and planning are overlooked, pushed aside, or delegated.

Representation involves the ceremonial, symbolic, and image-building tasks of top managers. Public appearances, meetings with outside groups, breakfasts with clients, and other occasions comprise organizational representation. Some managers spend most of their time here. Others, usually lower in the hierarchy, spend little or no time here—at least formally. Informally, all managers have representation functions, for they are almost always in contact with some group or individual. Formal representation is the job of top managers, but every manager has a part to play. Even a casual lunch with someone from another agency contributes to the agency image.

Strategic planning is the third element of the manager's job. It involves examining what the agency is doing, deciding what it should do, and making plans to move toward long-range goals. Since long-range planning is relatively uncommon in public agencies, this function is often ignored. Organizational responsibility for strategic planning is ultimately a top-level job, although any manager must examine the implications of what he does. Frequently, strategic planning is assigned to staff individuals or specialized agencies such as a planning division. In this case, the individual or section often recommends policies or suggests alternatives to the top manager.

Maintenance, representation, and planning are dry concepts. Aren't managers more interesting? Yes and no. People are always more exciting than intellectual abstractions, but in all honesty, public managers are no more exciting than other citizens. They have to be, for low-key and self-effacing behavior is usually more effective than aggressive or flamboyant acts. Even so, while most managers blend into their surroundings, a few are dashing. Most wear pin-striped suits or dark wool suits, but some wear Nike running shoes.

As a class, managers include people as diverse as the functions of their agencies—from small special districts such as the Sacramento-Mission Oaks Park District to the United States Defense Department. City managers, county managers, heads of large special districts, career state agency officials, departmental heads at all government levels, and federal supergrades from GS–15 to GS–18 are some of the job titles that indicate the diversity of public management.

Yet, public managers share similar qualities. They are all career public managers, although many do not have civil service protection. They are all professionals, which means they share a commitment to their occupational specialities and to the quality of public services in their agencies. They are, or expect to be, long-term employees of their agencies, such as the Federal Bureau of Reclamation, or of a level of government, such as city managers serving several cities. They have all invested years of training and education preparing for their careers. Finally, they share, in varying degrees, a managerial point of view. This managerial ideology favors expansion of existing programs, is protective of managerial rights, believes firmly in hard work, and generally supports existing social and political arrangements. There are few radicals in management positions. Managers, as a group, are marked by the capacity for and the acceptance of organizational life.

This book is about public managers: who they are, what they do, how and why they manage, and what their satisfactions and problems are. The emphasis is on the public manager, not on the broader fields of public administration and American government. The American public manager is hired, with rare exceptions, to manage public affairs under the direction of legislative or executive superiors. Sometimes, despite the biblical injunction against serving two masters, he serves both legislative and executive masters, as Chapter 5, Politics in Management, makes clear. Even in these cases, however, the public manager is hired to manage programs.

Since top management also involves giving advice to policymakers, managers are also involved in policymaking, although they usually try to downplay this role. Some top managers hold staff positions which have little management content and much policymaking content. This book, however, concentrates mostly on managers with line or program responsibility, such as city managers and state bureau chiefs.

Chapters correspond to some of the divisions in a public administration textbook, because top managers perform some of those activities, such as budgeting and personnel. The activities are discussed, however, from the public manager's point of view.

Decision making constitutes an important aspect of the public manager's time. Chapter 2 discusses the decision-making process and the manager's part in it, from broad societal policymaking to organization routines. Chapter 3 reviews the goals that different individuals seek through the decision-making process, and it examines the individuals. Chapter 4 completes the decision-making discussion by looking at quantitative and qualitative aids to organizational decision making, most of which are used in organizational maintenance. Strategic planning is often involved as the manager becomes involved in the decision-making process at top policy levels—as outlined in Chapter 2. However, lower-level decision-making, as mentioned throughout part of Chapter 2 and all of Chapter 3, is more accurately described as an application of organizational maintenance.

Chapter 5 describes the political side of organizational life. Effective management (maintenance) of the organization is the best protection against political pressures, although effective representation is often crucial. To the extent that key decisions are called for, the fate of the organization rests on top-level, strategic decisions.

Chapter 6 discusses the intergovernmental system in which each manager operates. You might think that organizational management, representation, or planning ability is necessary to manage intergovernmental affairs effectively, but this is only partially correct. Chapter 6 suggests that an understanding of the intergovernmental system is the key to all aspects of effective management—all management activity occurs in an intergovernmental setting.

Chapter 7 outlines the governmental budget process. Budgeting, as a technical process, primarily involves organizational maintenance. It also has significant representational aspects, and over time it demands long-range planning to advance or at least maintain the agency's position during the budget process.

Chapter 8, Managing Public Personnel Systems, discusses the type of personnel matters facing top managers. To the extent that the broad personnel issues discussed there involve techniques, organizational maintenance skill is called for. However, with some exceptions, these personnel issues involve larger questions that ultimately call for long-range strategic planning.

Chapter 9 discusses cutback management, a fact of life that public sector managers have faced with mixed success, for a decade. Cutback management will be a public management issue in the next decade as well. Handling the technical aspects of cutbacks is an exercise in organizational maintenance. The long-range implications of continued cutbacks illustrates the importance of a strategic plan, as perhaps no other part of public management does. Here, also, one sees the difference between managerial ability to plan ahead and cajole an organization into following a prescribed plan, and a lack of that ability.

Chapter 10 deals with the nature of the public manager. It covers the personal values, beliefs, and how representative an individual manager is of both the general public and of organizational peers. It also suggests how managers rise in organizations, and how future careers will develop.

The theme of this book is that top-level manager jobs are divided into organizational management, organizational representation, and organizational planning. The theme, as Chapter 1 stresses, is also that maintenance takes the majority of managerial time and energy, with representational activities a distant second.

Some managers never consider strategic planning, either because their job doesn't require them to or because they never get past the day-to-day obstacles that prevent long-term plans. Some managers try to plan strategically but fail, often for reasons they cannot control. However, managers who succeed make a significant difference in the fate of their organizations and for public management as a whole.

ACKNOWLEDGMENTS

I want to acknowledge many people, all for rather different reasons. My wife and children, to whom the book is dedicated, put up with my absence from a good deal of family life over the past few years while I wrote the book. They also made room in the family budget for a computer and word processing program, without which this book could not have been completed.

This book benefits from professional support I have received from Denny Putt, who was always available for help and counsel; the School of Business and Public Administration at California State University, Sacramento, who provided much-needed release time for work on the book; five book reviewers—including Irene S. Rubin (Northern Illinois University), David E. Schmitt (Northeastern University), and Robert J. Waste (San Diego State University)—four of whom gave me positive comments about specific suggestions for improvement and one who made severe criticisms and made me think more clearly about what purpose this book serves; a graduate class in Public Management where students extensively commented on the book and provided some useful examples; and the help of Dorsey Press editor Leo A. W. Wiegman and his staff.

Finally, this book emerges out of 30 years of teaching and administrative experience. Of particular importance during this period were my friends and colleagues from the cities of Pico Rivera and Palm Springs, California, as well as other public executives in the states of California and Illinois, all of whom taught me much about public management over the years.

John Rehfuss

Contents

List of Exhibits

List of Tables

CHAPTER 1

Maintenance, Representation, and Planning—an Overview

INTRODUCTION

The preface briefly outlined the three managerial jobs of organizational maintenance, representation, and planning, describing some of the main characteristics of managers and revealing the general plan for the book. This chapter describes the three managerial functions in more detail so that readers may understand these functions in sufficient depth to apply them in specific situations. Since maintenance requires the most managerial energy and time, this chapter places it in some theoretical and historical perspective and includes a range of illustrations.

Representation is considered as formal and informal interaction with the environment. Even though many top managers do not get directly involved in media relations, the issue is crucial, and so Chapter 1 covers this topic of media dynamics. It also discusses the use of outside communication channels to speak to the organization.

Three kinds of planning are identified: operational planning, restoring equilibrium, and strategic planning. This section identifies the major roadblocks to strategic planning, and it includes some suggestions for improving managerial planning. This chapter opens with Case Study 1–1, a sample day in the life of the city manager of Aurora, Colorado. It shows how activities can be divided into maintenance, representation, and planning.

ORGANIZATIONAL MAINTENANCE

Managers spend most of their time on organizational maintenance. Employees have to be hired, trained, promoted, and evaluated. Different programs in the department have to be coordinated to avoid duplication and overlap. Legislative and executive political leaders must be briefed constantly. Budgets must be prepared and expenditures controlled. Staff meetings must be held so that all members know what is happening. All kinds of mundane problems must be dealt with, from personnel issues such as disciplinary appeal to program issues such as staffing a new regional office.

Most traditional public management activities are included within maintenance. Personnel management, including recruitment, selection, promotion, training, safety, and labor relations, is part of maintenance; so is budget preparation and execution. Auxiliary functions such as inventory control, purchasing, and internal communications also are included, as are routine supervisory and management jobs such as discipline, supervision, and delegating authority. These aren't glamorous jobs, but they are important for two reasons. First, if they aren't done well, the agency won't get much accomplished. Second, most managers—by design, accident, or circumstance—spend most of their time on them. These two reasons alone make the maintenance job well worth studying.

Case Study 1–1

SAMPLE WORKDAY (MAY 1987) FOR JAMES GRIESEMER CITY MANAGER, AURORA, COLORADO

7:00 A.M.–7:50 A.M.
Breakfast with Marshall Kaplan, dean of the Graduate School of Public Administration, University of Colorado–Denver. Discussed an intergovernmental negotiating effort which is being facilitated by Kaplan and the University of Colorado dealing with planning and annexation of a 40-square-mile area south of Aurora. This is a complex intergovernmental effort involving a county, three municipalities, and several large landowners and developers.

7:50 A.M.–8:20 A.M.
Coffee with a foreman in the Parks Department to discuss innovations in his work group, problems which he is facing, and answer questions on general city policy. This is part of a regular program of meeting two times per week with supervisors at all levels in the organization. These half-hour morning meetings over a cup of coffee provide an opportunity to meet with supervisors. They are part of the city's overall effort at participatory management. They also represent a valued opportunity for me to keep in touch with the internal organization. (The city is organized with three deputy city managers who actually handle line operations and two assistant city managers who manage staff responsibilities.)

8:20 A.M.–8:30 A.M.
Review daily press packet. Each morning at 8:20 A.M., the city manager receives Xeroxes of articles and editorials from the two daily papers (*The Denver Post* and

Rocky Mountain News) and the weekly paper (*Aurora Sentinel*) covering Aurora. This news digest packet is provided daily by the Communications Office to the city manager and key staff and weekly to council members.

8:30 A.M.–9:00A.M.
Weekly policy meeting with deputy and assistant city managers, as well as the city attorney, to review upcoming policy items being prepared by council policy committees and to discuss major policy issues that are emerging. This meeting provides an opportunity to share information on policy issues and coordinate the policy process. Council policy committees are staffed by deputy and assistant city managers to provide a functional linkage between the development and implementation of policy. The city manager sits as ex-officio on all policy committees but actually attends meetings only as required on an "exception" basis. The city manager facilitates these weekly policy meetings with most of the substance provided by deputy or assistant city managers.

9:00 A.M.–9:30 A.M.
Meet with appointment secretary to review appointments scheduled for the day, and be advised of changes occuring during the week. Scheduling my time is a major function handled by a high-level secretary/administrative assistant. Since time is the most valuable resource that any executive has, the management of my calendar assumes a high-priority

status. Managing the calendar is a difficult and dynamic job. Also during this half hour, I quickly review incoming mail, *The Wall Street Journal*, and sign several letters dictated the previous afternoon.

9:30 A.M.–10:00 A.M.
Call council members. As a part of my regular routine, I attempt to call each council member at least once a week for several minutes simply to touch base on odds-and-ends items.

10:00 A.M.–10:45 A.M.
Meet with the deputy city manager for operations. This deputy city manager has managing responsibilities for the Public Works, Parks, Utilities, and Planning Departments. Each week, I meet individually with the three deputies and two assistants for 30–45 minutes. These are totally structured meetings with an agenda developed by the deputy or assistant. At these meetings, they present items for general direction and, organizationally, for specific decision making. In addition, they use this time to brief me on significant pending matters.

10:45 A.M.–11:00 A.M.
Return two phone calls, review odds-and-ends paperwork.

11:00 A.M.–11:30 A.M.
Meet with personnel director to receive an update on major changes in the city's personnel classification and compensation system. This item will come to the council in about six months and the per-

sonnel director will brief me on the early stages of the project.

11:45 A.M.–1:00 P.M.

Meet for lunch at a local restaurant with the director and the president of the city's economic development agency and a council member to talk about specific economic development issues. At the meeting, we decide to include the establishment of an Office of Tourism as part of the city manager's recommended 1988 budget.

1:15 P.M.–1:45 P.M.

Dictate the weekly "manager's memo" communication to the city council apprising them of current developments; dictate several letters and memorandums; sign congratulatory letters to citizens and employees based on newspaper articles and other information. The city's press secretary provides the city manager with brief congratulatory letters based on newspaper articles and a number of other sources. These letters are sent to citizens, local business leaders, and employees.

1:45 P.M.–2:00 P.M.

Schedule a dentist appointment and a haircut.

2:00 P.M.–2:30 P.M.

Meet with a task force coordinating the "21st-Century city" project. This is a major, year-long community goals project designed to look closely at the city of Aurora, its strengths and opportunities, and develop a clearer identity and community focus for the city. The group briefs the city manager on an upcoming seminar involv-

ing national speakers that will examine economic, technological, and social forces affecting cities today.

2:30 P.M.–3:30 P.M.

Meet with the budget officer and the revenue coordinator to review the current status of city revenues and establish monthly spending targets for departments. Although Aurora is a rapidly growing city, it suffers the same difficult resource limitations as other cities. In addition, being highly dependent upon sales tax, the current adverse economic climate in Colorado has driven revenues downward for several years. The organizational adaptation has been the establishment of a consolidated revenue office and the development of close revenue monitoring and economic projection systems. The city manager meets monthly with the revenue coordinator to monitor planned versus actual revenues and to receive expenditure pattern information from the budget officer. This meeting also includes deputy and assistant city managers. Spending and cash-flow decisions for the coming months are made by this strategy group and communicated to city departments.

3:30 P.M.–4:30 P.M.

Meeting with a major developer and his attorneys concerning a proposed 1.25 million square-foot regional shopping center planned for a piece of property currently being annexed by the city. The meeting involves discussions of general concepts with respect to how the city can assist the development and benefits that this project will produce for the city in terms of revenues and job creation. Some general directions are established and directions are given to city staff and the developer's consultants to plan jointly alternative proposals.

4:30 P.M.–5:00 P.M.
Meet with appointment secretary to update the calendar for the remainder of the week and review the city manager's comments at an evening meeting to be held.

5:00 P.M.–5:30 P.M.
Read additional mail for the day. Sign several letters.

5:30 P.M.–6:00 P.M.
Leave for reception with county commissioners.

6:00 P.M.–6:30 P.M.
Attend reception with county commissioners at new county airport.

6:30 P.M.–9:30 P.M.
Joint dinner between the Aurora City Council and the Arapahoe County Commissioners. Both the city manager and county manager make presentations to the group on the discussion topic for the evening, which is managing social service demands, an increasing problem for both the city and the county.

Analysis of Case Study 1–1

Item	Maintenance	Representation	Planning
University of Colorado annexation	x	x	
Coffee with supervisor	x		
Daily press packet	x		
Weekly policy meeting	x		
Appointment secretary	x		
Council member calls	x	x	
Deputy manager for operations	x		
Return phone calls	x	x	
Personal director	x		x
Luncheon	x	x	x
Dictation	x	x	
21st-Century project		x	x
Budget officer meeting	x		
Shopping center developer		x	x
Appointment secretary/read mail	x		
Reception/joint dinner		x	x

This outline covers a day in the life of the city manager of Aurora, Colorado, a large (population 170,000) suburb in the Denver metropolitan area. It shows that time schedules of busy executives can be divided, for purposes of analysis, into organizational maintenance, representation, and planning. As expected, most activities such as meetings with supervisors, secretaries, and lower-level managers, as well as handling mail, involved organizational maintenance. Even financial matters, which could involve long-term planning, are described in terms of day-to-day decisions.

Representation, involving personal appearances or letters to outsiders, is also involved in many activities, even routine ones such as phone calls to council members. The top executive is always on display, and people are always making judgments about personal style and effectiveness of representation.

Events noted as strategic planning, such as the city's proposed new classification and compensation plan, are only *opportunities* for long-range planning. Good managers have long-range plans that guide the activities noted above, but it is impossible to ensure that long-range goals or strategic plans actually guide the meeting.

The pace of this schedule also underlines a point made in Chapter 10, that one characteristic of a good executive is energy. Only someone with much psychic energy and good health can maintain Griesemer's schedule.

Academic Studies

Academic studies of management devote most of their attention to jobs that are part of the maintenance function. Most academic publications involve the private sector, although many, if not most, authors claim that their studies have universal application. Some of what is written is empirical, describing what actually occurs. Much is normative, involving value judgments, although the values often masquerade as descriptive statements.[1] In either case, the descriptions are generally abstract, since the activities of busy men and women are so varied that only general statements cover them. Perhaps the most famous description, at least for the public sector, is POSDCORB, a made-up word coined in the 1930s to describe the major management functions.[2]

POSDCORB includes the following elements: planning, organizing, staffing, directing, coordinating, reporting, and budgeting. Planning means outlining the things to be done and how they will be done. Organizing involves establishing the formal authority structure. Staffing refers to the personnel function, just as budgeting refers to the fiscal aspects of organizational life. Coordinating is interrelating the parts with the whole, while directing is giving orders and making decisions. Reporting is keeping one's supervisor informed. Together, the first letter of each function makes up POSDCORB.

POSDCORB became popular among management scholars as a way to describe the essence of management in one catchword. It came to stand for the view that management could be summarized in those principles. POSDCORB ignored any human or behavioral elements in the work setting. To most modern scholars, POSDCORB is shorthand to describe a simpler world where management could be reduced to simple descriptive terms. Even so, POSDCORB was the intellectual grandfather of public administration because it was the first comprehensive attempt to define public management.

Massie, writing about business management, describes the key functions of a manager as follows:

- Decision making, or the choice of a course of action from available alternatives.
- Organizing, or the process of determining allocations and structures of jobs.
- Staffing, the process by which managers recruit, train, and promote subordinates.
- Controlling, or measuring performance and guiding it toward established goals.
- Communicating, or the process of transmitting ideas to others to obtain goals. (Note that this does not include listening, even though most managers spend more time listening than giving orders.)
- Directing, or the process of guiding subordinate performance toward established goals.[3]

While Gulick's POSDCORB was written for the public sector and Massie's description was for the private sector, both have much in common. Both focus on internal management and both are highly structural—choosing to deal with the formal part of the manager's job. There isn't room for much about human behavior in their schemes, although both would protest that their works imply a concern for how managers actually behave. In defense of Massie and Gulick, it is inevitable that most descriptions of the manager's job become abstract. True, it's easier to explain how one spent the day planning a new Boston regional center and a San Antonio recruiting trip than it is to say that you spent the day controlling and directing. But each day is different, and each manager's job is different. That's why descriptions have to be general to be inclusive.

There are more specific (and more recent) descriptions of work in the public sector. A recent study of civilians in the navy identified four basic factors: supervision, information gathering and dissemination, planning and decision making, and resource allocation. This study of research and development managers, although a specialized group, clarified some tasks that all managers perform. Leadership and supervision proved the most crucial for effectiveness on the job, followed by executive decision making.[4]

Table 1–1 outlines the activities illustrated in Lau's study. Most tasks involve organizational maintenance. Information gathering, the major activity involving outside contact, primarily involves keeping informed about the outside environment. Attending conferences was one way of doing so, at least for these research and development officers. Such outside contact may involve strategic planning, since new ideas help managers look ahead in their own organizations. These outside contacts can also involve organizational representation, since the manager's presence reminds others of her organization. Nonetheless, Lau's list focuses primarily on internal management.

Lau's study also reveals the heavy and fragmented workday of these executives, which involves many interruptions and unscheduled events. They are unable to establish a schedule and stick to it. Meetings take excessive amounts of time. To keep abreast of their jobs, they spend an average of 52 hours a week in the office and eight more hours at home. About 90 percent of all respondents reported moderate to great stress due to frustration over the effort required to accomplish anything,

TABLE 1–1   Sample Elements of Navy Executive Job Content

Supervision and leadership	Evaluating the quality of subordinate job performance. Attending to training and development needs of employees. Attending to staffing requirements such as hiring and firing.
Information gathering	Attending outside conferences or meetings. Keeping abreast of who is doing what in your unit or command. Staying tuned in to what is happening with outside organizations.
Technical problem solving	Providing technical quality control through the review process. Consulting with others on technical matters.
Executive decision making	Implementing the directives of higher authorities. Evaluating the outcomes of internal improvement projects. Resolving conflicts.

SOURCE: Alan Lau, Arthur Newman, and Laurie Broedling, "The Nature of Management Work in the Public Sector," *Public Administration Review* (September/October 1980), p. 518. Reprinted with permission from *Public Administration Review*, © 1980 by the American Society for Public Administration, Washington, D.C.

the lack of staff support, and outside pressures.[5] One respondent commented:

> Your questions really don't address the real problems encountered by a line manager, i.e., the total frustration with personnel, contracts, and legal support offices who assume that line organizations exist to serve them. Also hiring freezes, high ceilings, additional staff, and layering of organizational levels. I can commit vast sums of taxpayer money, but can't get an operable typewriter for my secretary.[6]

The frustration of this manager is common. Hiring freezes, staff conflicts, and additional levels of hierarchy are compounded by other difficulties. Public agencies rarely provide extras for their managers—preferring to maximize jobs at the expense of office supplies, travel, and small capital equipment. Another problem is that in public agencies it is sometimes better to follow the prescribed procedures than to be "right." It takes much "massaging the system" to complete projects. Approximately 90 percent of the managers in the study allude to this problem. The requirements for following innumerable rules are a result of the demand for accountability in public agencies. However, the virtues of high levels of accountability in a democracy are often lost on managers who feel heavy organizational pressure to finish a project. This pressure drives out the time that should be spent on representation and strategic planning. It's the major reason that managers often shortchange representation and planning.

Shortchanging long-range planning is also common in the private sector, as Mintzberg's work shows. He notes that "job pressures drive managers to be superficial in their actions" and that managers gravitate to specific activities rather than to general planning. These job pressures demand a grueling work pace for long hours on a wide variety of short-lived activities, with little time for reflection.[7]

Pressures on managers come from both inside and outside the organization. Inside pressures are from subordinates or higher-level managers, usually involving resource demands. A department head, for example, wants to expand his program but there isn't enough money. The department head must give the unhappy news to subordinates, whose expectations caused much of the original pressure. Outside pressures come primarily from legislators and, to a lesser degree, client groups. Legislators and client groups generally want information, but sometimes they also want special treatment for applicants, favorable interpretation of regulations, or preferences among programs. While legislators get the highest priorities, no manager ignores constituent groups. As a result, managers spend much time seeking money for subordinates or information for legislators or clients. This time often comes at the expense of long-term issues.[8]

Managerial Activities in the Words of Managers

Managers react to legislative demands, for not to respond is to invite budgetary reprisals. They respond to subordinate's demands for resources as best they can, for not to favor expansion endangers agency morale. In addition, all managers attend many meetings, both within and outside the organization. They resolve conflict by choosing one set of opinions over another. They ration scarce money and plead at higher levels for more funds. Most managers in all the agencies surveyed had similar activities.

Among agencies, however, there is considerable variation among management jobs. While many of the activities mentioned involve organizational representation to some degree, many officials have little to do with outside forces. A ranking federal executive once reported:

> A large percentage of my time is devoted to my function as staff officer to the Secretary and Undersecretary. I have a relatively small staff—about 300 people. I spend perhaps a quarter of my time supervising the staff and the other three quarters in a staff capacity to my bosses. I probably spend less than five percent of my time with Congress, with industries, and other outside groups.[9]

This incumbent was head of a large staff unit for a major department. He supervised policy research, prepared policy papers for the secretary, evaluated programs, and so on. The agency may have been charged with long-range planning for the organization. If so, the maintenance responsibility of this executive was to assure that the long-range planning job was done.

Many programs have heavy contact with outside groups of clients, legislators, or the general public. Here, the maintenance and representation functions are closely linked. A California Department of Education official notes:

> My present assignment is that of Chief of the Office of Consolidated Management Services. This office has three operation units. One unit has responsibility for doing the developmental work for our Consolidated Program's Applications, processing complaints against this program's applications . . . Another unit is a program review unit with responsibility for reviewing school programs to determine the quality of those programs. The third unit has a primary function of maintaining a library of materials that our consultants and managers need to work effectively with our clientele.[10]

The internal management responsibility of this education office is primarily organizational management. In addition, the manager's responsibility is heavily laced with organizational representation. To the extent that concern for the effectiveness of the office of consolidated management makes him ponder the nature of education and the role of the Department of Education, he engages in some long-range planning. Thus, the three functions are joined, although maintenance takes the most time and energy.

Another executive from the California Youth Authority described his job as follows:

> I supervise the staff level functions of the medical and dental section as well as the education section, the Volunteer Coordinator, the staff training functions, and a whole bunch of other kinds of assignments that come through—like legislative bill analyses, developing budget material, and responding to a massive amount of correspondence.[11]

This manager's job involves miscellaneous staff duties necessary to keep the organization operating. The jobs of bill analyses and budget preparation are internal management, but they involve outside visibility. Like many managers, this youth authority manager cannot easily separate maintenance from representation.

The three managers quoted above have both similarities and differences. Since their jobs are in varying agencies at different levels of government with different clients and programs, the jobs have little in common. Yet, in another sense, the jobs have much in common. They are maintenance jobs with plenty of outside contacts. They operate under the same difficulties—a rigid personnel and budgetary ceiling and a heavy layer of rules and regulations to assure accountability. The work load is heavy in all agencies, for there are no ceilings on client demands. One California city manager spoke for all executives when he said: "The extremely heavy workload (sic) placed on the city manager is a perennial frustration. In a small city, you have no staff to delegate to . . . I am a paper flunky."[12]

Most public executives work hard at their jobs and all have, at one time or another, muttered comments such as these. Generally speaking, the hardest working group is at the peak of the hierarchy. Unlike top private executives, public managers find it difficult to delegate responsibility. Since increased responsibilities do not bring increased time to reflect on them, most public executives are too busy to think about what they are doing. And, over time, this attention to program details incapacitates executives for higher-level planning. Managers refer to this situation as "when you are up to your ass in alligators it's hard to remember you set out to drain the swamp."

Why do managers work as hard as they do if there are few rewards and great pressure? Usually it is because they are deeply committed to program goals. To them, better public health in Connecticut through better training of health inspectors is an end in itself. For managers in an agency with strong program goals, such motivation is important. Managers in charge of a nuclear power plant can dream of lower rates for customers. Managers of a local recreation district can plan more programs for senior citizens. National Park Service managers might look forward to more public utilization of lesser-known parks.

Most managers aren't near enough to the top to share these goals directly, or they aren't in agencies with such visible goals. And, many managers who eventually reach the top see their ardor cool. Something else must explain why managers keep managing. Primarily it's the joy of accomplishing management tasks. Recruiting a new staff for the organization, for example, is something tangible and significant. It is even more meaningful when it moves the organization toward its program goals, but it can stand alone as a major task well done. These are the tasks that managers take pride in doing well, and they spend most of their working time in such activities.

These tasks are known as *economy and efficiency* goals. Economy and efficiency are powerful symbols in public and private management. All managers bow to them. Rare is the manager who does not believe in them. In operational terms, they mean conducting public business at low cost (economy) while maximizing the use of resources (efficiency).

While managerial beliefs in economy and efficiency are held at all levels of government, some of the truest believers can be found at the local level. In one study, 70 percent of San Francisco Bay Area city managers reported economy and efficiency accomplishments. One manager noted, in response to a question about his accomplishments:

> I would say a high level of administrative performance in city government . . . I mean efficiency, economy, and professionalization of various departments, viz. engineering, works, fire and police. . . . Economy covers a lot of things. I try to promote an economical government, to provide the highest amount of services for the lowest cost.[13]

It's a long way from the California city manager paper flunky to the federal executive of 30 years ago and back to the navy research and development officer who was frustrated with budget and personnel ceilings. However, all three managers devoted enormous energy and time to maintaining their organizations. If time devoted to a job measures its importance, maintenance is overwhelmingly the major job of the public executive.

ORGANIZATIONAL REPRESENTATION

Organizational representation is the second job of the public manager. Sometimes representation is as an official spokesperson for the organization, generally for public consumption in a news conference, or while acting as a public information officer. Sometimes top public executives gain public notice because of their position, such as a long-tenured city manager, or because of their personality and the job they hold, such as the late J. Edgar Hoover of the Federal Bureau of Investigation (FBI). Sometimes individuals become highly visible when public attention is attracted to a special function, such as in a deportation hearing for a well-known figure. These are rare, however.

The public manager usually receives sporadic public attention. Many contacts, while formal, involve events of minor significance between the agency executive and a range of outside groups and individuals. A city manager may address the local Chamber of Commerce, the Lions Club, and the Garden Society on consecutive days. State and federal officials, although less visible, still make speeches to professional organizations and occasionally to local groups. Examples of this are a park ranger explaining the state park's Nature Trails program, a local social security director explaining social security law changes, or a state Department of Corrections official explaining prison crowding.

Other types of contacts are less formal. The local bureau of reclamation manager may breakfast with a local Sierra Club member, lunch with a group of farmers, and thrash out water-use requirements with the city manager in the afternoon. The city manager may leave the afternoon meeting to attend an evening meeting with subdivision residents furious about the lack of a stop sign. If she survives this meeting, the next morning she may call the regional office of the State Parks Department to check out the progress of a grant application for a community building.

In each meeting, the official represents her agency. Any one meeting may mean little, but the hundreds of meetings each year add up to an important opportunity for promoting agency programs and strengthening agency image. These meetings constitute the first of two general categories of representational activities. In formal representation, such as testifying to a legislative committee or giving important speeches to client groups, the presence of the chief executive officer is necessary. For other events of lesser symbolic importance, lower-level officials are equally desirable, particularly if they have intimate knowledge of the program in question.

Thus, the latter category is more common. It is the thousands of phone calls made and meetings attended during a year by every executive. Most, although not all clients, are with counterparts inside the government but outside the agency. These activities are largely unknown to the public, but they create the image of the agency. A senior analyst, for example, may negotiate joint actions among several agencies, arrange exceptions to a personnel ceiling or request budget changes with her counterparts in other agencies. Obviously, the image she presents is important to the agency, for she represents the agency.

A public works director needs to repave a street. Successful completion of the project is not just technical supervision of the fleet of gravel trucks and maintenance personnel on the job. This project also requires that the director give advance warning to utility companies, notify (well in advance) businessess along the street, and obtain approval of other units of government if the paving material was jointly purchased or if the street is in more than one city.

From budget hearings to street paving, the life of the public executive is made up of thousands of individual contacts with individuals both inside and outside the agency. Here, organization maintenance and organization representation are linked. A manager with a strong management record can use this maintenance record to become more effective in his representation function. Conversely, a manager with a poor performance record often has trouble gaining cooperation.

Personal integrity of the executive is essential. Trust and respect, rather than power or money, are the oil that lubricates interagency relations. A chief executive officer must gain legislative respect to testify effectively. His deputies must convince the agencies and groups they deal with that their word is their bond and that, while negotiating a solution to a problem, they can bind their organization. Both the chief executive and his aides must be people whom others trust and can deal with.

There are some troubling exceptions to the question of executive integrity. Robert Moses, parks and transportation czar of the New York City metropolitan region for many years, and J. Edgar Hoover, chief of the FBI, were lionized by the press and public for their administrative and political successes. Yet, both achieved success by trampling the rights of less powerful people and by coercing or shouting down equals.[14] Their careers suggest that a few unique and highly placed individuals can achieve power and influence without achieving the trust and respect that lesser managers require. Moses and Hoover achieved this through public relations campaigns touting agency accomplishments while brushing other issues under the carpet. Most public executives, however, cannot advance their programs by public relations campaigns that cover up duplicity or coercion.

Dealing with another agency's manager involves playing reciprocal roles. Chapter 3, Goals and Actors, and Chapter 5, Politics and Management, deal extensively with these roles. Managers are used to dealing with partisans from other agencies who strongly represent their agency's position. The system works on the assumption that all interests are represented, and the public interest emerges from a tussle between interests. Thus, all managers must be partisans for their agency, a rule known informally as *Miles Law*. Miles Law posits that "where you stand depends upon where you sit," meaning that executives will advocate proposals or positions that their agency favors. Miles, a former high-ranking federal official, notes that "in order to be effective within his organization, he had to be its strong advocate in external relationships."[15] Furthermore, "no person should ever be put in the position of being asked to be objective about the life and death or expansion and contraction of the organization to which he owes primary loyalty."[16] Applied to organizational representation, Miles's Law shows that executives will take positions supportive of their agency, and that this is expected. Although this sounds like unvarnished bureaucratic imperialism, others in the system anticipate such behavior. It manifests itself in the competitive arena of public managers.

The Audience Is the Agency

Many messages from organizational leaders are only ostensibly aimed at the general public. The real target is organizational members. The executive speaks, through the media or via prepared speeches, to the *agency* rather than to the public.

One example of this is when the top manager is dependent on support from his agency for new programs or for his continued tenure in office. Often subordinates have some control over the appointment or retention of an executive. In these cases, speaking effectively on their behalf or saying what they want to hear is a factor in their continued support. College faculties are a good example. Faculty support is crucial to a college president. Therefore, presidential statements ostensibly directed at alumni, the community, or others are often aimed at faculty members. Ringing statements supporting high academic standards are as much to reassure the faculty about presidential values as to convince listeners.

Even when a top manager is not dependent on lower-level support, however, widespread perception that the chief "doesn't fight for us" will damage morale in the agency. In these cases, public or private statements associating the top manager with lower-level values are important, no matter to whom they are directed.

A common practice in large and complex agencies is the *reverse leak*. It's called a reverse leak because it leaks information into the organization rather than out. Here, the manager makes a public statement that signals to employees what her priorities are. The statement may signal new program directions, certify that a bureaucratic struggle has been settled and announce the result, or provide general information about new management directions. The formal statements, which are read avidly by an agency person with a stake in the decision, serve as a public bulletin board. Since large organizations are cumbersome, this is a faster and sometimes much more efficient way of getting the word out.

A top official may say, in effect, "This is a good program and I'm proud of it. Anyone trying to sabotage it will be punished." This is both representing the agency effectively and warning potential internal dissidents. Often, the chief executive uses a public forum to make his position clear. Particularly at the federal level, direct comments to the media or the public are effective ways to address organizational members.

> Officials at all levels depend to some extent upon their immediate supervisors for career advancement. Giving the boss what he wants, or at least avoiding the appearance of insubordination, is a bureaucratic way of life. Because of his constitutional authority, if not his power, the President is the one official whose preferences matter most to bureaucrats. He often finds it efficient to tell the press what he wants, to ensure that all officials find out quickly and to tell them openly through press releases and press conferences.[17]

This tactic is limited in its application, since most career executives don't have access to press conferences. When they do, such as with small town newspapers on local matters, variations are common. A city manager may emphasize budget limits to his department heads, signaling that protests to the city council in formal hearings should not be too vigorous. Department heads may lament these shortfalls publicly, but they will not push hard for city council approval of increased budgets. This public lamentation tells their subordinates and client groups that there is no money but that they support the programs of the agency. Members and client groups follow these cues and word circulates inside and outside the organization as effectively as in a formal memorandum.

Top-level managers closely follow public statements of their chief, particularly political appointees. Despite the chance to send messages downward, chiefs are not always aware of what this attention may imply.

> We read (the appointee's) address (to an outside conference) pledging to meet the needs of these people. Then when we loosened up the program, word came down complaining that things were out of control. Everyone here was dumbstruck. It showed his ignorance about what he himself was doing.[18]

In this case, the executive (a federal political appointee) was representing the agency before a group of clients. He may or may not have meant what he said literally. It was taken literally, however, by his staff as a signal. Staff might prefer direct orders, as noted here in a negative comment about a federal office of personnel management director:

> We read in the papers what Devine is thinking and wants—managers have no directions from him. He refuses to tell us what he is thinking and wanting.[19]

However, getting specific direction is not always easy. At all levels, bureaucrats must get used to operating with subtle cues.

The Media

Despite anything that has been said, no executive "uses" the media, at least not for long. Managers with experience laugh at such a notion, for they often feel "used" themselves. Many dread or stolidly endure the media, which seem poised to pounce on bureaucratic errors and ignore successes. Experienced managers treat the press as a force to be regarded with care, but not one that is malevolent. These managers have certain expectations for the media. They expect that the media will inform the public fairly, that they will not be quoted out of context, that if they are interviewed, they will be able to speak off the record, and that the media are really interested in news (as defined by the press, not the manager). One study showed that public officials expected the media to communicate demands to the government, to try to protect the public by guarding against laxness and corruption, and to interpret the news as well as report it.[20]

Political officials deal more with the media than administrators. They have more responsibility for the representation function than for maintenance or strategic planning. Maintenance is done by lower-level officials, while strategic planning has often become the job of the lower-level staff officials in budget and planning offices. Whenever representation involves direct media contact, it usually falls to political leaders or high-level careerists. Many executives aren't ready for this responsibility, not having experienced the full glare of publicity in previous experience. The difficulties for politicians also arise from a lack of detailed agency knowledge.

Perhaps the major problem, however, is that the previous experience of many political executives hasn't been useful. Frederick Malek, a Nixon administration official, notes three differences between business and top-level government experience. Government officials (1) live in a fishbowl, (2) must influence and gain the confidence of Congress, and (3) must deal with partisanship, which prevents proposals from being judged on their own merit.[21] The first two points apply equally well to careerists who reach top levels in their organization. The importance of effective communication to the media and to clientele groups is essential. Malek quotes a former cabinet officer and businessman:

> Success in government depends on the attitude of the people you deal with—the bureaucracy, the Congress, the media, the public. To shape this attitude there is a much greater need for ability to communicate than exists in any business I can think of, including advertising.[22]

These successes in dealing with the press do occur, sometimes almost in the form of media manipulation. One case, occurring at the highest level, involved White House staffer Robert Kintner. Kintner tried to persuade Jack Gould, a *New York Times* reporter, to support Rosel Hyde, President Johnson's choice to head the Federal Communications Commission (FCC). Gould had been critical, so Kintner arranged a meeting between President Johnson and Gould and briefed Johnson on how to overcome Gould's skepticism. Gould did not mention Hyde in later articles, but he did write a glowing article about the Johnson administration's communication policy.[23]

Successful managers, whether political or career, have mastered the ability to communicate; Malek suggests political appointees must also master communication. They know how to speak effectively, when to speak or write, and who to communicate with. Few have as spectacular experiences as Kintner had with reporter Gould, but most know how to effectively handle the press.

An Honest Broker

A top public executive will normally spend much time mediating between two or more interests. Her role is rather analogous to a real estate broker bringing two individuals together. A city manager, for example, may have to coordinate a grant application among an adjacent park district, the federal granting agency, a state local affairs department and several community groups. To drain a swamp, a state official may have to work with a state and federal legislator (both of whom represent that area), a water district, and a mosquito abatement district. The manager acts as a catalyst to get different parties to agree on something of benefit to each of them. One city manager agrees:

> I think the city manager has assumed the role of a broker in many ways in Union City (California). I was the middle man in working with the school district and some developers recently. I explained to the developers that the school district could not handle the number of children that the new homes would bring into the schools. We were able to convince two developers to pay the entire costs for a new school in the area where they wanted to build.[24]

Since cities like Union City are small and the city manager has little staff help, projects often become the manager's personal responsibility. Even when underlings negotiate contracts, the manager's hierarchical position often makes her presence necessary to "bless" the arrangement. A senior career official in a California state agency related this tale:

> We have had, recently, some unresolved issues with the Ways and Means Committee. We received a call from the consultant of the Committee and

he needed some information very rapidly . . . he wanted to discuss some issues. So myself, the head of Business Services and the Director went over to the Assembly Offices and met with the consultant. In the meantime, I briefed the Director on details of various pros and cons, etc. We met with the consultant, resolved the issue, and within five minutes we were before a legislative committee, and we turned this issue into a consent item, which means that there was no discussion, and ran it out of there in two minutes.[25]

Situations like this one happen more smoothly if the top manager is present. Here, the top career manager did not bring the parties together, but did provide the information that made a negotiated settlement possible. Getting the parties together, as in Union City, and providing information, as in the consultant case, are part of the brokering aspect of representing the agency.

Sensing the Environment

Organizational representation is a major means of sensing environmental changes affecting the organization. Forces and pressures outside the organization usually become clear to the top manager as he confronts outside agencies, clients, and legislators in his role of organizational spokesperson. Opposing views become clear when he interacts with outsiders during committee meetings, press conferences, and professional gatherings. Good managers sense support for programs while meeting outside groups—not when sitting behind their desks.

Every organization falls upon hard times. Budget cuts, like God's rain, fall on the just and unjust. Personnel ceilings are a fact of life; programs fail. Thus, organizational policies must change, and it is crucial for top managers to sense how the environment will react to new policies or program changes. Active organizational representation is the primary means of judging how adaptations will be received.

Peter Drucker comments that a major corporation executive:

inevitably lives in an artificial environment and is almost as isolated as if he were in a monastery. This isolation is necessary. The executive of a big corporation—like the executive of any organization—is too busy to see people except on business. . . . Hence, executive life not only breeds a parochialism of the imagination comparable to the "military mind" but places a considerable premium on it.[26]

No top-level public executive could survive long in such splendid isolation. In fact, it is doubtful if most private executives conform any longer to Drucker's description. Interaction with the environment can no longer be avoided, if it ever could. Effective interaction with the outside environment is probably the most crucial reason for the importance of organizational representation.

ORGANIZATIONAL PLANNING

Organizational planning, or strategic planning, as it is known in the private sector, is the third major job of the public executive. Broadly defined, planning means assessing where the organization is going, what its relationship is with its environment and what it ought to be, and what changes ought to be made.[27] This job, which only top management can perform, is often not done at all.

Strategic planning involves a conscious attempt to take environmental forces into account and to direct organizational resources and strategies in directions that complement outside forces. It is aligning the inside strengths of the organization with outside environmental forces, particularly forces that will dominate the future.[28] This is tricky because it is difficult to precisely foresee future environmental forces.

Strategic planning is also called strategic management, indicating that the process is both an act and a process. It refers to both the management decisions that comprise a strategic plan, and to a set of premises that guide the management process and shape specific decisions.[29] Exhibit 1–1 illustrates this complex process. The exhibit seems to imply a one-time decision, but it also represents a continual reevaluation of strategy by testing it against the environment.

Exhibit 1–1 shows that the strategic management (planning) process begins with the identification of a desired strategy, followed by (1) a scan of the environment for support, (2) a review of the organization's internal capacity and strengths, and (3) an assessment of the resources necessary for the desired strategy. The latter two reviews often involve the same matters, since resource adequacy may be clearly linked to organizational capacity. The environmental scan and the internal review(s) may be done simultaneously or in sequence. Once the scan and the review are completed, the desired strategy is compared to the results. If management is satisfied, the strategy is implemented. If the strategy is inadequate to the task, the process begins again.

Most plans fail at the implementation stage because it is easier to plan than to struggle with opposing forces to make the plan a reality. Even so, the importance of strategic planning is that a conscious, deliberate attempt is made to adjust inside resources of the organization to outside environmental forces.

Lynn regards the strategic management process as both highly individualistic and highly political. The executive must scan the political environment and must identify the organizational strengths, but executives must also "reflect on their own values and beliefs."[30] This is necessary for political leaders to choose a set of operating premises under which they can feel comfortable directing and focusing organizational decisions.

EXHIBIT 1–1 Strategic Management Process

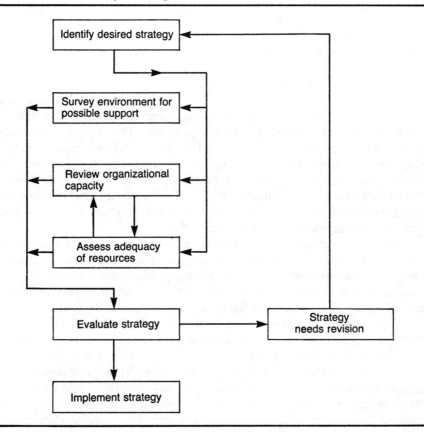

Lynn also indicates that strategic management in government is "ferreting out limited spheres of autonomy" since freedom to act is more limited than in industry, and that in government, "recognition and therefore incentives go to those who formulate policy and manuever legislative compromise."[31] Thus, in government, planning is limited to narrower issues of organizational turf and autonomy rather than the more dramatic and global activities of private businesses.[32]

Even if government actions are more limited, they can be significant for organizations that have put a strategic plan into effect. The following two cases are illustrative.

The Port of Seattle adapted its terminal to changes in the technology and economics of steamship lines, which were changing from cargo ships to large container ships. The steamship lines could no longer make Seattle a first port of call before other ports such as San Francisco, because idle or partly loaded ships cost too much per day. The Port of Seattle took 12 years to convert to terminals that enabled ships to load completely in Seattle. This required new sets of labor relations, new types of financing, and new and different equipment; not the least of which was a sophisticated computer system to maintain and control the larger inventories required. As a result of this long-range planing, Seattle expanded its share of West Coast shipping.[33]

The Naval Torpedo Station at Keyport, Washington, with inspired middle management strategic planning, convinced their superiors to maintain budget support for their operation. The nuclear age made torpedoes outdated technology, and Keyport suffered severe budget declines. However, the station developed a complex strategic plan that carefully and laboriously linked its existing strengths and capabilities to the navy's new global strategy. This involved a service goal of maintaining the navy's fleet of nuclear submarines and matching it with internal physical resources and human talents.[34]

In a large corporation, strategic management involves considerations such as product mix, market diversification, and financial alternatives for obtaining new capital. In a large public agency, strategic planning involves matters such as increases or cutbacks in service levels, assessing legislative support for new programs, and decentralizing operating programs to central or regional offices. In the late 1970s and early 1980s, many public agencies were faced with actual declines in revenues and the need to severely reduce service levels. This forced those agencies perhaps for the first time, to give real thought to questions of alternative service levels and revenue systems—in brief, they needed to think seriously about strategic management. This has resulted in greater interest for operational planning and attempts to restore equilibrium, as will be explained later, but strategic planning has not become a significant part of governmental management. Why not? Primarily because there are many institutional roadblocks to long-range planning in government.

Roadblocks that Prevent Strategic Planning

One of the main reasons for roadblocks is that most agencies don't control their destiny. They can't focus resources and programs to make the necessary changes, even if their managers see what needs to be done. Budget ceilings limit spending. Separate accounts can't be combined to increase flexibility. Personnel ceilings not only rule out hiring new staff, they may even dictate how the present staff can be used. Legislators and their staffs demand roles in agency plans and often veto new options. Top management, changing with each new administration, is often unsympathetic. Client groups have much to say about proposals they don't like.

Under the best of circumstances, planning is fragmented in government. The best managers find it difficult to concentrate their efforts—lesser managers give up trying. In contrast, large companies routinely expect top managers to devote their efforts to planning, although all companies are not successful. Donald Rumsfeld, secretary of defense in the Ford administration and now president of a pharmaceutical firm, contrasted public and private strategic planning in the following manner:

> Planning in business is more analytical and thoughtful than in government. You are in a less reactive mode. For example, if it evolves in the Pentagon that a weapons system doesn't work, it may have international implications, it becomes a Congressional problem, an OMB (Office of Management and Budget) problem, as well as one having national security implications. Suddenly you have a multiplicity of public pressures that wouldn't show up in a boardroom. In business the first task would be to work out the problem. In government, the time is taken up dealing with the pressures.[35]

Because planning is difficult, policymaking fares no better. George Schultz, after service in the Nixon administration and before becoming President Reagan's secretary of state, wrote with Kenneth Dam that "policymaking is necessarily a piecemeal affair; policymakers are under the constraint that they are not permitted to view problems whole."[36]

When top political leaders such as Schultz and Rumsfeld feel these pressures, it's not surprising that their subordinates, the career executives, don't do much strategic planning.

Another difficulty is that strategic planning is a shared responsibility. The same check and balance system in the process of representation and maintenance is at work here. Top managers can't act alone. They must convince all groups in and outside of the agency that long-term agency plans are necessary and useful. Since no proposal will have universal appeal, every proposal will face some opposition.

Another reason that strategic planning does not receive more attention from managers is that it involves raising long-term issues that many groups would rather not face. These issues may divide the constituency of an organization. Often, political leaders are uninterested because the issues extend beyond their terms of office. Finally, basic changes have an unsettling effect on people within the organization, and declines in morale are always a possibility; of course, if the organization is already in trouble, employee morale is of less consequence—but it may be too late for long-term planning.

Perhaps because the need for long-term planning extends far beyond the perspective of most officials, leadership occasionally is taken by business or community groups. Sometimes strategic planning is too important to be left to managers and politicians. A recent example occurred in San Francisco. There, business leaders working with city hall began in 1981 to "use proven business strategic planning methods and apply them to the future direction of the City."[37] The study identified four key issues: housing, transportation, city finances, and job and business opportunities. Nineteen strategies were chosen for implementation in the four areas. Housing, for example, called for rezoning certain areas for higher-density housing, streamlining the state environmental quality law (this takes state action), creating secondary housing units, and establishing a prohousing coalition. Business leaders report that "To the best of our knowledge, this effort represents the first comprehensive strategic plan developed for a major United States city."[38]

The ability of top managers to reevaluate the operations of their organizations and propose new goals may be even more limited than this section implies. It is easier for small agencies to reevaluate their activities because there are fewer people involved on the inside and fewer powerful interests outside. Hence, it is easier for local agencies to comprehensively review their operations, and easier for state agencies than for federal agencies. The lower the level and the smaller the unit of government, the more likely that immediately concerned groups and individuals will sense the need for change. Thus, managers have more flexibility to act at lower levels and in smaller units of government.

Some years ago, a high-level federal career executive fingered the reason more time isn't spent on strategic planning. He did this in dismissing the importance of having political leaders define objectives for their agencies:

> By and large, the objectives of agencies are spelled out in law and practice prior to the appointment of executives, who have to spend a good deal of their time finding out what these objectives are. Moreover, as quickly as political executives come into office, they have to resist pressures that would make them prisoners of their agencies. They have to meet so many demands, make so many contacts, process so much paper, and attend so many meetings all at once that they have little time for such matters as defining objectives.[39]

His reasons are still valid. These reasons suggest that managers don't get involved in strategic planning because: (1) managers don't have time for it, and (2) if they did, they would find little opportunity to change objectives, which are set by tradition or actual legislation.

Only modest changes in operational policies are likely to occur. A top career official in the California Department of Corrections noted, in reference to a question about planning and research:

I'm attempting to give some direction, (to) implement change. So rather than do some scholarly type of academic research, we're trying to focus on the type of research we need to administer this department and make the decisions we have to make.[40]

STRATEGIC PLANNING IN GOVERNMENT

Despite roadblocks, strategic planning in government really occurs, but in different forms than in industry. It involves three loosely connected activities. The first type of strategic planning is operational planning. It's the constant effort by public agencies to improve their services by becoming more efficient and economical. It receives considerable managerial attention because it is closely related to the organization management function. Indeed, some strategic planning scholars would dismiss it as good but basically routine management.

Operational Planning

A public works department, for example, is constantly evaluating its operations. How often should center lines be repainted? Should they be replaced with rubber or plastic at greater initial cost but less maintenance cost? Should the city purchase one-operator containerized refuse collection trucks? How much will the city save? The health department may be concerned about the mental health program. Should new facilities be leased or purchased? What population area should be covered? Should higher requirements for attendants be imposed, or would they simply drive up personnel costs with little change in patient care? The police department may debate at length over one- versus two-person cars and the trade-offs between officer safety and beat coverage.

These are important operational questions. They engage the attention of public managers and their research staffs, and they are a natural outgrowth of the agency's work. Mid-level engineers will advocate rubber or plastic center lines. Police officers will advocate two-person cars for safety's sake. Recruiting problems will force the health department to consider pay levels of mental health attendants. In this manner, operational planning issues arise from the nature of the program being managed and cannot be avoided for long.

Restoring Equilibrium

The second kind of strategic planning is restoring equilibrium. This means monitoring the directions that public agencies take, correcting them (or trying to correct them) if they have strayed off course, and maintaining stability during emergencies. Programs must be evaluated and sometimes disagreeable actions must occur. Perhaps client relationships must be changed. Performance must be upgraded or expectations changed. Since the late 1970s, this has meant that expectations must be lowered, as Chapter 9 outlines. Employees may have the wrong mix of skills for new technologies. Service delivery systems must also be adapted to new technologies. These are adjustments to changes in public demands for the program's services or changes in resource allocations.

An example of restoring equilibrium was in California after Proposition 13, involving the gradual switch of most local agencies to new methods of operation at lower budget levels. When voters limited local revenues to 1 percent of property values in 1978, the state used its surplus to bail out local government with increased subventions, grants, and increased controls over the use of that money. As the surplus declined in succeeding years, local governments turned to alternate ways of cutting costs and raising money. Some services, particularly parks and libraries, were slashed because they were considered the lowest priority. Volunteers were recruited for many programs, particularly libraries. Fees and charges were levied for the first time and in other cases fees sharply increased. Some employees were laid off. One city even published a catalog of public tax-exempt gifts for citizens to donate. In subtle ways, citizen expectations were dampened. After slow and uneven progress, California local governments are leaner and somewhat more efficient now.

Creating Institutions

A third case of strategic planning involves creating institutions. In a few cases, organizations change from neutral tools that provide a public service to institutions that are valued for themselves. A famous example of the institutionalization process was the Tennessee Valley Authority (TVA). The TVA was created in the 1930s as part of the government takeover of a nitrate plant. From this modest beginning, it became the instrument by which the Midsouth region developed dams, created navigation channels, improved transportation, and spurred economic growth. The TVA, an organization created by national action, became a model of grass roots local control in its eight-state regional development area, as well as a model of regional economic growth.[41]

Selznick claims that leadership was the key factor in institutionalizing the TVA. Generalizing from the TVA case, he claims, "The executive becomes a statesman as he makes the transition from administrative management to institutional leadership."[42] Institutional leadership, which made the TVA a powerful social instrument, means to "infuse with value beyond the technical requirements of the task at hand. The organization is changed from an expendable tool into a valued source of personal satisfaction."[43] Selznick concludes from the TVA example that leadership is required to make institutions important to the personal lives of people when those organizations once were simply a means to perform a service.[44] The same process applies to Harvard University, the Marine Corps, the Peace Corps, and the TVA.[45]

Unfortunately, beyond the work of Sargent Shriver with the Peace Corps or David Lilienthal with the TVA, examples of strategic planning that create institutions are rare. Selznick argues that leadership is unnecessary in most organizations, because routine activities (maintenance, representation and routine planning) can be left to technicians and ordinary managers. He prefers to limit leadership to the creation of institutions, although it's difficult to determine if true institutional leadership will make a difference to a specific organization at a particular point in time. Limiting leadership to institutional creation doesn't do much, moreover, for public managers who are constantly being exhorted to exercise leadership.

IMPROVING STRATEGIC PLANNING

Why isn't strategic planning done more effectively or at least more often? Lack of managerial incentives, lack of support from political leaders, and opposition from client groups have been mentioned. It's possible, however, to remove some institutional barriers.

Changing the length of the management cycle would help. For most managers, this is the fiscal year. The almost universal annual budget originally was designed to assure accountability and control, but it works against long-term planning. Biennial budgets would double the time horizons of most managers. California has met the constitutionally mandated date for budget approval only three times in the past decade. The federal government has operated continuing resolutions in recent years because of Reagan administration loggerheads with Congress. Managers have less than a year to put any new or changed programs into effect. Biennial budgets would let managers do more thinking about their programs, and would halve the time spent formulating and testifying on proposed budgets.

Creating stronger planning and research divisions is another solution. The Department of Housing and Urban Development had a $60-million budget in the 1970s administered by an assistant secretary for policy development.[46] California has a governor's office of research and planning plus offices of planning and research in both legislative branches. There is much variance between levels. Some city or county budget offices are large and well-staffed. In large local units, some departments such as police even have their own planning and research units. Many small units, conversely, are limited in analysis to the time their chief executive, if they have one, spends driving to work in the morning.

Unfortunately, a strong research or planning unit won't assure a flow of strategic information to the chief executive. The world is not that simple. The odds are better, however, that effective planning will be done with a planning agency than without one. Furthermore, size is not the crucial factor. It is the willingness of the chief executive to use the unit that makes the difference.

Planning or research units would be more effective if more care was taken in choosing their members. Many planning staffs, such as police or fire research units, have a bias toward existing organizational policies and programs. Most ideas from planning and research agencies (and sometimes their marching orders) come from inside the organizations they work for. One way to partially avoid this problem is to select staff from outside the organization and bring new ideas into the unit.[47] Of course, even if the ideas are good, the difficulty still lies in convincing the chief executive to use the plans and to take planning seriously.

The most basic noninstitutional way to improve planning is to develop incentives for managers to spend more time thinking about their operations. While maintenance and representational activities take much time, time is not the major stumbling block. If more attention to planning was required by superiors, managers would find the time. Management by objective (MBO), a popular management evaluation device, is one possibility. Perhaps public executives should operate under a MBO system that demands a yearly or quarterly list of strategic alternatives to the way services are presently provided. MBO-required lists resemble a "cookie cutter" approach to strategic planning, but simplistic lists may be better than none.

Zero-base budgeting systems (ZBB), which had their day under President Carter, work in the same way as MBO. They require a formal alternative way of providing a service, with each alternative presented in the annual budget. Alternatives include contracting out, reducing, or redesigning the service.

Budget proposals could list a range of options without the formal analysis that ZBB required. The chief executive can require a yearly list of alternative strategies, to be proposed by research unit staffs after consultation with departmental officials.

Top managers and political executives bear some of the responsibility for encouraging strategic behavior. They need to do more formal and informal program experimentation. An example of this sort of experiment was tried in Kansas City. There, certain areas received heavier than normal police patrols, some areas received less than normal, and some areas received normal amounts. Police officials usually argue that heavy surveillance by officers reduces crime. However, in this case, it didn't.[48] Sacramento County tried to require that general assistance welfare clients use a county-provided boarding home instead of welfare payments to reduce total costs.[49] The plan worked, but a court case ruled that it violated the right to privacy of welfare recipients.

The most effective chief executives encourage such experimentation whenever possible. To a large degree, it is a mark of professionalism. Such experimentation is riskier to a politician, since failure is fair game for opponents. Hence, managers who work for a political executive may have a more difficult job in encouraging strategic behavior. But even then, concern for strategic behavior is one way that managers let their political superiors know that they care about improving services.

SUMMARY

Occasionally the need for good managers is clearly recognized. Economist and scholar, J. K. Galbraith, noted the need for strong public management:

> The solution is without novelty; it is highly professional public management. The democratic left must now address itself to the development of a force of public managers of the highest level of proficiency. There must be men and women who believe in public enterprise, take pride in seeing performance that improves upon private capitalism, and take a substantial part of their personal reward in their accomplishment.[50]

This chapter provided an analytical look at how highly proficient professional public managers make their organizations work. Their jobs have three parts: organizational maintenance, representation, and strategic planning. Maintenance is, briefly, operating the organization from day-to-day and from month-to-month. Representation is the public and ceremonial part of the manager's job, carried on outside the organization. At its worst, representation is mere public relations; at its best, it is public validation of the organization's commitment to public values. Planning is gaining agreement over long-range goals that guide day-to-day organizational activities.

This chapter treats three parts of the manager's job separately for analytical purposes. The Aurora case study described these activities and some of the organizational dynamics that affect them in reference to an actual executive's day. However, in real life, managers don't divide their time or efforts into maintenance, representation and planning—actually, they don't even think of their job in those terms. They do whatever is necessary to get the job done. The rest of this book examines different parts of the public manager's job, using these three analytical tools. The next chapter provides an overview of the way large-scale policies are made and how these policies affect the organizational decision-making process. The prism of maintenance, representation, and planning helps clarify the manager's part in organizational decision making.

NOTES

1. For example, Robert Simmons and Eugene Dvorin, *Public Administration, Values, Policy and Change* (New York: Alfred A. Knopf, 1977) is openly critical of "value free" public administration.

2. Luther Gulick, "Notes on the Theory of Organization," in Luther Gulick and Lyndall Urwick, eds., *Papers on the Science of Administration* (New York: Institute of Public Administration, 1937), pp. 3–46.

3. Joseph Massie, *Essentials of Management*, 3rd ed., (Englewood Cliffs, N.J.: Prentice-Hall, 1979), p. 7.

4. Alan Lau, Arthur Newman, and Laurie Broedling, "The Nature of Managerial Work in the Public Sector," *Public Administration Review*, (September–October 1980), pp. 513–20. This work was heavily influenced by the work of Henry Mintzberg, *The Nature of Managerial Work* (New York: Harper & Row, 1973), and found that Mintzberg's work on private executives could largely be extended to public executives.

5. Ibid., p. 517.

6. Ibid.

7. Mintzberg, *The Nature of Managerial Work*, p. 60.

8. For a further discussion of pressures on managers, see Thomas Clark, Jr., and William Shrode, "Public Sector Decision Structures: An Empirically Based Description," *Public Administration Review*, July–August 1979, pp. 343–54.

9. Marver Bernstein, *The Job of the Public Executive* (Washington, D.C.: Brookings Institution, 1958), pp. 50–51.

10. These quotations are from personal interviews during 1981 with California state executives holding career executive assignments (the highest-ranking permanent members of the civil service), referred to hereafter as Rehfuss, CEA research.

11. Rehfuss, CEA research.

12. Ronald Loveridge, *City Managers in Legislative Politics* (Indianapolis, In.: Bobbs-Merrill, 1970), p. 74.

13. Ibid.

14. Robert Caro, *The Power Broker* (New York: Random House, 1975); and "The Truth About Hoover," *Time*, December 22, 1975.

15. Rufus Miles, "The Origin and Meaning of Miles Law," *Public Administration Review*, September–October 1978, p. 399.

16. Ibid., 401.

17. Leon Sigal, "Bureaucratic Objectives and Tactical Use of the Press: Why Bureaucrats Leak," a paper presented to the American Political Association, Chicago, September 1971.

18. Hugh Heclo, *A Government of Strangers* (Washington, D.C.: Brookings Institution, 1977), p. 206.
19. Irene Rubin, *Shrinking the Federal Government* (New York: Longman, 1985), p. 183.
20. Delmer Dunn, *Public Officials and the Press* (Reading, Mass.: Addison-Wesley Publishing, 1969), pp. 59–85.
21. Frederick Malek, *Washington's Hidden Tragedy* (New York: Free Press, 1978), p. 55.
22. Frederick Malek, "Mr. Executive Goes to Washington," *Harvard Business Review*, September–October 1982, pp. 64–65.
23. Francis Rourke, "The Presidency and the Bureaucracy," in Frederick Lane, ed., *Current Issues in Public Administration* (New York: St. Martin's Press, 1986), p. 79.
24. Karen Smith, quoted in "The Nature of the Job," *Public Management*, January–February 1980, p. 11.
25. Rehfuss, CEA research.
26. Peter Drucker, *The Concept of the Corporation* (New York: Mentor Books, 1964).
27. For examples of strategic planning, see Charles Sumner, *Strategic Behavior in Business and Government* (Boston: Little, Brown, 1980).
28. Mary Louise Hatten, "Strategic Management in Not-For-Profit Organizations," *Strategic Management Journal*, September 1982, pp. 90–104.
29. Laurence Lynn, Jr., *Managing Public Policy* (Boston: Little, Brown, 1987), pp. 131–34.
30. Ibid., p. 146.
31. Ibid., p. 137.
32. Ibid.
33. Sumner, *Strategic Behavior*.
34. Ibid., p. 293.
35. Interview with Donald Rumsfeld, "A Politician Turned Executive," *Fortune*, September 10, 1979, p. 91.
36. George Schultz and Kenneth Dam, *Economic Policy Beyond the Headlines* (New York: Norton, 1977), p. 173.
37. Arthur Anderson and Company, *San Francisco's Strategic Plan* (San Francisco: Chamber of Commerce, February 1983), p. 1.
38. Ibid.
39. Marver Bernstein, *Job of the Public Executive*, p. 13.
40. Rehfuss, CEA interviews.
41. The TVA also has been accused of walking hand-in-hand with wealthy land owners and of being biased against blacks. In any case, it adjusted nicely to the area power structure, which is why it survived and grew.
42. David Lilienthal, *Democracy on the March* (New York: Harper & Row, 1944).
43. Philip Selznick, *Leadership in Administration* (New York: Harper & Row, 1957). See also Selznick, *TVA and the Grass Roots* (Berkeley: University of California, 1949).
44. Selznick, *Leadership in Administration*, p. 17.
45. Ibid., pp. 26–64.
46. Michael Moskow, *Strategic Planning in Business and Government* (New York: Committee for Economic Development, 1979), p. 20.

47. See Aaron Wildavsky, "The Self-Evaluating Organization," *Public Administration Review*, September–October 1972, pp. 509–20.
48. Robert Pursley and Neil Snortland, *Managing Public Organizations* (New York: Duxbury, 1980), pp. 389–90. See the section on program evaluation in Chapter 4 for more details on this experiment.
49. Interview with Mel Simonson, assistant director, Welfare Department, Sacramento County, California, December 1983.
50. John Kenneth Galbraith, *The New Republic* (August 16, 1975; August 23, 1975), p. 20.

CHAPTER 2

The Decision-Making Process

This chapter and the next two chapters describe different aspects of the public decision-making process. This chapter is about the process, Chapter 3 outlines the major actors in the process, and Chapter 4 discusses the use of managerial techniques in decision making.

The process of administrative decision making is not a series of crucial decisions that shape the organization. Dramatic decisions such as "You're fired!" or "Build the Supersonic Transport!" don't routinely occur during a chief executive's tenure.

In reality, administrative decision making resembles the broader U.S. policymaking process, which is why this chapter begins with an outline of the process. Managers who don't understand how this macro system works often have trouble in their organizations. The manager normally plays a judgmental role as proposed policies rise to the top of the hierarchy ("bubble up").

The maintenance role assures that the organizational decision-making job operates smoothly, that it can be modified when necessary, and that lower-level decisions are evaluated periodically. The manager knows that decisions are not rational (in a scientific sense), but incremental, and the manager judges the process from this perspective. Directing, observing, and coordinating the decision-making process are done in many different ways that demonstrate leadership in organizational management.

In administrative decision making, the issue of leadership and rationality in the decision making process are crucial, and this chapter devotes a section to each item. Understanding the complexity of decisions and demonstrating leadership over a range of decisions is part of how managers maintain their organizations.

Leadership involves organizational representation before hostile and friendly audiences or committees, as well as maintaining a public image that advances organizational objectives. Representation also includes convincing outside groups and individuals that the organization is making effective decisions and implementing top-level policies. This is the job of maintenance, but if it is done well, outsiders should know it.

Finally, leadership combined with awareness of the decision-making process makes strategic planning possible. The top executive can consider the organization's decisions and the direction in which they move the organization, modifying them as necessary and as politically, economically, and administratively feasible.

POLICYMAKING IN THE UNITED STATES

Policymaking in the United States involves four successive stages: initiation, persuasion, choosing (deciding), and implementation.[1]

Initiating Policy

Initiation is largely a "bubble-up" process for top-level decision makers. For large issues such as tax policy at the federal level or health care reimbursement at the state level, a wide range of groups propose numerous programs, suggest solutions to real and imagined problems, and advocate new legislation or revised administrative regulations. These groups come from inside and outside the government. With health care, they might include a range of professional groups that provide medical care such as: nurses and physician associations; private health insurance companies; contractors involved with hospital construction; hospital financing institutions; and racial, religious, or other private-citizen groups. Once a problem is identified, many of these groups and their legislative representatives present a plethora of solutions and comments. Michael Blumenthal, secretary of commerce in the Carter administration, described this process:

> In the government no one has the power to decide that this is the policy he wants to develop, these are the people who are going to develop it, this is how it's going to be decided, and these are the folks who are going to administer it. No one, not even the President, has that kind of power.
>
> Take . . . the framing of a U.S. economic policy toward Japan. If the President said to me, you develop one, Mike, the moment that it becomes known there are innumerable interest groups that begin to play a role. The House Ways and Means Committee, The Senate Foreign Relations Committee, the oversight committees, and then the interest groups, business, the unions, the State Department, Commerce Department, OMB, Council of Economic Advisers, and not only the top people, but all their people, not to speak of the President's staff and the entire press.
>
> So it's assigned to me, but I can't limit who gets in on the act. Everyone gets a piece of the action. I'm constantly amazed when I have the lead responsibility to find two people talking to each other and negotiating something–when I haven't assigned them any responsibility. They're not in the loop. But everyone wants to be in the loop.[2]

In state government, the following groups might be involved in the process of proposing solutions: legislative staffs, financial control agencies such as the Finance Department and the state treasurer, employee organizations, and program agencies such as Health Care Facilities Planning. Other levels of government, such as counties with hospitals, also will be involved.

Political leaders are less active in suggesting solutions than the groups just mentioned. While a legislator, governor, or agency head might initiate proposed legislation, it would probably be drafted by or in connection with one or more interested groups. Direct action by any policymaker without extensive consultation among interested groups is unusual. In this sense, policy formulation takes a strong judicial cast. Top leaders normally do not initiate solutions, but judge the value (defined as the amount of support) of proposals that "bubble up" from below.

The bubble-up process has evolved in the United States over many years. It's in marked contrast to a hierarchical system where decisions are handed down to citizens. There are several reasons for this behavior. First, the United States is a legalistic nation and top policymakers view their jobs as including "judicial" reaction to proposals that bubble up from others. The merits of ideas are judged against other proposals or against the status quo.

Secondly, U.S. citizens regard government as responsible for responding to needs expressed by groups or individuals rather than simply mandating solutions. Most officials wait for outside interests or actors to propose action. If no one asks for changes in a program or policy, its assumed that the program or policy is acceptable. Former Defense Secretary Donald Rumsfeld gave indirect credence to the reactive nature of most policymakers when he said:

> It is useful to ask whether you are working off your "in" basket or whether the organization is working off your "out" basket. If it's the former, you may be reacting rather than leading the organization toward agreed-upon priorities.[3]

When political leaders "work off their 'in' basket," they are implicitly waiting for issues and problems to bubble up from the organization rather than initiating action and "making the organization work off the 'out' box." Rumsfeld, by his proclaimed propensity to initiate action, prided himself as different than traditional political executives. Cabinet officers such as Rumsfeld or Robert McNamara, who played an initiating role as secretary of defense under Presidents Kennedy and Johnson, are viewed as "a strange phenomenon, because of their activist behavior."[4]

Persuasion

After policy initiation, the second step in the policymaking process is persuasion, which involves consensus building for a policy proposal and mobilizing support for it. This step precedes the actual choice of a policy. Many groups and individuals must be consulted. For large issues, the majority with some influence must support the proposed policy or at least be neutral. The existence of these interests is a fact of life for every policymaker. They can halt or drastically modify most proposals although they cannot necessarily get their own policies approved. No policymaker, for example, would dream of proposing specific gun control legislation without meeting at length with the National Rifle Association and the International Chiefs of Police. Therefore, many proposals are initiated in a loose, general form so they can be modified to attract support during the consensus-building stage.

Choice

The third step in the policymaking process is deciding among the feasible alternatives. Often the consensus-building process narrows the choice to one alternative, perhaps with some permutations. Thus, the choice becomes whether or not to select the alternative presented. Clearcut choices occur only when the consensus-building process results in a substantial preference for one choice. Frequently, proposals are vetoed by policymakers because they have insufficient support. In most cases, the decision stage is postponed for considerable lengths of time, either until a consensus is reached or until outside events force a decision to be made.

Policy choices are correct because they gather wide support. The social security system, adopted in the mid-1930s, reputedly was acceptable because liberal forces wanted to provide for the needy and elderly, while conservative forces wanted to reduce pressures for private pension plans. This suggests that social security was a good program because it had widespread support. Likewise, at the local level, an upperclass community may impose architectural controls on new commercial development to maintain its image. Such a decision is correct because most residents and the chamber of commerce like it, not because these controls are good planning practice.

Implementation

Implementation is the last step in the policymaking process. It often consumes more energy and time than all other steps combined. If the policy is complex or has many ramifications, execution will take months or years while quirks are ironed out, bottlenecks eliminated, and procedures developed. Delays are common and understandable. One reason for delay is that interest groups attempt to influence implementation. Conflict often arises when regulations will be written. It may take years to propose, publish, and revise controversial regulations. Failing here, disgruntled opponents may try to bar action by lawsuits.

The ambiguous nature of legislation often accounts for the snail's pace of implementation. The legislature may not be able to, or even want to, make hard choices between competing groups or interests. Small and large banks, for example, may be divided over a branch-banking proposal. Not wishing or able to choose one side or the other, the legislature may pass enabling legislation but leave to the executive branch the controversial and time-consuming task of writing the rules.

As mundane a subject as corner visibility can illustrate, in a small way, how the bubble-up process of policymaking works at the local level. The issue of visibility, a traffic safety issue, will arise from the traffic safety commission, from driver or pedestrian complaints, or from individual concerned citizens, some of whom may be politically ambitious and looking for an issue. The issue will bubble up to the council through Kiwanis Club debates, reports of accidents by the engineering staff, calls to council members from angry citizens, and by delegations of parents concerned about school children's safety.

The council, in formally hearing complaints and proposals, allows consensus to build and suggests a solution such as cutting shrubs back 20 feet from the street. Any opposition can be heard from homeowners, and the council can gauge the depth of support for a solution. The council then chooses among several alternatives.

At this time, the city manager and the traffic engineer will implement the policy. If the proposal is controversial but popular, these administrators may have to decide how high shrubs can remain, how far back from the street they must be reduced in height, which are the most dangerous corners, and where the city will begin enforcement.

As noted, policies can falter at the point of implementation because legislative bodies seeking a political compromise, deliberately pass vague laws. This is usually due to compromise, but it is occasionally designed to place the burden of handling situations that are unpredictable or controversial on the administration. This is true of corner cutbacks as well as branch banking and foreign policy.[5] When this occurs, managers and their agencies struggle to develop regulations and design operating procedures for legislation that does not deal with the problem clearly.

When implementation raises major problems, the process begins again as groups and officials propose solutions to the problems. Occasionally, environmental changes such as public opinion swings, tastes, or economic conditions cause reexamination of the issue, in which case the process begins anew, as Exhibit 2–1 indicates.

From Major Policies to Administrative Decisions

The policymaking process is the same at all levels of government and for most issues, from the U.S. policy toward the Middle East to a small park district's tree-planting program. Most of the same steps are taken, the same sequences appear. While policies and issues vary from level to level, to an onlooker from Mars, the process looks similar.

Organizational decision making, of more interest to most managers, differs from major policymaking primarily in the scope of matters considered. Organizational decisions primarily concern issues involving a department, agency, or other specialized unit. They involve smaller and more limited issues than major policies. It is here that managers become involved with decisions, since most rarely become deeply involved with major policies other than through implementation. Even so, every effective manager should understand societal policymaking, for organizational decision making follows the same steps.

THE MANAGER'S JOB IN THE ORGANIZATIONAL DECISION-MAKING PROCESS

Introduction

When people anticipate, observe, or participate in societal or organizational policymaking, they have become accustomed to a certain sequence of actions. Over the years, interested publics have come to expect that governmental decisions will be made in certain ways consistent with broad cultural values. These expectations are held by groups ranging from organizational subordinates to citizens and interests outside the organization. These groups presume that certain processes will be followed in making a decision, and that observing them is as important as the decision itself.

These expectations arise from the common method of making broad societal decisions described earlier. This process includes, for example, widespread participation and publicity. If these basic societal mores are not followed in making individual decisions at the managerial level, any given decision will be seen as invalid, regardless of content. The policymaking process legitimizes the process followed in public-sector decision making. Failure to follow it is dangerous for a manager.

Organization members and outside parties expect the manager to follow the same procedure for organizational decisions as in societal policymaking. Most managers use a bubble-up system of management; are satisfied with policies that are satisfactory to most groups; attempt to build consensus over specific decisions; and accept wide support as a definition of a correct decision. Of course, there are many exceptions, but these behaviors are typical of most managers. Readers who are disappointed at these "herd" tendencies should reflect on the fate of a manager who aggressively pushes his policies regardless of support, doesn't bother to build consensus, and doesn't care about support for his decisions.

EXHIBIT 2–1   The Policymaking Process in the United States

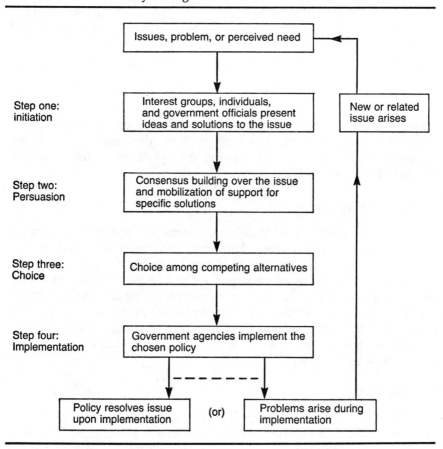

Step one: initiation	
Step two: Persuasion	
Step three: Choice	
Step four: Implementation	

Consider, for example, a tough manager who insists that "something has to get done." She may be right, and her vigorous stance will draw praise from persons who lionize "hard-chargers." Yet, in most cases, she runs a risk of alienating subordinates and outside supporting interests accustomed to more deliberate executive action. This will weaken the organization: all because she was not "judicial" enough. True, when the situation calls for aggressive leadership, failure to take charge also will be criticized. Thus, the life of an executive consists of walking a narrow tightrope between activism and caution.

Managers aren't condemned to a life of inactivity just because aggressive actions usually don't work. Most long-time managers learn to use the bubble-up management system. When they become convinced that more ideas need to come up through the hierarchy, they structure the organization to send them up or they plant ideas with lower-level executives. Clever, proactive managers create a bubble-up system instead of merely reacting to one that develops on its own. In this light, when managers need to move rapidly and aggressively but are afraid of resistance, the cleverest managers see that subordinates will demand action from above—negating potential opposition from below. The same approach can be taken with interests and groups outside the organization.

The top manager's primary job is to assure that administrative decision making occurs smoothly. Subordinates usually initiate the process, manage the details, help persuade others, have the day-to-day responsibility for implementation, and help evaluate the results. This is the process of organizational maintenance, and decisions are the more visible part of the process.

Persuading

Managers spend considerable time persuading others to approve ideas, programs, and policies. They may react judicially to ideas, but once they find a good idea, they become aggressive in promoting it. Legislators and administrative superiors and peers must be convinced. Clients must be informed, and their assent must be obtained. Subordinates often have to be mollified, for their failure to support the decision could ultimately sabotage it at the implementation stage. Once the support of most parties is assured, the decision can be made and the implementation stage will begin.

Delegating

Practically speaking, the public manager is rarely the significant decision maker in his or her organization. Why? The executive's job in the decision-making process is to assure that decisions are made by the right people at the right time. The manager is a facilitator, a monitor, a conflict resolver, one who announces decisions frequently not made by himself, and when decisions must be made at his level, a judge of last resort.

The public manager facilitates the administrative process by letting other actors make the minor decisions that affect their subunits. This means decentralizing authority. It means encouraging subordinates to settle their own problems. Sometimes it means refusing to let them pass difficult issues upstairs for the top manager to settle, because too much top-side decision making eventually destroys subordinate initiative.

Resolving Conflict

The public executive resolves conflict. Rather than decision making, this usually involves setting parameters within which subordinates must act, assigning responsibility for certain activities to one person, and listening while subordinates talk out their problems. Good managers motivate subordinates to achieve subunit goals, encourage their aspirations toward higher service levels or lower cost solutions, and console them when they feel low. Motivation involves both setting examples and providing solace and support. Experienced managers blend these elements expertly. This assures that decisions, 90 percent of which should be made at lower levels, are made by subordinates.

Announcing Decisions

Top managers often announce decisions that, while formally made by the executive, were actually made by a group, by subordinates, or by consensus. Announcement legitimizes them, because the chief executive is ultimately responsible. This process, seemingly artificial if not dishonest, is necessary. If the manager insists on making or becoming involved in every minor decision, she will soon find that action has slowed as subordinates push problems up to her for solution. Meanwhile, subordinates' commitment to their jobs weakens as their responsibility declines.

City planning is an example. A city manager may be responsible for the town zoning ordinance. However, if he overrules the planner on technical zoning issues, he risks losing that planner's commitment. If he insists on making each decision in implementing the ordinance, he may lose the planner and multiply the number of poor decisions. Excessive top-level involvement in lower-level decisions destroys subordinate initiative and slows operations by bucking matters up an additional level. In addition, it generally results in poorer decisions because top-level policy considerations have been injected into purely technical considerations. Sometimes, rather than providing top-level considerations, the executive simply substitutes his own opinion. In such cases, the city has one too many planners.

This is why good managers usually content themselves with announcing or ratifying lower-level decisions even though they might not have made the same decision. They don't flyspeck lower-level decisions because this destroys morale and wastes time. While these are primarily administrative reasons, there are also sound policy reasons. Wise managers know that too much involvement in minor decisions often incapacitates them for important policy decisions.

Certain situations demand top-level decisions. Two subunits may struggle over authority for a program. A choice among projects may be so delicate that the decision can only be made top-side. A key subordinate position may have to be filled. These decisions call for top-level judgment. However, experienced managers try to reduce the number of decisions they make. They refuse to settle issues that could be well-settled at lower levels. They act on consensus from subordinates whenever possible. They solicit information and advice from other sources, from peers, and from subordinates, and attempt to make the decision reflect the best judgment of the organization. One way to do this is to reduce the number of top-level decisions and increase the number made at lower levels.

GENERAL MANAGERIAL DECISION-MAKING BEHAVIOR

Managerial actions in persuading, delegating, resolving conflict, and announcing decisions are specific examples of a more general process. This process falls into three parts. The first part is ensuring that the process is initiated or, when necessary, modified. Decisions must be made at the right time and by the proper persons (persons at the right level in the organization). Second, the manager must control the decision-making process, ensuring that subordinates implement previous decisions effectively. This means that while close communication with the subordinate is important, the manager must have an independent means of monitoring lower-level performance. Finally, since monitoring performance is too important to be done occasionally or randomly, top managers must create a system that evaluates program accomplishment regularly.

The significance of this cycle for managers is that when done properly, it creates a system that allows, even forces, subordinates to make decisions at the right time. No experienced top manager ever tries to manage subunit programs alone or make all the decisions about those programs.

This keeps managerial attention riveted on major issues rather than on routine operations, which is what top managers are paid to do. Managerial decision-making responsibilities call for the creation and maintenance of an organizational system that decentralizes decisions to the lowest possible level. This is hardly news by now, but the point is crucial for effective organizational maintenance. Thomas Edison once said that genius is 99 percent perspiration and 1 percent inspiration. Managerial effectiveness is also 99 percent hard work in ensuring that the system works well—not the 1 percent brilliance of a spectacular decision.

Initiating the Decision-Making Process

The first step in the manager's decision-making task is to ensure that subordinates make effective and timely decisions. The manager is often a prod. Deadlines always have to be met. One joke is that the only person who can force Congress to make a decision on the federal budget is the government printer—through printing deadlines. However, there are real deadlines. Timeliness in a program involves hiring staff, developing client linkages, creating positive relationships with other agencies and individuals, creating a reporting system, and buying equipment.

The task is to galvanize subordinates into action—to prod, support, encourage, and if necessary, coerce them into making decisions that move a program along. A subordinate such as the director of public works (DPW) will spend time scheduling street paving and cleaning, digging water wells, and replacing traffic signals. The task of the manager is not to ask how well these jobs are done. This question comes later. The first task is assuring that the DPW has a management system (i.e., a decision-making system) in place. In small cities, citizen complaints and lack of staff often inhibit long-range planning by the DPW. In larger cities, supervision of a large staff may distract the DPW's time from long-term planning. With no long-term planning for operations by the DPW, it's unlikely that services will be maintained over time. The job of the manager is to serve as a motivator, confidante, supporter, and whatever else is required to refocus the DPW's attention on the long- and short-term decisions he needs to make at that level.

For every subordinate who puts off decisions or tries to "buck" them upstairs, there is another subordinate who manages the department well and becomes a strong advocate for more resources. Most managers prefer aggressive subordinates. It's easier to review decisions for comprehensiveness and balance than it is to cajole a subordinate into making decisions. One reason that managers prefer such subordinates is that it provides a better opportunity to examine their decision-making system. Their requests for additional resources provide this opportunity.

Controlling the Decision-Making Process

Controlling the decision-making process is the second managerial job. This establishes a program monitoring system for which the manager is ultimately responsible. The purpose is not to look over a subordinate's shoulders, but to assure that her decisions are reviewed periodically. The first step, initiation, ensures that subordinates make the decisions necessary for managing their programs. This second step, controlling, frees the manager from dependence on information the subordinate chooses to give. Independent checks must be available.

Many techniques provide a basis for evaluating subordinate decisions, although they are not generally known as decision-making techniques. Chapter 4 covers them in detail. Management by objective (MBO) is a way to periodically appraise subordinate performance. Evaluation commonly is based on mutually agreeable criteria that represent actual performance, such as miles of streets swept, or in more sophisticated cities, cost-per-mile of streets swept. Accomplishment of the goal presumes that the proper decisions were made, while failure to perform starts discussions of what happened. This highlights which decisions were made.

Program evaluation review technique (PERT) and the critical path method (CPM) are administrative techniques to control and monitor the progress of projects. As far as the decision-making process goes, these techniques provide a series of check points that inform decisionmakers if the project is on schedule. For simple projects, they can be used to schedule activities as diverse as notifying citizens of street closings, the acquisition of salt for winter months, and similar ideas. Failure to meet schedules causes a review of the decisions made to date.

While MBO and PERT or CPM serve different purposes, they have similar results. These techniques allow managers to monitor subordinate decisions without being too obtrusive.

Evaluating

The third part of the public manager's job is to create some process to evaluate programs or projects after completion. This is the final management step of the organizational decision-making process, which follows initiation and monitoring.[6] Program evaluation is covered more fully in Chapter 4.[7] It's important here because of the decisions that it may call for. A formal evaluation point naturally leads to a decision about continuing, modifying, or abandoning the program. Thus, the triad of initiating, monitoring (controlling), and evaluating continues.

With permanent programs, evaluation is a simple review of operations and costs. The chief executive may be satisfied that operations are periodically reviewed at lower levels. For new or modified programs, however, the chief may ask for a formal evaluation. Usually, a formal evaluation compares costs to comparable programs, accomplishments to program goals, and so on. Often a formal research design compares actual program achievements with achievements prior to the new program. Decisions about the program follow this evaluation.

All evaluations are not cold-blooded, analytical comparisons of costs to benefits; some are much more judgmental about the basic nature of decisions. These are often part of strategic planning, somewhat like the concept of restoring equilibrium in Chapter 1. Gordon Chase, who held top positions in all three levels of government, speaks of his evaluation policies as administrator of the New York City Health Services Administration:

> I can remember, when I first became administrator of the New York City Health Services Administration (the first nonphysician to hold that position), that I would call in my commissioners and senior managers and ask

them what they'd been doing—what their agencies or units or programs had been up to in the last few weeks or months or years.

Some of these senior officials would start by telling me how many meetings they had attended, how many memos they'd written, how many staff they'd hired, and similar benchmarks of bureaucratic activity. I'd look at them and say: "But whom did you make healthy today (or last week, or last year)? Did you make anyone in New York healthier—and how do you know?"

In short order people came to realize where I wanted my emphasis—not on the mechanics of running public agencies but on the outcome of the services we were there to deliver. It's not that I didn't understand the importance of dealing with the chief, overhead agencies, and the rest of the characters in our daily fare; it's just that I wanted my managers to be conscious of the fact that we were there to make people healthier, and not to lose sight of that fact in the daily squabblings that we all had to endure.[8]

HOW RATIONAL IS THE DECISION-MAKING PROCESS?

The quote from Gordon Chase shows that managers are human beings filled with emotions, commitments, and values. They are cool, calculating machines on rare occasions. They don't calculate and plan every step in the decision-making process. Chase did not calculate from his first day on the job just how managers would make New Yorkers healthier. Intuitively, most people recognize this. It's a bit surprising, then, that traditional theories about decision making, until as late as the 1950s, didn't completely take the human factor into account.

At one time, theorists believed that the decision-making process was an orderly, step-by-step consideration of alternatives followed by a final choice. Now there is debate over whether the decision-making process is, can, or should be truly rational. Almost everyone agrees that many shortcomings exist in the decision-making process and that it could be improved. Not all agree that more formal rationality would improve the process, although this view is held by many scholars, who want the process more aligned with scientific method.

The scientific method generally involves the following pattern:

1. Identify the problem.
2. Clarify the values and preferences of the decision maker and rank them in order of importance.
3. Examine all possible alternatives for dealing with the problem.
4. Identify all consequences, costs, and benefits associated with each alternative.
5. Evaluate each alternative and its consequences in comparison with all other consequences.
6. Select the alternative that maximizes the decision maker's values.

Unfortunately, life isn't arranged into six tidy sequential steps. Problems are fuzzily defined, sometimes in contradictory ways. Values and preferences of decision makers are ill-defined. Managers don't know what they want until they know what they can get. As an example, consider whether a police chief wants a salary hike of 10 percent for members of his department or eight new patrol officers with no payhike, if he has no idea of the probability of getting either. No one, including the chief, will be able to decide. The chief will hedge, and search for more information, rather than clarify his choices or identify the consequences.

No decision maker has time, energy, or staff to study all the consequences of any action, let alone all alternatives. Thus, she cannot compare them. Even if comparison were possible, it would be little help if objectives were not prioritized—and most decision-maker's objectives and values are not prioritized. Actually, the public manager reviews only the most obvious solutions, spending most of her time identifying their costs and consequences.

The following considerations catch the manager's attention. Is a new proposal politically feasible, or at least unlikely to rouse opposition? Can it attract budgetary support? Can it be staffed and managed if it is approved? Does it solve a problem for the manager, her superior, or the legislature?

These are crude, inexact questions—a far cry from pure rationality. In fact, the executive *satisfices*,[9] meaning that he searches for the first solution which suffices to meet the decision and satisfies the decision maker. This strategy is called *incrementalism*. It handles problems in a way that doesn't prevent later reversals. The decisionmaker avoids radical solutions in favor of small, sequential steps. It is easier to solve unforseeable bottlenecks when they arise than to spend time planning how to avoid them. The decisionmaker also expects to make continuous mutual adjustments with other decisionmakers and environmental forces at each point along the way.

Incrementalism is recognition of the limited power of the human mind and the lack of information on most topics. It is called incremental because changes occur in small increments from the existing policy rather than in large movements constituting a sweeping change in policy. Since few policies or programs are suddenly changed significantly, incrementalism describes both the real world of policymaking in the United States and routine organizational decision making. Thus, individual decision makers are psychologically and organizationally predisposed to consider issues incrementally. The debate between scholars is not over whether decision making is incremental but whether this is desirable. Some scholars laud this, while others are distressed.

Lindblom argues that it's more reasonable to make continual incremental adjustments than to try to predict in advance all possible results of a decision.[10] Wildavsky argues for a partisan adversary system in which affected interests argue for their own advantage in administrative or legislative decisions.[11] This will most likely account for the multiplicity of values involved. It also assures that the system remains incremental, since powerful contending interests make it difficult for sweeping change to occur.

Critics such as Dror regard the incremental method as likely to: (1) overlook further needed information, (2) ignore comprehensive decisions when the situation calls for them, and (3) needlessly perpetuate the status quo. This may be true, but it's largely an academic plea for theoretical rationality.[12] Whether Dror is right or not, managers don't operate in this way. "Managers are in an ambiguous environment requiring reaction rather than reflection."[13]

A modified form of incrementalism called *logical incrementalism*, has been suggested by James Quinn. It is called logical partly because it does not rely on political or power interactions.

> The most effective strategies of major enterprises tend to emerge step by step from an iterative process in which the organization probes the future, experiments, and learns from a series of partial (incremental) commitments rather than from global formulations of total strategies. Good managers are aware of this process, and they consciously intervene in it. . . . The process is both logical and incremental. Such logical incrementalism is not muddling, as most people understand that word. Properly managed, it is a conscious, purposeful, proactive, executive practice.[14]

Quinn puts forth the best possible case for incrementalism. His position is justified, since incrementalism has proven a rational system for managers. Without time, energy, or intellect to look for the best solution, managers happily accept a better solution. In many cases, however, neither muddling through or logical incrementalism succeeds in finding an acceptable decision. Exhibit 2–2, discussing Red Dye #3, indicates that managerial decision-making environments sometimes ensure that only marginal changes are possible.

Persons who wish to improve the decision-making process usually have in mind the errors, miscalculations, unintended consequences, wrong premises, and blunders associated with national policy decisions. These include the Cuban Bay of Pigs invasion, the Vietnam War, the series of miscalculations about Great Society programs, and the tax revenue from supply-side economics. Critics of such decision-making processes want to improve problem identification, reduce the impact of the "group-think" phenomenon,[15] widely examine alternatives and their consequences, and so on.

EXHIBIT 2–2   Incrementalism and Red Dye

On February 1 (1985) the Food and Drug Administration put off a decision to ban six artificial colors that have been found to cause cancer in test animals. To those who haven't been following this proposed regulation, the delay could hardly have been a surprise: it was the 26th time that the agency had postponed action since the proposal was first made, in 1960. . . .

The proposal dealing with the six coal-tar or petroleum-based colors, which include Red Dye No. 3, used extensively in baked goods, beverages, dessert powders, cereals, maraschino cherries, ice cream, candy and vitamins, has had a particularly stormy—and to many, frustrating—journey through regulatory channels. It has involved many animal experiments, several lawsuits, a special hearing by a Congressional oversight committee and pressure from both consumer groups that want the food colorings banned and from industry lobbyists who seek their continued use. . . .

Those in favor of the proposal argue that Red Dye No. 3 has been proved to cause cancer in animals; citing provisions of the Delaney Amendment, they argue that it should thus be summarily banned. Enacted into law in 1960, the amendment to the Federal Food, Drug and Cosmetic Act states that any substance whose ingestion has been linked to cancer in either humans or animals must be banned. It leaves no room for assessment of risk. . . .

Industry lawyers, some officials at the Department of Health and Human Services and the Office of Management and Budget, however, contend that the Delaney Amendment is too dogmatic and have suggested that it be reinterpreted to allow for risk assessment in humans. . . .

In October 1984, Representative Ted Weiss, Democrat of New York, conducted a Congressional oversight hearing on why action on the proposal to ban the colors was taking so long. Mr. Weiss, Chairman of the Intergovernmental Relations and Human Services Subcommittee, questioned Dr. Brandt, a number of FDA officials, including Dr. Novitch (acting FDA Commissioner) and Dr. Miller (Director of the FDA Center for Food Safety), and representatives of the industry's trade association. At the end of the daylong hearings, Representative Weiss concluded that industry pressure was responsible for keeping all the colors on the market. . . .

FDA Scientists and commissioners, as well as the assistant secretary of Health and Human Services, have recommended that the additive be banned. Mr. Weiss said in a telephone interview, "But there has been tremendous pressure from the Office of Management and Budget, from industry and otherwise on Secretary Heckler's office to delay the recommendation from being implemented. . . ."

The "other" pressure cited by Mr. Weiss included two letters sent to Margaret Heckler, Secretary of Health and Human Services, in May, one signed by eight senators and the other by 30 House members. They asked that a decision to ban Red Dye No. 3 be deferred until further studies are completed. The legislators, many of whom represent states where canned fruits and maraschino cherries are produced, said the ban would "cause an immediate economic effect—the public will shun any substance for which a ban has been proposed."

EXHIBIT 2–2 (*concluded*)

January 22 the Health Research Group once again sued the FDA to ban the dyes. The suit is pending. February 1 the FDA again extended, until April 1, the provisional listing of the colors. . . .

SOURCE: Excerpted from Marian Burros, "The Saga of a Food Regulation: after 25 Years, Still No Decision," *New York Times*, February 13, 1985, p. C1. Copyright © 1985 by the New York Times Company. Reprinted by permission.

Top career officials rarely have to deal with these types of questions. Occasionally, some issues require a Bay of Pigs type of organizational decision. These include choices of whether or not to ally the agency with a new interest group, whether or not to initiate a new program or whether a sweeping reorganization would solve management problems. There have been cases where managerial decision making has been guilty of the same group-think phenomenon or miscalculation of consequences that have occurred with larger national policy decisions. But these are few, because public executives rarely deal with such global issues.

Even for major organizational decisions, managers usually are limited to (or, as critics would charge, limit themselves to) incremental decisions. Getting more information, avoiding group think, or making better calculation of consequences might improve decision making, but it would not make it rational. Decision making is still an art.

LEADERSHIP

An important element in the decision-making process is leadership. It, too, is an art, not a science. It cannot be taught, and while it is somehow learned, at least by persons who are good administrative leaders, the exact process is a mystery. As Secretary of State Dean Acheson once said of his distinguished career, "all I learned was at my mother's knee and other low places."

Leadership Is Situational

The key aspect of leadership is that it is situational—that is, it is best understood as an individual or group of individuals' response to a specific administrative situation. It is not a trait that some people possess, such as stature (although that may help), or wit (sometimes that helps too), or brainpower, or charisma, or even friends in high places. It is all of these at times, and none of these at times. It depends on the administrative situation at the time, and different issues and times call for different behaviors. A situation may call for leadership, but the need for it does not mean that it will appear, for leadership is elusive. It is even difficult to define leadership, other than describing it as social behavior designed to achieve organizational goals at a point in time.

Some scholars, unimpressed with what passes for leadership in organizations, argue that leadership is dispensable in all but the most unusual cases. Leadership is necessary only when the organization undergoes basic transformation. This occurs when the organization is becoming an institution, as described in Chapter 1. Short of these radical changes, most organizations can get by with good management alone.[16]

Arguing that leadership is only good management is arguing over definitions. No matter what one calls it, however, public executives have to exhibit it both in moments of organizational stress and over years of routine activity. In time of stress, it holds an organization together. In routine times, leadership sets standards of behavior that maintain the organization's equilibrium. Many executives need to exhibit high standards of behavior for large organizations to work—but if top management does not exhibit leadership, the work of underlings may be wasted.

Gordon Chase showed leadership as administrator of the New York City Health Services Administration by reordering departmental priorities toward the health of the individual. A small thing, but an act often not done. It also arose from a specific situation, and the combination of individual and situation was unique.

This chapter's case study of San Diego indicates that administrative efficiency and some organizational planning arose from a one-time decision to house all department heads in one place. Was that leadership or just good management? It's impossible to draw a clear line, but if leadership is pushing or forcing organizational decisions that might not be made, City Manager Fletcher was a leader.

Leadership Examples

Leaders come in a variety of sizes and shapes, with quite different qualities and traits, and demonstrates their leadership in a wide range of situations. Some leaders are truly charismatic, almost as if their leadership was based on some "gift of God."[17] Today's version of the centuries old Asian warrior-king who led by fear and example is the manager who develops a public agency from nothing but the force of his personality and hard work. Hyman Rickover, who drove the navy into the atomic age through his effective advocacy of the nuclear submarine, is such an example.

Some leadership by example is quiet and barely noticeable. Any agency undergoing stress needs calm leadership at the top to reassure organizational members and to keep the agency from flying apart. Confidence, optimism, and continuity are forms of leadership. One could argue that active rather than passive leadership is required, that the manager only demonstrates leadership by restoring the organization to a stable position. This ignores the fact that many organizations today will never return to their previous position of strength, and a definition limiting leadership to attaining or retaining organizational prominence rules out much behavior that most observers would call leadership. Most organization members would settle for managerial resoluteness and continuity while they try to ride out the storm.

In another case, the organization may desperately need public visibility and support. The manager, by her continuous participation in community activities, constant speeches to various groups, and appearances on radio or television, may achieve important organizational goals. This, too, constitutes leadership.

Leadership can be found in many organizational situations. While nothing guarantees that it will arise when needed, most observers would agree that the above managerial actions constitute leadership. However, each is quite different. Are there any consistent factors that constitute leadership, or any consistent behaviors that leaders exhibit?

Leadership Qualities and Behaviors

There are innumerable ways to describe the behavior of administrative leaders. Some emphasize traits, others emphasize skills, and still others emphasize behaviors. However, this diversity indicates that leadership is so complex that it cannot be reduced to a simple set of qualities, traits, or behaviors.

One view looks at the roles that organizational leaders play.[18] The first role is a director, who is responsible for reconciling organizational and personal goals. Directors try to make personal and organizational goals overlap, and to bind organization members to organizational goals. Their role is like an organizational sociologist. Convincing ambitious staffers that organizational growth, an organizational goal, will help their personal goals is an example of this process. The convergence of organizational goals of growth and influence with personal goals of power and security are explained in Chapter 3.

The leader is a coordinator of organizational activities. This is, using an old phrase, making a "mesh of things." Since these activities are increasingly complex and the manager cannot know much about each one, it means that he must be able to work with a wide range of specialists—binding their disparate activities to the larger organization.

The leader is a catalyst and innovator for the organization. This sparkplug role varies greatly from organization to organization. Essentially, the leader is responsible for seeing that the organization moves ahead, for stimulating group action, and for being the focal point for new ideas. He is the yeast in the organizational bread loaf, responsible for growth and vitality. A more sophisticated view suggests that growth and vitality are crucial for all organizations, and that effective leaders find a way to spur this growth.

The leader is also the external spokesperson for the organization. This role is largely identical with the job of organizational representation. This role is important to organizational members, who often expect strong agency advocacy before outside groups such as legislative bodies or the press.

The last leadership role is crisis manager. The leader has to deal effectively with various crises that beset each organization, such as changes in mission, revised expectations of outside interest groups, and the occasional charge that the agency fails to provide adequate services to clients. Recently, crises have arisen because of budget cuts, and the question becomes how the agency should respond to a seemingly permanent problem. Chapter 9 discusses this question in terms of cutback management.

Traits and Skills

This view interprets leadership as a set of roles. Just as common is the view that leadership is a set of traits. This is not the traditional view that certain traits, such as height or intelligence, are associated with leaders. Traits are closer to skills, which largely involve complex behaviors. Lynn suggests that leaders:

1. See problems in a different way (their perspectives are different than their subordinates, perhaps because of their different hierarchical positions).
2. Convince and teach their subordinates.
3. Perform symbolic acts for their organization (perhaps thus reaffirming the organization's value).
4. Deal effectively with people and with centers of power and influence (this is true almost by definition since no one ascends to top positions without such skills).
5. Solve problems both of substance and process. The methods vary depending on the situation, but the key is that leaders involve themselves with problems rather than avoiding them.
6. Define and represent the values and aspirations of the organization. (This is the job of organizational representation.)[19]

Another similar approach is that of Harry Levinson, who focuses on "dimensions of leader's personalities." His emphasis is on choosing chief executives for large corporations, whose jobs include leadership.

Paraphrased and simplified, his dimensions include:

1. Having the ability to conceptualize and synthesize a range of data.
2. Having a tolerance for ambiguity.
3. Possessing practical as well as abstract intelligence.
4. Showing good judgment in knowing when to act.
5. Being comfortable with authority.
6. Demonstrating proactive approaches to organizational problems.
7. Being achievement-oriented toward organizational goals.
8. Being sensitive to interpersonal behavioral cues.
9. Having a deep involvement in the life of the organization.
10. Possessing personal maturity.
11. Remaining independent while accepting criticisms and comments from others.
12. Being articulate.
13. Possessing personal stamina.
14. Being adaptable and flexible.
15. Having a sense of humor.
16. Having a clear idea of the organization's goals and how one's career fits into those goals.
17. Persevering in a task.
18. Being well organized.
19. Possessing personal integrity.
20. Willingness to assume social responsibility.[20]

These dimensions were developed with corporate managers in mind, and many are simply measures of an effective manager, such as being well organized. However, some have a significant impact on the ability of public managers to become organizational leaders. The ability to tolerate ambiguity, to operate in an unstructured situation without losing confidence (to keep your cool in a tough and unsettling situation) is crucial in public agencies that are in increasingly turbulent and stressful situations.

Personal stamina is becoming more important, as situations become more stressful and long-lasting. The ability to perform well under pressure for long periods is a significant requirement for effective leadership.

Another dimension of behavior receiving more emphasis in contemporary times involves personal integrity. The newspapers are full of examples of aberrant personal behavior, from Watergate through Irangate, and there are examples of organization members who have failed themselves and their organizations. Personal rectitude is badly needed, both because is is intrinsically important and because it can help restore public confidence in government agencies. Chapter 10 discusses ethical behavior in more detail.

A final desirable characteristic of leaders is a sense of humor. A sense of humor, in Levinson's phrase, includes behavior that eases tensions, which contributes to more effective management. A sense of humor can do more than that. In pressure-filled organizational settings, it also can preserve the psychological balance of the top executive. It means being able to laugh at the incongruity of position limits and increased workloads. Someone who cannot laugh at such situations and themselves will probably crack under pressure.

The need to identify leadership talent is crucial to public agencies. Whether one approaches it from a trait or a behavioral point of view, a study of leadership is intimately intertwined with effective management in today's public organizations. Managers, by personal example, coolness under fire, commitment to the organization, and integrity, keep organizations from unraveling under pressures and bind their subordinates to the organization. These behaviors and attitudes constitute leadership in today's organizations.

SUMMARY

Organizational decision making is a complex process—far from the image of some heroic leader charismatically choosing a single alternative. In reality, few decisions are actually made by top-level executives, and many times the executive ratifies or announces either joint decisions or decisions that were made lower in the organization. Good managers spend much of their time assuring themselves that lower-level managers are making effective operating decisions. They are also concerned that only top-level decisions wend their way up the organization, so that subordinates settle those matters for technical rather than policy reasons.

These concerns about the smooth operation of the decision-making system are the task of organizational maintenance. To the extent that they must be defended or explained outside the organization, they involve organizational representation. Finally, as reviews of the decision-making process reveal larger issues than the decisions themselves, managers hopefully are forced to deal with strategic planning issues.

The decision-making process, contrary to some views, is not a rational exercise. Attempts to portray it as scientific miss the mark. Decision making is both an art and an incremental process. Decisions are made sequentially in bits and pieces after reviewing a limited number of alternatives.

Organizational decision making mirrors the entire policymaking process in the United States. National policies are developed out of a bubble-up process in which subordinates or public groups identify problems and suggest solutions. The initiation process is followed by a persuasion period in which solutions compete for political support. Top leaders engage in a support-building process which, if successful, results in some acceptable policy being ratified by leaders. The decision is followed by an implementation stage, which may consume as much time as the first three stages.

This, with some exceptions, is the process followed at organizational levels. Perhaps the major difference is that aggressive managers may initiate more organizational action than top-level politicians. Inside the organization, more aggressive managers frequently play an advocacy role and a judicial role in policy initiation.

The manager's job is not primarily to make decisions, but to assure that lower-level managers make them at the right time for the right reasons. The manager is generally a reviewer of lower-level decisions. She must make sure that subordinates have initiated the program review process so that lower-level decisions are timely. Controlling the lower-level decision-making process is the second responsibility for managers. This involves creation and maintenance of an ongoing monitoring system to review operations. This action prevents the manager from complete dependency on subordinate information. The final step is formal evaluation of ongoing and new or modified programs.

Through the whole process, the ability of the manager to lead subordinates is crucial, whether leadership comes from force of character, skill, or example. Good managers exhibit leadership as they pursue organizational goals through one means or another. Leadership, a slippery concept, emerges from specific situations in unpredictable ways. Yet, some constants remain, such as managerial ability to tolerate ambiguity, to manifest high ethical standards, and to maintain a sense of humor. These skills and behaviors make managerial leadership possible and facilitate the decision-making process.

Case Study 2–1

HOW TO GET DEPARTMENT HEADS TO DO LONG-RANGE PLANNING

Tom Fletcher, assistant manager of San Diego, California in 1961, looked at the relationship between department heads and their assistants:

I found that traditionally the position of assistant department head was not a line but a staff position. If they had a choice, division heads and departmental employees would always go straight to the department head rather than to or through an assistant. This created two problems. The department heads were so involved in the administrivia of their departments that they didn't have time to do the more important things that they really wanted to do as department heads. Frustration was the obvious result—for assistants as well as department heads. All these assistants, appointed from line positions, were disgruntled to find themselves in a staff role.

But how to correct these frustrations? Simply telling people to change their role and habits doesn't work. Given a choice between taking your problem to a department head or to an assistant, there will always be a tendency to go to the top person. Heading off that option when the department head is sitting right there frustrates everyone. The need was to clearly differentiate the two positions. The logical way would be to make the assistant responsible for day-to-day administration and let the department head be responsible for longer-range departmental affairs.

Fletcher became city manager later in 1961, with his first project to assign space in a new city hall. Recalling the department head assistant problems, he took an unusual step. Department heads were moved into the same suite of offices with the city manager. The assistants were to stay with the departments in charge of day-to-day affairs. The department heads were enthusiastic. Only the police chief,

fire chief, and librarian, whose departments were not moving to city hall, stayed with their departments.

Why were they willing to leave their departments to be in the same offices with the city manager? Fletcher recalls three reasons. First, they would get freedom from day-to-day responsibilities so they could function more as department heads; second, they would get to work more closely with other department heads, and third, they would get closer to the city manager and his staff. The manager, in return, pledged to deal only with them and not the assistants.

The experiment worked. The auditor/controller later remarked:

I've never worked so hard in my life. Getting me out of the routine problems of my department has meant that I have been able to concentrate on the more important problems of the department, and that's tough but very productive work. You couldn't get me to leave now with a twenty mule team.

The suite of offices for the department heads was occupied in 1965. Later the police and fire chiefs and the librarian chose to join the other department heads on the ninth floor. Fletcher believes this idea worked partly because the department heads had to move to a new city hall anyway. In addition, three of the department heads had previously had experience working together in a

superdepartment and had enjoyed
the experience of working closely
together.

SOURCE: Thomas Fletcher, "Cloud Nine," in LeRoy Harlow, ed., *Servants of All* (Provo, Utah: Brigham Young University Press, 1981), pp. 215–20.

NOTES

1. The basis for the discussion about U.S. policymaking is from Zbigniew Brzezinski and Samuel Huntington, *Political Power: USA/USSR* (New York: Viking Press, 1963), chapter 4.

2. Michael Blumenthal, "Candid Reflections of a Businessman in Washington," *Fortune*, January 29, 1979, p. 44.

3. Interview with Donald Rumsfeld, former secretary of defense and current president and chief executive officer of G. D. Searle and Company, "A Politician Turned Executive Surveys Both Worlds," *Fortune*, September 10, 1979, p. 91.

4. Brzezinski and Huntington, *Political Power: USA/USSR* p. 203.

5. See Chapter 5, legislative oversight, for an expansion of this point.

6. Jeffrey Pressman and Aaron Wildavsky, *Implementation* (Berkeley: University of California Press, 1973). They show how the process of control review and evaluation often fails at evaluation.

7. See Harry Hatry et al., *Program Analysis for State and Local Governments* (Washington, D.C.: The Urban Institute, 1976).

8. Gordon Chase and Elizabeth Reveal, *How To Manage in the Public Sector* (New York: Random House, 1983), pp. 177–78.

9. Herbert Simon, *Administration Behavior* (New York: Macmillan, 1957), preface to 2nd ed.

10. Charles Lindblom, *The Policy Making Process* (Englewood Cliffs, N.J.: Prentice-Hall, 1968).

11. Aaron Wildavsky, *The Politics of the Budgetary Process*, 2nd ed., (Boston: Little, Brown, 1974), pp. 166–67.

12. Yezhekial Dror, "Muddling Through—Science or Inertia?" *Public Administration Review*, September 1964, pp. 153–57. Also see Amatai Etzioni, "Mixed Scanning—A Third Approach to Decision-Making," *Public Administration Review*, December 1967, pp. 385–92.

13. Thomas Clark and William Schrode, "Public-Sector Decision Structures: An Empirically Based Description," *Public Administration Review*, July–August 1979, pp. 434–54.

14. James Quinn, *Strategies for Change: Logical Incrementalism* (Homewood, Ill.: Richard D. Irwin, 1980), p. 58. Quoted in Grover Starling, *Managing the Public Sector*, 3rd ed. (Homewood, Ill.: Dorsey Press, 1986), p. 183.

15. Irving Janis, *Victims of Group Think* (Boston: Houghton-Mifflin, 1972).

16. Philip Selznick, *Leadership* (New York: Harper & Row, 1957).

17. H. H. Gerth and C. Wright Mills, *From Max Weber* (New York: Oxford University Press, 1946), provides a good outline of Weber's famous discussion of charismatic leadership.

18. George Gordon, *Public Administration in America*, 3rd ed., (New York: St. Martin's Press, 1986), pp. 274–97, provides additional details on these roles.
19. Laurence Lynn, Jr., *Managing Public Policy* (Boston: Little, Brown, 1987), pp. 119–24.
20. Harry Levinson, "Criteria for Choosing Chief Executives," *Harvard Business Review*, July–August, 1980, pp. 114–16.

CHAPTER 3

The Decision-Making Process—Goals and Actors

Chapter 2 showed that decision making is far from a rational process. It's not done in sanitized laboratories by people coldly calculating their alternatives and weighing the consequences on a precise scale. It's a messy, unpredictable process in which managers, groups, interests, chief executives, and legislatures struggle. While these parties contend for power, it alone doesn't explain everything. Effective leadership, for example, accounts for much of what happens. Other forces than leadership and power are at work. Nevertheless, it's useful to think of the decision-making process as a struggle in which each party tries to achieve certain objectives. Therefore, this chapter is about the actors in the administrative decision-making process and their goals.

Chapter 2 emphasized how important it is for public managers to make the organizational decision-making system work effectively. Most of the job involves delegating, monitoring, encouraging, and controlling middle-level managers. This is primarily organizational maintenance, although all three managerial jobs are involved.

In contrast, this chapter is more closely related to the top manager's representation and strategic planning functions. In contending for power and influence, managers face actors from different perspectives and values based on their organizational position. Some of these perspectives, such as from line versus staff positions, from specialized versus generalist positions, from inside versus outside the organization, and from political versus career jobs, are covered in this chapter. In these bureaucratic struggles, the manager must be as effective in representing the agency as possible.

Strategic planning and representation are involved. Managers occasionally can advance their organization or subunit by taking advantage of the interaction of goals, personalities, agencies, and groups in the decision-making process—if they have a long-term objective. Without some long-term plan, bureaucratic struggles and the ensuing decisions are just that—bureaucratic struggles—full of sound and fury with little significance. With some long-term objective, the struggles, debates, and decisions fall into a coherent pattern.

Don't expect high bureaucratic drama at every conference. Dramatic actions come infrequently. Most effort is expended in rather minor and often meaningless interbureaucratic struggles. Most of these struggles are within agencies, with the collection of zealots, advocates, and conservers committed to the narrow goals found in every agency. Even so, managers who have a long-term strategic plan and are effective representatives of their organization are more effective than other managers, and they usually are more effective in advancing their personal and organizational interests.

GOALS

Goals are both personal and organizational. Personal goals are the hopes, ambitions, and drives that one brings to work or that develop from work and affect work decisions. Acquiring power and influence is one common personal goal. Organizational goals are behaviors associated with organizations, such as growth. There aren't organizational goals, actually, since only humans can have goals; however, individuals in an organization often engage in patterned, predictable behavior that is associated with the organization they work for. We refer to these behaviors as organizational goals, as if the organization is a living, breathing thing.

Organizational Goals

Organizational goals are a complex mix of legislative programs, history, commitment to clients, and individual preferences. This mix becomes a set of institutionalized values called the organizational culture. This culture is a social and psychological mind-set found in most members of the organization. It predisposes them to look at issues from similar perspectives and to make decisions accordingly.[1] Growth, service to clients, survival, and symbolism are the most common organizational goals. Most organizations, through the actions and decisions of managers, exhibit many of these goals.

Organizational commitment to programs and clients runs deep and strong. Offices of economic opportunity have underprivileged clients, while the Bureau of Indian Affairs serves Native Americans. A state Department of Public Education ministers to the educational establishment of teachers and administrators, while libraries serve the book-reading public.

Much clientele service involves symbolic organizational goals. The mere existence of some organization may indicate that some constituency is recognized as legitimate and that its programs have social legitimacy. The Forest Service is in the Department of Agriculture instead of the Department of the Interior because conservationists remember a dispute from early in this century and still distrust the Department of the Interior.[2] Attempts to move it to the Department of the Interior, a more logical organizational arrangement, face opposition because the present location has become a symbolic issue. The Interstate Commerce Commission (ICC) represents a historic victory for consumers, created to regulate railroad monopolies. As with many regulatory agencies, unfortunately, the ICC has been captured by its industry, and the railroads control appointments to the commission.[3]

Agencies try to expand their activities to serve their clientele more effectively. This normally occurs through attempts to increase their share of the budget or by gaining functions at the expense of another agency. Growth provides more resources, more services to provide, and more opportunities for personal advancement. Personal advancement is one point where personal goals and organizational goals coincide.

If organizational goals conflict, agencies generally opt for improved services to existing clients rather than adding new functions, particularly if new functions are controversial. New York City agencies:

> compete to avoid program assignments that are especially difficult and controversial. The Commissioner of Hospitals and the Commissioner of Corrections have both tried to prevent lodging responsibility for narcotics addicts in their Department, and the Department of Health has been restive under the burden of inspections the Commissioner and Board of Health would generally prefer to have placed entirely on the Department of Buildings.[4]

Desire for survival almost always takes precedence over other goals. Even when agencies appear to have no goal or objective to speak of, their goal is survival. A reviewer of this chapter noted that "Most of the public agencies I have been involved with have no organizational goals or if they do, nobody seems to know anything about them." The organizations she knew were probably concerned only with survival.

An example of survival as a primary goal occurred in 1968 when the California Golden Gate Bridge district realized the bonds that had financed the Golden Gate Bridge would be paid off in 1971. The District would then serve no purpose, since the state highway district would then operate the bridge. The bonds were originally supported by a property tax on several Northern California counties to improve commerce and tourism by linking San Francisco and the North Coast. The district convinced the state legislature to allow it to provide bus and ferry service across San Francisco Bay to relieve suburban automobile commuter traffic. These new services were expensive. Bridge tolls were hiked from 50 cents in 1968 to $1.25 in 1981 to finance the new activities. Nevertheless, the district faced a projected loss of $28 million in 1985.[5]

When the issue of adding new and unrelated services arose, district representatives from counties far from San Francisco supported traffic reduction activities inconsistent with the district's original intent. Why? Survival of the district is the only explanation. In this case, it was necessary to change organizational goals from building a bridge for commerce to another goal—relieving traffic congestion on the bridge. Providing a service, or at least providing the original service, was less important than survival.

Personal Goals

Personal goals are much more complex than organizational goals since they are so varied from individual to individual. The most common personal goals are power, security, status, autonomy, and money. These goals are interdependent since they rarely are achieved separately. While drives toward goals such as security were brought to the workplace by individuals, opportunities and situations in the workplace provide an opportunity for individuals to manifest them. Organizational life is essentially a game in which players try to win (Chapter 5 outlines the process in detail). Since organizational life is a game, the decision-making process is also gamelike. Managers try to succeed by improving services to clients, obtaining higher appropriations, hiring more subordinates, and increasing their power over programs. As they succeed, their status, power, salary, and influence increase. These increases tell us who the winners in the game are. Increased influence or autonomy are personal goals that affect the organizational decisions made by managers. This is a universal aspect of executive behavior, public or private, although it is culturally more acceptable for private executives to admit.

Public executives seek a wide range of goals. Some managers are altruistic. Their basic commitment is to a clientele, idea, service, or program—even at the cost of some personal benefit. Consider public housing, for example. Managers fight vigorously for the program, for their clients, and for their agency (the agency, after all, is the instrument for more public housing). Should the agency be abolished or cut back seriously, the more seriously committed manager might move to another agency or organization advocating public housing, perhaps moving outside of government. Some managers will decline lucrative offers from, say, the building industry, to join advocacy groups for public housing. Their commitment to the program is based on a deep, personal belief in public housing.

At the other extreme are managers unconcerned about their program and primarily motivated by private concerns. To them, public management is just a job—interesting but a basic way to earn a living.

Between these two extremes are managers with a range of views.

Some love public management as a process but have little or no commitment to programs. Some managers believe their job is deeply significant to society. Most managers are neither purely self- or program-oriented. One California city manager commented:

> Calling a city manager a professional is like calling construction an industry. To be a city manager you need a certain amount of experience, a certain amount of savvy. There are no particular courses you take in school to make you a city manager. A city manager is not a professional in any sense of the word.[6]

This manager, who must have loved his work enough to tolerate the difficult life of a city manager, still rejected the highly professional view of his job that many managers profess. His view is between the extreme of purely personal goals held by some managers, and the advocate of public housing at the other extreme.

Downs's typology of bureaucrats provides the basis for a useful and entertaining list of bureaucratic goals. Downs refers to bureaucrats as nonmarket managers, indicating that their behavior results from not having direct interaction with marketplace economic incentives. Bureaucrats include public sector managers and, say, librarians in a private corporation. Downs assumes that managers seek their ends based on a rational, economic model. Even though it is a caricature, his list captures much of the behavior of public executives.[7]

Climbers seek to improve personal position by increasing the power and prestige of their present job or by moving to a higher level in or outside the organization. They try to add new functions, capture existing ones, or expand their present job.

Conservers are not sure that change will benefit them, so they conserve what they have by maximizing present salary and prerequisites. They vigorously oppose any loss of influence or power, but do not try to aggrandize their present position. They fit popular views of the typical bureaucrat.

Zealots regard the public interest as synonymous with their sacred policies, such as solar energy, nuclear submarines, or fully computerized traffic signals. Zealots fight hard and implacably for these programs. Because they are so committed, they dislike constraints such as the opinions of political leaders and they often can disrupt an organization. However, every agency needs zealots such as Edward Bergin (Case Study 3–1), because their commitment overcomes organizational inertia and they provide an impetus for change.

Advocates are loyal to a broad cause—usually an agency or agency subunit. Advocates take a long-term perspective toward their unit and become the major force for agency expansion.

Statesmen, according to Downs, are the least self-interested class.

Case Study 3–1

A ZEALOT IN OSHA

Edward Bergin has chosen a unique way to challenge his superiors. He has written a book which could serve as a training manual for workers who have been chemically injured on the job—telling them how to demand government action and how to find useful information in government files. The book also castigates several federal agencies and the Reagan administration in general for failing to protect the public from chemical pollutants.

In 1980, Bergin took part in a Labor Department study of workers disabled by workplace chemicals. The study estimated that nearly 2 million persons are totally disabled by workplace chemicals, dust, and gases. Bergin says that ". . . only 1 out of 20 people suffering from occupational diseases received anything from the state workers' compensation system which is supposed to take care of work-related injuries and diseases." Since most state laws preclude worker suits against employers for diseases contracted on the job, "The only thing they can get is workers compensation, but the laws are rigged to prevent them from collecting."

Bergin and his colleagues, with Labor Department blessing, designed several programs at a New York hospital to train physicians in recognizing and treating chemical-induced diseases. Bergin headed a new program to teach workers in selected states about toxic substances and their rights, but the Reagan administration killed the programs and transferred Bergin to the Occupational Health and Safety Administration (OSHA). "My experience convinced me that the American people were genuinely concerned about birth defects, chemicals in drinking water, toxic waste dumps, and food additions," noted Bergin. ". . . I wrote my book to give people who have problems with chemicals the information they need to help themselves until the government gets its act together."

Bergin, 42, is now a senior policy adviser in OSHA where he is keeping up the fight to restore the programs he once worked on in the Labor Department. "I'm expecting trouble, and I know I'll be subjected to tremendous pressure, . . . But I'm sick and tired of our government agencies continuing to act as if chemicals have more rights than people."

SOURCE: Excerpted from Jack Anderson, *Washington Post*, March 14, 1981, p. B16.

They are loyal to society or to an entire level of government as contrasted to a single unit. They are representatives of the public interest in bureaucratic garb. However, the statesman role is inherently unstable. If statesmen wish to retain their position, organizational pressures for expansion or influence force them to become advocates for their department.

Since the system is based on strong advocacy of programs, the role of advocate may be the most functional bureaucratic role. One needn't subscribe entirely to Downs's typology to see that managers have many

---

EXHIBIT 3–1 Idealized Types of Bureaucratic Behavior

Robert Presthus types:

Upward Mobiles. Upward mobiles emphasize control and dominance over situations and people, and they deeply respect authority. They identify with the organization and since they do well in hierarchical situations, they achieve a good synthesis of personal and organizational goals.

Ambivalents. Ambivalents dislike authority and do not easily accept organizational goals, particularly at the expense of personal autonomy. They are tender-hearted and thus have trouble making decisions. Creative, they often find large organizations stifling.

Indifferents. Indifferents are found primarily among rank-and-file organization members rather than among managers. They neither worship the organization nor let it create personal anxiety. The job is an individual economic/psychological trade-off that most indifferents accept easily.

Leonard Reissman types:

Functional Bureaucrats. Functional bureaucrats are interested in achieving status and recognition through professional groups (e.g., accountants, lawyers, foresters). Government agencies are essentially just another place to practice their profession.

Specialist Bureaucrats. Specialist bureaucrats identify both with professional groups outside and within the agency. The organization has more leverage over them than functional bureaucrats. They can be meticulous about organizational rules.

Service Bureaucrats. Service bureaucrats are imbued with personal values about rendering services to a group or groups. They enter civil service to achieve these goals. They are concerned primarily with the services that the agency provides.

Job Bureaucrats. Job bureaucrats are committed to the agency as a mechanism for advancement. They care nothing for job recognition outside the agency. They are materialistic and status-oriented and, being strongly committed to the agency, are rather rule-oriented.

SOURCES: Robert Presthus, *The Organizational Society,* rev. ed. (New York: St. Martin's Press, 1978), chapters 6, 7, and 8; Leonard Reissman, "A Study of Role Conceptions in Bureaucracy," *Social Forces,* 27, March 1949, pp. 305–10.

complex goals. Exhibit 3-1 demonstrates this by outlining two alternative bureaucratic categories to Downs's scheme. Downs's typology, which comes closest to actual behavior, includes the desire to possess influence, the love of competition, and the need for security. These and other personal goals contribute directly to organizational goals.

Organizational goals such as agency growth, stability, and better service to clients are furthered by managers who find personal satisfaction, achieve recognition, or gain power through administrative or program responsibilities. Most public managers cannot achieve their legitimate personal goals without strengthening the organization—nor can organizations become stronger without benefiting individual managers.

ACTORS IN THE DECISION-MAKING PROCESS

Examining personal and organizational goals is only one way to view human behavior in the decision-making process.[8] Another way is to consider the roles played by different parties. An emphasis on roles focuses attention on the behavior patterns that each actor (manager, politician, lower-level civil employee, and so on exhibits in organizational positions. Looking at personal goals clarifies the orientations that each group member will bring to the decision-making process. Looking at the organizational goals illustrates how managers' personal goals are modified by the organization.

The most useful categories of roles that actors play in decision-making are insiders versus outsiders, line versus staff, "careerists" versus political executives, and generalist managers versus specialists.

Insiders versus Outsiders

Insiders are organizational members with responsibility for ongoing agency operations. Outsiders are persons with few or no formal ties to the organization who may be called on to evaluate, discuss, and help make decisions. Frequently outsiders are consultants or citizen groups nominated by the agency or self-chosen to look at organizational issues and policies from a neutral or outside perspective. U.S. public organizations may be unique in their openness to outsiders. They receive a constant flow of opinions, viewpoints, and information. Making some sense of this information barrage is a major managerial responsibility.

There are several reasons for the influence of outsiders in public decision making. Often it is impossible to recruit highly qualified persons for full-time positions, but these same persons will periodically consult with the agency or will serve on formal advisory boards. In these cases, their prominence may result in great weight being placed on their views. The National Science Foundation, for example, relies heavily on outside consultants both to perform their research and also to judge competitive proposals for funding.

Another reason for the use of outside agents is that they are freer to speak their minds—not being subject to organizational pressures to conform. The availability of an outside point of view may strengthen the hand of those advocating unpopular inside opinions. Thus, a few organizational members will always want outside opinions in the hopes of finding support for their views. In other cases, top managers, unsure of action in the face of opposition inside or outside their organizations, frequently seek formal outside views.

Outsiders don't necessarily have different views, but they have different thought patterns. Organizational life breeds certain ways of looking at issues based on long immersion in organizational values and operations. To outsiders, things look different. The same information may point to different conclusions.

Often advisory groups are institutionalized to provide technical or nonpolitical advice to prominent decisionmakers. A local planning commission, made up of amateurs who devote large amounts of time to becoming expert in planning issues, fulfills this function. At the national level, the council of economic advisors serves a similar role, although its members are frequently picked as experts and for partisan reasons. To be effective, these groups must be independent enough to provide unpopular advice yet supportive enough so that their advice is followed by the administration. This is no small task.

The ability of outsiders to provide unbiased information about policy issues keeps agencies and public executives alert to opposing views. This reduces the likelihood that official actions will be isolated from reality. Outside advice, although sometimes unrealistic, point to potential directions for future policy. For this reason, advisory committees are more likely to push for comprehensive rather than incremental change. They thus not only provide information, but also provide pressure to innovate and change. Such pressure is useful, but frequently policymakers won't accept such advice. This is frustrating to outsiders who have freely given their time and energy and feel that the least the policymaker can do is take their advice. A federal budget bureau official commented on the dilemma faced by persons who provide advice at the pleasure of the chief executive:

> Thank God I'm here and not across the street. If the President doesn't call me, I've got plenty I can do right here and plenty coming up to me, by rights, to justify my calling him. But those poor fellows over there, (members of the Council of Economic Advisers) if the boss doesn't call them, doesn't ask them to do something, what can they do but sit?[9]

Line and Staff

Different views arising from different organizational experiences in line versus staff positions commonly shape the organizational decision-making process. Line people work directly with a clientele. Staff individuals provide support to line staff but generally do not work directly with clients. A federal Bureau of Indian Affairs (BIA) agency head has a line job, while a budget examiner or a personnel officer holds a staff position.

At the local level, a police chief heads a line agency while the purchasing agent holds a staff position. At all levels of government, a common type of staff aide is personally responsible to the chief executive for a range of administrative duties as needed. The White House staff, special assistant to the governor, and the assistant to the city manager are examples of personal staff.

Line people have close contact with agency programs and client reactions to them. They are concerned with maintaining long-term working relationships with clients and are sensitive to the difficulties in implementing programs. They have continuous, institutionalized responsibility for program management and are often suspicious of proposals for change. They develop deep loyalties to their program, clients, and department. Line people, therefore, take technical and programmatic issues seriously. Committed to specific ways of approaching problems, they want to behave in a professional way, and they want to avoid intellectual arguments over the value of their service. Basically, they want to get on with the job.

Staff members have different perspectives. Personal aides to the top executive are loyal to him. Technical staff such as budget or personnel experts tend to move from agency to agency in their field as better positions in their specialty develop. In either case, staff members have shorter-term interests in the agency. These differences in orientation toward time have significant effects.

Struggles between the White House staff and cabinet officials illustrate the different points of view. True, cabinet officials are not career line officials, because they can expect only a few years in their post. They do, however, have responsibility for their programs while they are in office. This is quite different from the White House staff, faithful to the president alone. Cabinet officers have split loyalties—to their program, to the presidency, and to others such as Congress. They also have a role as advocates for their department. Wilbur Cohen, secretary of Health, Education, and Welfare under President Johnson, pointed out these conflicting roles:

> If you're the Secretary of HEW, you're responsible really to the Ways and Means Committee, and to the Interstate Commerce Committee and the

House Education Committee. And, boy, they can tell you in the White House, they can tell you in the Office of Management and Budget, and they can tell you everywhere, do this, that and the other thing. But if you come back next time to Capitol Hill, and you've violated what is their standard for their delivery system, you're not going to get what you're asking for.[10]

Cohen explains that officials with program responsibilities, such as secretaries, have conflicting responsibilities because they manage departments with long-term, ongoing relationships with congressional committees. They can't do the president's bidding. The conflicting commitments of secretaries such as Cohen cause a strain. Staffers have no such mixed responsibilities, and may feel, as did John Ehrlichmann, President Nixon's chief of staff, that cabinet secretaries "go off and marry the natives" (adopt departmental viewpoints).

Staff officials are less tied to the status quo and are more likely to consider significant, even radical alternatives to present programs or practices. If you equate rational behavior with the willingness to consider extensive changes, staff members behave more rationally than line officials. After all, line officials have committed their working life to the program and they don't take lightly proposals to change. The matter is not that simple, however. Rationality in decision making also includes calculation of long-term consequences and results. Line officials put less weight on short-term gains or benefits and more on long program consequences. Thus, resistance of line officials to change can be functional or it can merely be dislike of change. Neither line nor staff have a monopoly on rationality.

Generalists and Specialists

A third set of roles involves generalists and specialists. Their struggle pervades most organizations. It is a perennial issue in public management, partly because government hires many professionals (usually these are specialists). Generalists such as a city manager or the head of a large agency have responsibility for the well-being of the entire city or agency, rather than for the library system or the environmental sanitation division. The hierarchical level of generalists gives them a broad view of the organization. Among other things, this makes coordination possible. Without generalists, specialists such as highway engineers and recreation supervisors would soon leave each other alone and do their individual jobs—at the expense of coordinating their activities.

Specialists are highly trained and educated. They have a deep and abiding commitment to their profession or specialty and to its codes of conduct. This provides the expertise needed for high levels of service. Specialist programs are usually linked to a specific bureau, division, or department, such as highways, education, or mental health. When the department is large, bureaus or divisions become the point where services are delivered, and they are headed by specialists. For example, the Department of Agriculture has, among others, the Forest Service, the Soil Conservation Service, the Agriculture Marketing Service, the Food and Nutrition Service, the Rural Electrification Service, the Farmers Home Administration, the Federal Crop Insurance Corporation, and the Federal Grain Inspection Service.[11] President Robert Hutchins of the University of Chicago reportedly once said that the university was a group of individuals held together by the heating plant (or was it the parking lot?). Perhaps the Department of Agriculture, like the University of Chicago, is held together only by the parking lot, even though the secretary is formally responsible for coordination.

Thus, the need for specialization is matched by the need for coordination. How are these two contradictory needs met? Sometimes specialists are responsible for coordination, particularly in single purpose agencies. Here, specialists occupy all management and operational positions. They often form an elite corps that dominates decision making throughout the organization.[12] In a state Highway Department, for example, the director is normally a civil engineer who specialized in highway construction. Key spots, except for staff positions in finance or personnel, will be held by civil engineers. In mental health agencies, psychiatrists frequently control the decision-making pattern. This sets the dominant pattern for treatment and establishes the assumptions, values, and context for agency decisions. Not surprisingly, many agency heads are psychiatrists, although this pattern is less frequent now.

There is nothing wrong with specialist domination at the operating level. Most of us would rather have our highways designed by civil engineers than by finance directors, or our mental health clients cared for by psychiatrists rather than personnel analysts. Problems may arise when the decisions to be made involve broader considerations than technical questions about asphalt depth or personality problems. Professional specialists approach decisions from a narrow speciality, demanding that decisions be correct or based on professional standards.

Technical issues often raise, in turn, both broader policy issues and political short-term issues. Broader mental health issues might involve the results of the treatment of patients, and whether release to the community or continued institutionalization is desirable. The long-term implications range from community preferences to long-term care costs. For example, does a hospital design foreclose future changes in capacity? Freeway construction through or around a city involves much more than technical questions. Will off-ramp locations affect adjoining street design and influence development patterns? Short-term political repercussions would involve the location of off-ramps, the names on signs, and so on.

It is probably wiser for generalists to make these decisions, for by definition their positions in the hierarchy expose them to broader perspectives. This does not mean that nonengineers or nonmedical generalists should direct these agencies. Rather, specialists must quickly become generalists if they ascend to top management positions. The technical content of their decisions rapidly becomes less important than policy or political content.

The question of who makes decisions is not entirely remedied by placing generalists at the apex of organizations. For many reasons, specialists, at lower levels than generalist superiors, still hold effective decision-making power. In one case, program specialists in the Department of Health and Human Services (HHS) controlled all regional activity. Their emphasis was on vocational education, mental health, and family planning rather than service integration or comprehensive human service delivery systems. The department could have created stronger regional centers—forcing lower-level field specialist decisions to be made by a regional director. However, HHS top management didn't favor this plan, for it also would have decentralized decisions being made in Washington to the region. Powerful interests in Congress and around the organization didn't want decentralization if it changed their influence. So, nothing happened. Decision making remained lodged with the regional specialists, although the decisions were minor and all important decisions remained in Washington. The result was that regions remained weak, but specialists retained apparent control of service delivery systems.[13]

The Reagan administration domestic cutbacks have made these kinds of issues less relevant, since few programs remain untouched. Hence, not only program content is at stake. So is power, and as long as social programs even have scraps to squabble over, the specialist-generalist struggle will continue. The debate between specialists and generalists is usually phrased, "should the expert be on tap or on top," implying that generalists should be in charge. This is based on the belief that higher-level positions, due to their location in organizations, see more issues and take more into account in making decisions. A World War II story clarifying this point suggests the view is different at higher organizational levels. The *San Francisco News* refers to the City Utility Department, which controls the City Water Department, the Hetch Hetchy Power Development, and other local utilities:

> While Utilities Manager Cahill was in Washington for 10 days that lasted a month, Nelson Eckart, head of the Water Department, filled his own job, the top Hetch Hetchy post of the late A. T. McAfee, and Cahill's overall job, too. Forrest Gibbon, executive secretary, had to tell who he was by the hat he was wearing. On Cahill's return, Eckart's first words were, "Here's the key to the powder room, here's the aspirin bottle, I quit." But it was some days before Cahill discovered all the triple-personality kinks which

had brought Eckart to the brink of madness. He discovered, in fact, a letter Waterman Eckart had written asking money for more water-works, another letter Hetch Hetchy Eckart has written asking for more HH dough, and a final letter Acting Utilities Manager Eckart had written denying both of his own requests. Naturally, Cahill asked what the devil. "From up here," Eckart explained, "Things don't look quite the same as they do down there."[14]

Political Executives and Careerists

Political and career executives make up the final set of actors and actresses. Political executives are persons directly elected or appointed by elected public officials. Common examples of appointed political executives include federal cabinet officers and some bureau chiefs, heads of large state agencies who change with the governor, or local officials such as a police commissioner who changes with the mayor.

Careerists are top-level civil servants such as a member of the federal senior executive system, a director of the bridge division of a state Highway Department, or a department head in a county government.

Defining a careerist is difficult. In one state, all top officials in a Highway Department change with a new administration, while in another state only the top position changes. City managers, who are far from traditional civil servants, usually consider themselves careerists—in local government rather than in a given city. Their stay in any one city may be short. Sometimes both careerists and political appointees occupy a given post over time. At the federal level, it is often difficult to tell careerists from political appointees. One assistant secretary declared that his job was:

> One of the most impossible in government, given the diversity of activities under me. Two offices are headed by political appointees. Two others are headed by civil servants. Two others are headed by Deputy Assistant Secretaries, but I'm not sure to what extent they're career people. I know that they come and go a lot as Assistant Secretaries change.[15]

The best way to distinguish one type from another is their approach to time. Political officials almost always expect to be short-timers who come in with a new administration. They have a short time to put their programs into place. Careerists have a long-term interest in their careers and usually their agency, and they have the luxury of taking a longer view.

In theory, political executives make policy for an agency—charting its course with the blessing of a popular mandate. Careerists carry out the policy directives they are given. This neat division of the administrative world into two parts, policy and administration, collapses in practice.

Careerists have a heavy responsibility for framing alternatives, analyzing the pros and cons of proposed policies, and shaping proposals before any political decision is made. The California Career Executive Assignment system (CEA), for example, selects top civil servants and places them in policy positions where they can be sent back to their previous civil service positions with 20 days notice. One CEA noted that:

> By and large, the things that distinguish CEA employees from regular civil service is that CEA employees tend to get involved with policy formulation, and advising superiors which policies ought to be considered.[16]

Careerists endure institutionalized and ritualistic political criticism from political candidates. After all, most new administrations come into power after having attacked the policies of the previous administration. The casual observer might assume that most government programs aren't working well and that new initiatives are needed to move government off dead-center. In reality, at the same time that politicians are announcing their search for new ideas, they use the same list of proposals that careerists have seen for years. Political executives really are looking for new ideas, and they also ask outside groups to suggest them. But almost inevitably they ask senior staffers to develop some lists of alternatives. True, some administrations, such as the Reagan administration, pride themselves on not using careerist ideas. But this is unusual. With Reagan, this reflects a desire for no programs at all.

Because most administrations ask careerists for new ideas, new administrations frequently rely heavily on careerists. Policymaking is shared between careerists and political executives. For careerists, this is a mixed blessing. It's satisfying to become involved in decision making; indeed, that is the major job satisfaction for many careerists. On the other hand, it's disconcerting to be charged with footdragging, as often happens. This charge occurs when: (1) the ideas of a new administration don't work quickly or at all, or (2) the careerist winds up defending existing policies against new ideas. In either case, careerists become associated with the status quo.

A classic case of commitment to the status quo or to established routines in the face of pressures for change was illustrated during the Cuban missile crisis. President Kennedy became concerned that the navy might blunder into an incident while blockading the Soviet fleet, particularly at the point where the first ship was to be intercepted. Defense Secretary McNamara interrogated the chief of naval operations and asked how the chief would handle a situation in which the Soviet captain might refuse to answer questions about the cargo. The chief's angry response was to wave the manual of navy regulations in McNamara's face and shout, "It's all in there!" McNamara riposted that he didn't care how John Paul Jones would have responded. The encounter ended with the naval chief's remark that the navy would run the block-ade when McNamara returned to his office.[17] A blockade with nuclear consequences was unheard of, but the navy had established general procedures for blockades, and it was committed to them.

Generally, careerists and political executives live in an uneasy truce with each other because neither can get the job done without the other. Political executives bring political legitimacy and a commitment to change to their jobs. Careerists supplement these assets with detailed knowledge of the agency system—how to most rapidly move new pro-grams or revised old ones through the agency and the government with the least controversial method. When these two functions work together well, little conflict arises. Most careerists get their major job satisfaction from this process.

There are forces that raise tensions, however. One is mistrust. The new administration or political head may distrust anyone associated with the previous administration. This distrust increases when new ad-ministrations try to change decades of policy with sweeping reforms. Then, short-time perspectives clash with the longer views of careerists. The root of this conflict is a difference in perspectives. Political execu-tives have short terms and must look for speedy results. Few political executives can look beyond a four-year term, and the actual tenure of federal assistant secretaries is under two years. Careerists, on the other hand, often think in terms of decades.

On occasion, careerists become associated with political positions when they are forced to explain policies or decisions to legislatures or interest groups. This usually happens when the political appointee has not learned the details about the job. "If the political executive cannot answer the question, Congress calls in the fellow who can, the career-ist."[18] This may make political leaders jealous and destroy careerist-political executive rapport. It also may make the careerist a political figure.

> If the careerist turns up a few years later with a new head of the depart-ment who is an appointee of the opposite political party, the same Con-gressman may now regard the careerist as a politician who cannot be trusted.[19]

Summary: Actors and Goals

There are four major sets of actors in the decision-making process. Insiders contend with outsiders, line with staff, generalists with special-ists, and careerists with political executives. Table 3–1 uses four catego-ries to contrast the perspectives that each set brings to the decision-making process.

Comprehensiveness of view refers to the number of alternatives considered and the amount of information used in a decision. Time orientation refers to the time in which consequences are considered. Attitude toward change refers to a willingness to consider new proposals, methods, and ideas. Responsibility to political or executive leadership refers to the perceived or actual need for the actor to respond quickly to the organization leader.

As Table 3–1 shows, line officials are less receptive to change than staff counterparts, perhaps because they are less dependent on the top executive. Line officials also have a longer time perspective about program issues.

Outsiders generally have a more comprehensive view of issues than insiders. They also take a longer time perspective and tend to be more receptive to change, but they feel less responsibility to top management.

Generalists likewise have a more comprehensive view of issues than specialists. More receptive to change, they are also responsive to top leadership.

Careerists have a longer time orientation than political executives. They also are less positive about the prospects of change and tend to be less responsive to top leadership.

Table 3–1 suggests that specialists and insiders (most often program persons) tend to take a more incremental approach toward decisions than their paired counterparts. Other than this generalization, no strong

TABLE 3–1 Perspectives of Different Sets of Decision-Making Actors

	Perspectives of Actors			
Actor (contrasting pairs)*	Comprehensiveness of View	Time Orientation	Attitude toward Change	Responsibility to Political or Executive Leadership
Line	Varies	Longer	Mixed	Low
Staff	Varies	Shorter	Positive	High
Insiders	Less	Shorter	Mixed	High
Outsiders	More	Longer	Positive	Low
Specialists	Less	Varies	Negative	Low
Generalists	More	Varies	Mixed	High
Political executives	Varies	Shorter	Positive	High
Careerists	Varies	Longer	Mixed	Low

* Comparisons are only between actors within each set (i.e., between line and staff), not between line and insiders.

or marked tendencies appear. The table indicates that in certain cases the decision-making balance can be tilted away from one dominant group or individual. For example, if it is desirable to have a recommendation that a top political executive can endorse, it might be wise to add more insiders than outside experts to persons considering that report. Insiders, after all, are interested in her approval. If a decision will affect a program for many years to come, it might be wise to add outsiders and line people to a recommending body.

SUMMARY

Personal and organizational goals are a key part of the decision-making process, not only determining objectives but also shaping the way that individuals perceive basic facts. The major organizational goals are survival, growth, service to clients, and symbolism. The major personal goals are power, security, status, autonomy, and income. Decision makers are actors in the decision-making process, each group playing different roles. Common sets of contrasting roles are organization insiders and outsiders, staff and line positions, generalist and specialist responsibilities, and careerists versus political leaders. Members of each set have different perspectives from the other. They also view organizational issues much differently than other role sets. This often results in diametrically opposed views and leads to rather different decisions.

This chapter's discussion of actors and goals highlights the maintenance, representation, and planning job of managers in yet another way. Managers cannot maintain, represent, or plan for their own organizations effectively unless they can assess the goals and motivations of other actors. Managers who do not possess the interpersonal skills and psychic energy to succeed in the rough and tumble world of the decision-making process rarely move to the top of their organizations or, if they do, remain there for only a short time.

Case Study 3–2

OAKLAND AND THE ECONOMIC DEVELOPMENT ADMINISTRATION

One of the major reasons projects don't always achieve success is that personal and organizational goals are at odds. Thus, matters that appear to be simple decisions may not get settled quickly or at all. The objectives of actors may seem similar, but short- and long-term interests can be quite divergent. Unless there is some convergence of long-term interests, a project will rarely be started—let alone completed.

The case of Oakland and the federal Economic Development Authority (EDA) points out how differing organizational and personal views can slow and even block action on a project.

In 1966, Eugene Foley, EDA head, envisioned a new goal for the EDA. It was creating a showcase project of how a private, local, and federal partnership could concentrate massive resources on economic development to eliminate unemployment. This vision was a crucial strategic decision. The EDA was an organization that made rural loans. It had little concern for, or expertise with, urban programs. Foley wanted to change the image, perhaps even the nature, of the EDA. Oakland, California was chosen as the pilot study because it was a racially-conflicted city with high unemployment.

The EDA poured an unprecedented amount of money into the unemployment relief plan through grants and loans for an airport/industrial park project. Table 3–2 shows the planned funding:

TABLE 3–2   Proposed EDA Funding for Oakland Project

Airport hangars and support facilities (Port of Oakland, leased by World Airways)	$10,650,000
Marine terminal and access roads (Port of Oakland)	10,125,000
Industrial park (Port of Oakland)	2,100,000
Access road to Coliseum area (City of Oakland)	414,000
Total	$23,289,000

This was in 1966 dollars. Three thousand jobs, primarily for minorities, were to be created by this program, which was supported from federal, state, and local sources other than the EDA. The project received national media attention. Unfortunately, it soon became bogged down. By 1970, only about 1,000 jobs were created, most went to nonminorities, and few projects were completed. The basic reason for failure was that the parties had different goals. This was not apparent initially, however, and the following series of events received most of the blame.

Foley had resigned as EDA director. The Mayor of Oakland was convicted of embezzlement (unrelated to the case). His successor could not work with ghetto leaders, who confronted city hall instead of supporting the program. Contracts for dredging and filling San Francisco Bay took three years to award because of objections from government agencies. These objections included navy fears that water currents in the ship entrance would be affected and Bay Area Rapid Transit fears that dredging was too close to their dikes. World Airways could not agree on leases. The Port of Oakland's architectural plan took two years to complete and then had a 55 percent cost overrun. After World Airways agreed on a lease, it was discovered that the minority employment goal would not be met. Meanwhile, costs went up another million dollars. The EDA had four regional representatives in five years, further delaying action. There were many other circumstances that delayed action.

The real reasons could have been identified as easily as a lack of consistent goals among all parties. Foley's zeal was not matched by his successors. EDA units had fuzzy lines of authority, with the Seattle office consistently trying to assert its "limited program authority" over the project. The Oakland project director had no power to approve grants or loans and Washington signatures took time. The Port of Oakland didn't really care about minority employment. Conservation groups informally fought agreements that they felt endangered the bay and its wetlands. The Health, Education, and Welfare Department (HEW) preferred to provide skills training through established centers. The Labor Department felt no urgency about another agency's project. Both HEW and the Labor Department had some control over employment training funds and were not anxious to see a rival agency, the EDA, move into their turf. The Oakland black community had broken with the city over local issues. So, while most actors favored the project in principle, none had any direct incentive to make the project work.

There were 30 decisions requiring 70 separate agreements among independent governmental and private actors between 1967 and 1971. Many were controversial, such as the EDA's decision to bypass the mayor and go directly to black community groups to avoid being labeled a tool of city hall. In general, however, the more controversial decisions involved relatively few decision makers. Less controversial decisions took as much time because they involved many participants. Implementing one training program involved nine actors at three levels of government: the local training agency, the mayor, both the California State Departments of Employment and Vocational Rehabilitation, both the regional and the Washington office of both Departments of Labor and HEW, and the Washington EDA office. This guaranteed delays, since many of the multiple required approvals involved reluctant parties. The major reason for delay was a lack of sufficient incentives among the actors to harness personal and organizational goals.

SOURCE: Jeffrey Pressman and Aaron Wildavsky, *Implementation*, 2nd ed., (Berkeley, Calif., University of California Press, 1973).

NOTES

1. For an example of how this phenomenon affected administrative behavior, see Herbert Kaufman, *The Forest Ranger* (Baltimore, Md.: Johns Hopkins Press, 1960). For a good discussion of organizational goals, see Charles Perrow, "The Analysis of Goals in Complex Organizations," *American Sociological Review*, 26, December 1961, pp. 854–65.

2. Harold Seidman, *Politics, Position and Power*, 3rd ed., Boston: (Little, Brown, 1980), p. 153. Also see Herbert Kaufman, *Are Government Organizations Immortal?* (Washington, D.C.: Brookings Institution, 1976).

3. Samuel Huntington, "The Marasmus of the ICC: The Commission, the Railroads and the Public Interest," *The Yale Law Journal*, April 1952, pp. 29–41.

4. Wallace Sayre and Herbert Kaufman, *Governing New York City* (New York: Russell Sage Foundation, 1960), p. 262.

5. *Sacramento Bee*, March 1, 1981, p. B6.

6. Ronald Loveridge, *City Managers in Legislative Politics* (Indianapolis, Ind.: Bobbs-Merrill, 1971), p. 63.

7. Anthony Downs, *Inside Bureaucracy* (Boston: Little, Brown, 1967), pp. 88–112.

8. This outline is from Francis Rourke, *Bureaucracy, Politics and Public Policy*, 2nd ed., (Boston: Little, Brown, 1976), pp. 109–42.

9. Richard Neustadt, *Presidential Power* (New York: John Wiley & Sons, 1960), p. 41.

10. *National Journal*, December 16, 1972, pp. 19–21.

11. *United States Government Manual 1980–81* (Washington, D.C.: U.S. Government Printing Office, 1980).

12. Frederick Mosher, *Democracy in America* (New York: Oxford Press, 1968).

13. Mark Yeserian, "The Generalist Perspective in the HEW Bureaucracy: An Account from the Field," *Public Administration Review*, March–April 1980, pp. 138–49.

14. Herbert Simon, *Administrative Behavior*, 2nd ed., (New York: Free Press, 1957), p. 214.

15. Hugh Heclo, *A Government of Strangers* (Washington, D.C.: Brookings Institution, 1977), p. 43.

16. John Rehfuss, 1981 interviews with California officials holding Career Executive Assignment posts.

17. Graham Allison, "The Power of Bureaucratic Routines: The Cuban Missile Crisis," *American Political Science Review*, September 1969, p. 707.

18. Marver Bernstein, *The Job of The Federal Executive* (Washington, D.C.: Brookings Institution, 1958), p. 43.

19. Ibid., p. 43.

CHAPTER 4

Quantitative and Qualitative Aids to Decision Making

The previous two chapters discussed the decision-making process as a broad social and organizational process. This chapter is also about decision making, but it deals with techniques managers use to improve the quality and quantity of information that decisions are based on.

Two basic types of techniques, quantitative and qualitative, are available to managers. Quantitative methods, often referred to as *management science*, rely on numbers, hard information, and some computation to sharpen the actual choice between alternatives or to seek the most precise definition of a given alternative. These techniques include program evaluation review technique (PERT), critical path method (CPM), cost-benefit analysis (CBA), and operations research (OR), which includes exotic practices such as queuing theory, inventory modeling, linear programming, simulation, and sensitivity analysis.

Top managers don't usually get involved in the direct use of quantitative data, but they rely on these techniques to generate better lower-level decisions. The top executive's role is generally limited to assuring herself that mid-level managers are using these techniques whenever feasible and appropriate.

Qualitative methods include techniques such as increasing citizen participation, management by objective (MBO), organizational development (OD), and information-gathering devices such as the nominal group method or the Delphi technique. While some managers don't consider nonquantitative methods as techniques, all these devices can improve decision making by increasing the amount and variety of information that the organization can use in making decisions.

The use of qualitative methods poses different and much more important questions than the use of quantitative data. Qualitative methods are often initiated by top management because the organization isn't operating effectively and changes in the organization's nature or in its information-gathering process are needed. This is primarily true of citizen participation, management by objectives, and organizational development.

The two methods deal with separate issues. Quantitative methods are generally techniques to manipulate data or improve analysis where the problems can be defined. Qualitative methods are necessary when problems are ill-defined or systemically linked to how the organization operates. Top management has to take direct leadership in the application of qualitative methods, while they can take a much more indirect role in using quantitative data.

Two other aids to decision making are covered in this chapter. One is the computer. Computers are capable of handling volumes of quantitative data and providing the base for routine operations and top-level decisions about operations. The use of computers is not technically a specific quantitative technique. However, their widespread use and the dependence of most agencies on them raise important managerial issues.

The other decision-making aid is program evaluation, which helps managers make decisions about program effectiveness. Program evaluation is a central element of top management control. Recent cutbacks in public programs at all government levels have made program evaluation even more significant; both career managers and elected politicians feel a greater need to allocate scarce resources to the most effective programs.

Quantitative and qualitative techniques and methods, program evaluation, and the use of computers are all part of the public manager's organizational maintenance job. Most of these issues deal with organizational management questions and the continued effectiveness and health of the organization. As the manager uses some qualitative methods such as MBO and OD to redirect the agency, long-range organizational planning is involved. And, as public explanations of matters such as program evaluation reviews are made, organizational representation often becomes more important. This again shows that all three parts of the manager's job are interrelated even if one, in this case maintenance, seems to predominate.

THE COMPUTER

Computer Uses

Computers are marvelous devices for operational and housekeeping functions such as these:[1]

1. *Storage of and access to information.* This usually includes a simple means to update data such as uniform crime reports and accounting ledgers.
2. *Manipulation of stored data.* Computers sort, calculate, and print stored data using high-speed data-processing capacity. Examples of this use include payroll processing and utility billing.

3. *Manipulation of routine data.* This often involves computer access to and search of the files. Police and departments of motor vehicles use this for parking tickets and record of warrants.

4. *Manipulation of complex data.* Examples of this are computer mapping and revenue estimating.

5. *Reorganization of data.* Diverse data sources are linked or large volumes of material are summarized. One example of this is a program budgeting system that pulls line items together into programs.[2]

6. *Systems monitoring.* Traffic signal and navigation systems fall into this category. Water and power distribution control systems are cybernetically controlled in this manner.

These uses are associated with large mainframe computers. Microcomputers extend managerial capacity even further—to any location with access to an ordinary electrical outlet.[3] Word processing on microcomputers saves enormous amounts of typing time as writers revise drafts on the screen. Microcomputers monitor operations directly and process housekeeping operations such as budget expenditure items, account billings, and accounting records. The public works director in Olathe, Kansas, has in his computer memory a block-by-block street-paving record, a record of operating costs for every vehicle, and a complete parts inventory.[4] Policy analysts can generate quality graphic presentations on short notice. Programs exist for critical path analysis involving time and costs (more about critical paths later). Welfare worker supervisors can use database programs to give quick answers to operational questions such as the number of clients with certain characteristics.

Computers are ushering in a new set of opportunities for managers. But their use is limited to the availability of good information in a usable form.

Management Issues

From the top manager's perspective, the computer system must generate useful information for top-level decisions. That's generally basic data such as current account balances, the status of work projects, and employee turnover. Most of this data can come from the manager's desk-top computer.

The system also has to generate information useful to operating managers. This is where the uses for mainframe computers are important. Operating-level decisions about traffic-light maintenance and parking-ticket enforcement depend on an effective system. Unfortunately, nothing guarantees this.

The first step in developing a working system is to ask operating managers what kinds of information they need and how they can use it.

When operatives aren't consulted, the resulting information system will often be of little use. Either it has useless information or the users weren't consulted and lack commitment to the new system.

Contrary to what some cynics allege, computer system designers generally ask operating managers what information they need before they design the computer system. Unfortunately, managers don't know what they need in many cases. Thus, their responses to "What information do you need?" aren't very helpful. Managers have to be shown what they can get from a computer system before they can make reasonable responses.

This lack of awareness by operating managers of what computerized information systems can do creates another issue. Who should make the decision of how a system should operate? While operating managers have to use it, they may not be the best judges of results. One study of 42 cities concluded that decentralized, user-based systems don't capture technological advances. Immediate access to large mainframe systems, for example, is the fastest way to get big returns from computerized traffic-ticket processing, budget-control reporting, or police patrol beat allocation. It isn't important whether the user had anything to do with designing the system or even trusts it.[5] On the other hand, the use of centralized systems in cases such as the use of accounting information results in less usage during operation. This is because operating officials don't understand the importance of centralized capacity. They often don't see that the system is designed for them. It may be crucial to have a centralized system that can integrate resources completely, but the system will limp along if operating managers lack the ability or inclination to use it.

GIGO

Probably the major computer system problem for most managers is the quality of information. GIGO (garbage in, garbage out) means that information from the computer is no better than the information fed into it. The question is quality, relevance, and usefulness. Useful data is information that managers use daily or must have for periodic reports or analyses. Most systems could be used even more fully by managers and their subordinates. In some cases, the system is underutilized because employees or managers either distrust the data it produces or do not know how to use it effectively. Stories abound about underutilized computer systems because the agency does not know how to use the system or because the system was designed improperly. For example, one eastern city had a billing system with no balance brought forward routines to credit partial payments on account.[6]

Computers give managers instant access to much information. Utilizing this information, however, is another thing. The use of computer systems to pull line items into program budget categories does not help the manager create meaningful programs for these categories. At operating levels, the speed of a system is critical for, say, driver's license checks. At top management levels, routine but relevant information such as a monthly report on traffic tickets written per watch or per individual is much more important. The existence of an automated data-processing system does not guarantee management information. Management decisions depend on common sense, the ability to test political and social environments, good judgment, and periodic relevant information. Computerized information systems help provide this information—and effective managers make sure the computer system provides it.[7]

PROGRAM EVALUATION

Program evaluation burst into managers' consciousness in the 1960s, spawned by the suspicion that many Great Society social programs weren't effective—or seemed to be ineffective. In the late 1960s, federal grants began to require periodic evaluation of the programs they funded. Many of them had to set aside a certain percentage of the grant for evaluation. Even after 20 years of experience, however, program evaluation is still not well established. Requiring it provides no assurance that it will be done well.

Program evaluation is a formal assessment of how well programs accomplish their goals. It is usually applied to social programs because there is usually an explicit or implied target population of individuals whose life is somehow to be improved, whether through higher quality housing, reduced crime, or improved education. Social programs are commonly evaluated, but so are municipal services such as street sweeping, garbage collection, and recreation programs.

Program evaluation is important to managers for several reasons. It is often a grant requirement. It is often required by political leaders in both the executive and legislative branches, and the evaluation results become the basis for political and top-level budgetary decisions. But program evaluation can also satisfy purely management concerns as well, since managers can always use feedback on program accomplishments. Every manager needs information to judge how well programs are provided to clients, what programs are developing or might develop, and details on program effectiveness. In addition, there are constant demands for resources and good managers are interested in allocating them to the most effective programs.

Why Evaluate?

There are three reasons why program evaluation is used. First, managers want to know what the program is accomplishing. This involves an attempt to monitor or audit program results against planned objectives. Sometimes these audits are to collect data such as the use of personnel and financial resources.

A second reason for evaluation is to find out how clients or citizens regard the program. This is an *outcome* evaluation. These evaluations can be compared to output evaluations, which involve efficiency issues such as measles vaccinations per $1,000 spent. Outcomes evaluations often use a survey to determine what citizens think about the program.

An increasing number of evaluation studies, particularly at the municipal level, involve citizen surveys. The use of surveys is due partly to a basic interest in eliciting citizen opinion, particularly if a grant requires citizen participation. However, most surveys are guided by an interest in determining which services are most popular. As long ago as 1974, the Urban Institute and the International City Management Association classic *Measuring the Effectiveness of Basic Municipal Services* relied on citizen surveys for measures of effectiveness in a third of all cases.[8] This technique is now often used by local governments.

A third reason for evaluation is to test whether the assumptions of a program are valid. For example, a special probation program may be designed to keep juveniles within their community rather than at outside institutions to reduce recidivism. Did it? And, if not, does the failure to do so suggest that the assumption is still sound?

Types of Evaluations

Most program evaluations are done in one of four ways.[9] The most common are simple before and after comparisons that compare accomplishments after a new program or innovation occurs with the results before the change occurred. It is the simplest and easiest, partly because it assumes nothing else intervened to affect the program other than the specific change or innovation. Results from changes in police patrol staffing patterns or welfare payments, such as reduced robberies or reduced welfare rolls, are examples.

A second evaluation method is to extrapolate existing program trends and compare them to the new data that a changed program created. The differences can be attributed to the new program. For example, if five robberies a month can be predicted from past years data, a new program associated with only three robberies can be credited with preventing two.

A third general type of evaluation compared similar jurisdictions without a program to the agency with the new or modified program. Any changes in the clients, outputs, or program outcomes under consideration are attributed to the modifications. Sometimes this research design is used to compare clients in a program with clients not covered or served, assuming that the two groups were matched in all significant ways.

A fourth form of program evaluation, which is powerful, sophisticated, and costly, is the controlled experiment. Only major programs justify such evaluations. Control and experimental groups are formed and the program is applied only to the experimental group. Postprogram changes then are attributed to the program alone, for both groups are identical—in fact, individuals are assigned to each group at random. This is difficult, for public opinion may not allow random selection, as in the case of convicted criminals.

One example of the use of an experimental design was by the Michigan Department of Social Services in 1979. Assessing an employment and training program, 231 clients were randomly assigned to an experimental program with education, training, and employment opportunities, while the control group had to find such opportunities themselves. After phone interviews six to ten months later, the experimental group was more successful in finding jobs than the control group, assuming the client had no barriers to employment (e.g., disabled).[10]

A second major evaluation program using a controlled experiment was the decade-long study of a negative income tax (NIT), concluded in 1978.[11] The NIT, by providing income to poor people who could supplement this income by keeping almost all extra income, was designed to help the poor move out of poverty. The Office of Equal Opportunity sponsored experiments in New Jersey, North Carolina, Seattle, and Denver. All factors were controlled with individuals assigned to groups at random and other factors such as age and income held constant. Experimental group members were given a three-year income floor whether they worked or not, while control group members received no extra income. Researchers concluded that the NIT reduced work effort. Employment dropped 9 percent for husbands and 20 percent for wives in Seattle and Denver. Hours worked dropped even further for young, unmarried males. Another disturbing finding was that NIT recipients had more marital instability than individuals receiving welfare. True for both black and white families, apparently the independent income from the NIT made spouses less dependent on each other's income. These results were probably responsible for the lack of interest in the NIT since.

Studies as extensive and expensive as the NIT study or the negative income tax experiment are done rarely. The methodological purity is not worth the time and money it requires in terms of the results for the typical program. The issue has to be of major importance. Even then, simplified designs will normally produce results that convince decision makers.

Managers, Organization, and Program Evaluation

One might get the idea that program evaluation is commonplace, that most or at least many programs are formally evaluated, and that the results of evaluations make or break programs. While evaluation is more common and more effective than it used to be, evaluators are not welcomed with open arms into many organizations. There are two reasons.

First, after all the time and effort for an evaluation, little evidence is gained to guide program managers. Most program managers are not interested in findings because they are inconclusive—neither giving a go-ahead to the program or suggesting beneficial changes. Some of this is due to program complexity, but much is also due to evaluation techniques that are too sophisticated for the available data. One experienced U.S. Labor Department official noted that:

> You get very bright people applying econometric techniques to limited data and, over and over, they come up with the conclusion that we can't say whether the programs are doing good or not. . . . The situation now is that the evaluator says "We can't tell" and the program people say "fine" and go on with the program."[12]

In this case, program evaluations failed because the results were too vague for management to use. Managers are pragmatists. They want something concrete that they can immediately apply to modify programs, to improve operations, or to justify what they do. As the Labor Department official noted:

> Program people want to hang their hat on specific hard data items. They don't want to say "you could do it better. . . . The dream is to have a three month study of CETA (Comprehensive Health Education and Training Act) which will say, "these things worked out for these reasons" so that I can go in and change the regulations to make it work.[13]

Second, evaluations are not welcome because they represent a real or perceived threat to the agency. "The lower level program administrator and her staff literally see their bread and butter at risk when the program evaluator arrives on the scene."[14] Administrators want to present the best possible face to the outside world. They suspect that, at best, the evaluator will do nothing for them, and at worst, the program's image will be tarnished. Program managers and specialists have invested their lives in a program, lobbied for its support, and shed blood to protect it. It's best to take no changes with evaluations. This attitude occurs whether or not the reviewing agency is in-house or from outside.

Inside agencies are tamer than outside groups, for they share some of the agency's values even if the analysts have a professional commitment to rigorous review. They represent less threat to program managers because their findings can be debated inside the agency without outside pressure for action.

Outside agencies—from the chief executive to the legislature—carry more weight. They are more of a threat to programs because the results become public. If the report is unfavorable, programs face more immediate adverse actions. Examples of outside evaluation agencies are the Federal General Accounting Office or the program evaluation unit of the California state Department of Finance.

Should managers opt for inside or outside evaluation? Outside evaluations are uncontrollable because demands for resolving program deficiencies are less controllable. Inside evaluations by an agency team or consultants are preferred because the dissemination of the report can be controlled and the program less disrupted by the results.

These generalizations are not always true. In large, weakly controlled agencies, the agency manager may seize upon outside evaluation to reduce the independence of the particular program or subunit. In this case, the manager of the independent program is rarely enthusiastic about outside evaluation. In other cases, outside evelution is necessary because the agency has to prove that its program is worth supporting and doing a good job. Internal evaluations rarely provide credible results to outsiders.

To reduce the threatening aspects of evaluations, Wholey proposes evaluation assessments (EA). Some EAs have already been completed.

> (EA) is a form of preprogram evaluations, designed to determine if the program is ready to be managed to achieve performance and outcomes, what changes are needed to allow results oriented management and whether evaluation is likely to contribute to improved program performance. If the answers are yes, program evaluation proceeds. It seems to be well accepted. Some federal Health and Human Service managers commented "We realized through EA that our goals were too broad, so we revised planning guidance to the field agencies to focus on four core areas." Furthermore, "The assessment confirmed our suspicions; it showed routine reporting was not really telling us enough about program performance. On the positive side, it showed that a wealth of anecdotal information about performance was available in the field. This data could be the basis for evaluation."[15]

EA may make agencies more receptive to evaluation and may even help them in nonthreatening ways. But agencies and programs still fear evaluation.

Why Are Evaluations So Often Negative?

Are evaluations always negative? No. If so, do most programs get a clean bill of health? No. Undeserved praise or complete damnation are rare, and most programs fall between these extremes. Unfortunately, anything short of universal praise gives critics a chance to be heard and even good reviews pose some threats to insiders.

There are several reasons why evaluations aren't generally glowing, positive statements. Reviewers aren't journalists—they are restrained in both criticism and compliments. Evaluations are often dry, methodology-driven documents. Statements are hedged. The evaluator frequently cannot come to a clear-cut answer.

Another reason is that public agencies have multiple goals and in striving to meet all of them, they often fall short of achieving any one. Indeed, multiple goals such as, say, both improving the competence of clients by quickly sending them back to school and returning them to economic activity may work against each other.

Federal aid programs to police for specialized equipment may not only be concerned with radios but with the use of minority contractors and citizen participation in governing the department—requirements that are part of many federal grants. Minority contracts and more specialized training for members of the department may be as important as radio equipment to the granting agency, and evaluation techniques should consider this.

In theory, evaluating agencies with multiple goals is not difficult. Evaluators should focus on a specific, clearly defined question. In the Michigan Social Service Department study, it was whether education, training, and employment opportunities helped find jobs. However, focusing on a single goal is not as easy as it seems. The evaluation may be criticized if it ignores any of the mandated public goals for the agency.[16] Furthermore, interaction between the goals may make it difficult to isolate accomplishment on any one of them. Isolating performance on differing and sometimes conflicting programs makes program evaluation difficult.[17]

MANAGEMENT SCIENCE TECHNIQUES

There are a number of quantitative techniques that provide specific answers to managerial questions. Applying mathematics or applied economics to the matter, they have precise solutions when specific constraints, limits, or schedules are provided. Infrequently applied by most managers to routine decisions, they are most helpful when they can be used. These techniques are dubbed management science because they apply scientific method to managerial problems with mathematical precision. The trick is defining the problem so that this precision is possible, such as with inventory problems.

Network Analysis

Network analysis is the most common management science application.[18] It includes program evaluation review technique (PERT) and the critical path method (CPM). PERT and CPM are managerial control systems used to monitor projects or programs that extend over time and involve a host of interconnected yet independent events and activities. These techniques were developed in the late 1950s to aid in the scheduling and development of weapons systems. They are designed to organize the sequence and timing of project activities.

Once a project is chosen, it must be planned completely. All activities and events that affect completion must be specified in the order that each will be done. This includes the estimated time, cost, and personnel for each activity. Once this is done, a diagram is constructed showing the interrelatedness of each activity. This is the network analysis. Events (the start or completion of a given task in the project) and activities (the time and resources necessary to complete the task) are identified. The diagram illustrates in graphic form the time required to complete a task and the effect that time has on succeeding tasks. It's ridiculously simple for jobs like "Check with Michaels on the Marketing survey before beginning to dictate memo" but more complex for jobs like "Get bids on landscaping plans before developing requests for proposals on building sites while at the same time create a list of potential bidders for both contracts (as part of a 30- or 40-event process)." PERT and CPM also focus the attention of managers on tasks that must be completed before the job can continue. Exhibit 4–1 outlines a simple PERT chart with expected times shown in parentheses and with each event shown in circles.

The critical path method (CPM) is the series of activities that take the longest time span. It is called critical because slippages will delay the project. There is no slack time to be "crashed" or used to catch up on an overdue project.

The strengths of PERT and CPM are that they require detailed planning before starting a project. If costs are added to the times for activities, the PERT chart becomes a cost-control device. A further advantage is that anticipation of bottlenecks is made easier and management control is simplified. Almost all large projects formally use PERT and CPM. Good managers use informal versions of it for all projects with any time consideration.

As is the case with most management science techniques, the actual use of PERT and CPM varies. In some organizations, even routine tasks

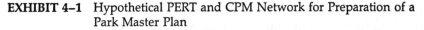

EXHIBIT 4–1   Hypothetical PERT and CPM Network for Preparation of a Park Master Plan

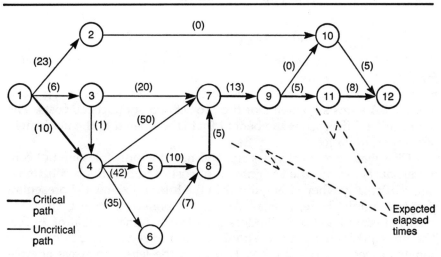

Critical path method (CPM)

1 Park budget authorized
4 Master plan consultant hired
5 Consultant report received
8 Consultant report reviewed by department
7 Recommendation to city manager
9 Recommendation to city council
11 Council consideration and hearing
12 Council approval

Uncritical path events

2 Park department review of all park master plans
10 Park director approval of departmental review
3 Review by park advisory board
6 Citizen unofficial comments on park planning and usage

Note: Not all elapsed times are described; expected times are shown in parentheses and events are shown in circles.

SOURCE: Grover Starling, *Managing the Public Sector* (Chicago: Dorsey Press, 1982), p. 216. As adapted from Air Force Systems Command (1963: 11–18).

get an informal analysis and a completion estimate. In others, some tricky projects don't have a formal PERT. There is some debate over how much top managers use PERT and CPM to "manage by exception." Critical projects with the risk of blockages may get more managerial attention than the use of network analysis implies. Sapolsky suggests that the U.S. Defense Department Polaris missile found PERT and CPM more valuable in convincing outsiders that the project was under control than it was in scheduling missile production.[19]

Cost Benefit Analysis (CBA)

CBA has been used for many years to compare costs and benefits for projects that require large sums of money, such as water projects, new towns, highways, and some social programs such as drug treatment. CBA sums all benefits of the project and subtracts all costs. The net positive difference is the benefit that is compared to the net benefit of competing projects.

CBA was developed years ago and now the principles are not controversial. However, the assignment of costs and benefits is controversial, particularly when either occurs in the future. Exhibit 4–2 presents a simple example. Here, a small dam is the preferred project, since the marginal cost of $6,000 is still less than the marginal benefit of $9,000. The principle is that projects should be authorized as long as marginal benefits exceed marginal costs. However, the least expensive alternative—an earth dam—has the best ratio of benefits to costs (two to one, or $8,000 to $4,000), which may make it an acceptable alternative if the money for the small dam is unavailable. Furthermore, the large dam still has a total favorable ratio of benefits to costs although it is less desirable from a marginal view than the small dam. Property owners who may benefit from the larger dam may lobby for it, and their interests coincide with the agency, which would like to build the large dam.

CBA is far from an exact science, even though the methods are straightforward. Costs and benefits are not always discounted over the years in which they occur. Money used to build the dam or, more commonly, benefits received from the dam, are both worth less in future years than now. Since many projects have a long-term stream of benefits with costs concentrated in early years, discounting future benefits may make many projects unfavorable. For example, at a 6 percent discount rate (equal to a 6 percent inflation rate), a benefit of $1,000 two years from now is worth only $890 now (in present day values). A high discount rate makes few projects feasible. The Army Corps of Engineers used a 2.63 percent discount rate for years, which made many projects appear desirable, when a 6 percent rate would have eliminated nearly two thirds of them.[20]

Calculating costs and benefits is also difficult. Costs are calculated more precisely than benefits. In addition, opportunity costs are not considered. The alternative uses of the $15,000 for the small dam in Exhibit 4–2 might go to, say, a drug prevention program. The real dam costs are the lost drug-prevention benefits.

EXHIBIT 4–2   Cost Benefit Analysis of Flood Protection Project

Plan	Annual Project Cost	Benefit (Reduced Annual Damage)	Marginal Cost	Marginal Benefit
No protection	0	0	0	0
Earth levee	$ 4,000	$ 8,000	$ 4,000	$ 8,000
Levee with spillwater	9,000	15,000	5,000	7,000
Small dam	15,000	24,000	6,000	9,000
Large dam	32,000	36,000	17,000	12,000

SOURCE: Adapted by permission of Prentice-Hall, Inc. Otto Eckstein, *Public Finance*, 4th ed., (Englewood Cliffs, N.J.: Prentice-Hall, © 1979), p. 21.

Tallying benefits is difficult. Dams, for example, have many benefits in addition to loss of flood damage. Navigation may be improved. Recreation benefits from boating may be created. Wildlife may be destroyed or enhanced, resulting in intangible costs and benefits.

There may be distributional benefits. These are political gains from spreading projects widely enough around the state, congressional district, or nation to gain overall support for reservoir projects. To build mostly cost-effective projects, some noncost-effective projects may have to be included to gain political support.

Cost benefit analyses are made by specialists, not by top-level managers. This doesn't mean that top managers aren't deeply involved with these studies—only that they don't do the studies themselves. Top managers need to examine carefully the assumptions that underlie analyses of costs and benefits. Are they too optimistic? Too pessimistic? Do they make sense so that political decisions supporting them are defensible? Does the agency want to justify its programs or projects with CBA analyses? There may be other nonCBA justifications more acceptable to legislators or executives.

CBA is a powerful technique for deciding among competing projects. The stakes are high to proponents and opponents of a project as well as to the agency that will design, operate, or build it. Enormous pressures exist to fudge the analysis one way or another, or to choose a more favorable discount rate, or to ignore certain costs and include other benefits. The job of top managers is to use CBA as originally intended. It is a quantitative guide to decision making, not an ironclad means to justify or rule out specific choices. In the latter cases, the credibility of the agency is at stake and only top management can provide the leadership to assure that CBA is a neutral means to an end, not an end in itself.[21]

Operations Research (OR)

Several management science techniques involve mathematical approaches to clearly defined problems. They include linear programming, inventory control models, queuing theories (waiting lines), and mathematical simulations of ill-defined problems. Simulations are included because of their mathematical basis even though the problem cannot be defined precisely as in the other models.

These are the basic OR techniques. They were developed during World War II by the British for purposes such as locating radar stations and fuse settings for submarine bombs. Some applications were used by the United States in the 1960s, mostly associated with the Defense Department's program-planning-budgeting system (see Chapter 7). These analyses included, for example, calculations of the mix of ships and cargo planes for maximum responses to various war threats in different parts of the world. A similar example involved studies about the kinds of weapon systems that maximized the destruction of bridges under specific conditions and topography.

These mathematical techniques are based on technical criteria where agreement on goals is assumed. No one wants to lose a war, waste bombs, or increase defense spending, and so the techniques are noncontroversial. Even when used for social programs, OR techniques don't usually precipitate major controversies about their validity.[22]

Linear Programming

Linear programming is a mathematical way of developing a solution to the problem of optimizing scarce resources when there are specific quantifiable constraints such as working hours or fixed costs. The U.S. Forest Service used a linear programming equation to maximize the number of cows and elk using a grazing range. The constraints were: (1) cows use twice as much range as elk, (2) the limits of range and feeding habits limit the total number of animals to 600, (3) there could be no more than either 400 elk or 200 cows. The optimal solution of 300 elk and 300 cattle depended on plotting equations graphically.[23]

Queuing Theory

Queuing theory[24] is an attempt to minimize client waiting time in lines and public expenditures for additional clerks or stations. There are trade-offs between customer convenience and public expense. Clients are not always people. They may, for example, be vehicles with minor repairs that will, unless serviced, be driven until major but preventable repairs occur. Questions asked of the queuing specialist are, for example, how much shorter would the average line be if an extra window is opened? How often do horrible examples occur, such as a 45-minute wait in a driver's license application line? What would happen to waiting lines if each application could be processed a minute faster? Most questions or problems such as these are usually handled by some simulation with random numbers.

Inventory Models

Inventory models deal with delivering materials of some kind to using departments. The rate at which goods leave the inventory is given, or can be estimated, and the decision makers control the supply by reordering. Control of the supply makes the process a set of operating rules rather than a random occurrence. Inventory managers try to increase order sizes to minimize the number of orders, while also trying to minimize the storage costs by keeping supplies at the lowest possible level.

Inventories include more than paper, paving supplies, or parts. Cash or employees, for example, are also inventories. Cash management involves an inventory model that keeps the minimum amount of cash for expenses and invests the rest. Executive replacement or new groups of fire department recruits are also inventories whose holding costs and ordering costs (recruitment and training) can be predicted by an inventory model. The key, other than estimating storage and ordering costs, is determining how quickly supplies, executives, or cash will be used by departments, administrative assignments, or expenses. The computations are straightforward. In the following commonly used equation, Q is the most economical quantity to order, Co is the cost of ordering a unit, Ch is the cost of holding a unit-per-time period, and D is the quantity of units used in a time period.[25]

$$Q = \frac{2\,Co\,D}{Ch}$$

Simulation

Simulations develop a mathematical model of the problem under consideration after the problem is defined (defining the problem is often the toughest part of the simulation) using equations to represent the interrelationships. The model is usually programmed on a computer.

One type is called Monte Carlo, named for the resort's roulette wheels. The simulation relies on random but probable events that are represented by random numbers such as fires per day when a small fire department is deciding whether to purchase a third engine. Using historical observations, a table of random numbers is used to simulate the number of fires each day. Then, total costs over a year are totaled, day by day, including both community fire loss and cost of maintaining the fire engines. The simulation indicates that a third engine will or will not reduce total department and community losses.[26]

A more complex simulation was used in Cleveland, Ohio in the early 1970s to develop sample routes for solid waste pickups by the Public Works Department.[27] The system collected data on routes, predicted changes in population and in the transportation system, used continuous data to feed back into the system, and used the model predictions to make management decisions. The model has master programs such as truck availability, disposal site location, and information such as distance traveled. The system monitored two routes and resulted in eliminating backyard collections and reducing collection crews by two persons, leaving a four-person crew reduced to two. On these routes, the cost dropped from $30 to $13 a ton and the project was expanded to an on-line solid waste management system for the entire city.

Summary of Management Science Techniques

With the exception of network analysis and cost benefit analysis, management science has not been used heavily in the public sector. It still mystifies managers even though the techniques are generally straightforward. Indeed, many managers distrust management science, believing that it only answers trivial questions. Thus, while some claim that management science results are oversold, other still underutilize it. Don't blame management scientists, who can only solve the problems that interest top managers. Blame for failures rests mostly on managers. Peter Drucker noted:

> Managers, by and large, have failed to take managerial responsibility for management scientists and management science. They have refused to accept the fact that the management scientist, like any high grade specialist, depends on the manager for direction and effectiveness. They have left the management sciences unmanaged—and are therefore largely responsible for their degenerating into a box of tricks, a "management gadget bag" of answers to nonexisting questions.[28]

QUALITATIVE TECHNIQUES FOR DECISION MAKING

Managerial decisions are usually based on qualitative judgments rather than quantitative data. First, hard data is not always available and is often unreliable. And, since many managers are unaccustomed to using it, they may not search for hard data or may be disinclined to use it even if it is readily available.

Another reason is that hard data or management science information is often irrelevant to the case at hand. Using the earlier linear programming example, the ability to maximize the elk and cow population on a given grazing area doesn't justify grazing if political leaders don't believe in leasing Forest Service lands to private parties. The ultimate critierion is political acceptability.

There are a number of qualitative means to improve decision making that many effective managers use. These means supplement the more quantitative methods when the latter are available, and they can often stand alone as the basis for decisions. These qualitative methods include organizational development, management by objective, quality circles, the nominal group, the Delphi technique, and citizen participation. They all either develop alternative choices for decisionmakers or else improve the flow of information—enabling managers to make wiser choices.

Organizational Development (OD)

OD is a deliberate attempt to open up an organization by breaking down interpersonal barriers between members or by creating teams whose members exhibit high degrees of openness and trust in each other.[29] OD makes the organization receptive to change by making members more aware of their values and more supportive of other members. OD programs have objectives such as reducing the tendency to avoid problems, increasing trust and openness of members, developing more effective problem-solving techniques, increasing communication, and supplementing role or status authority with the authority of knowledge and competence.

These objectives, stripped of their jargon, directly affect decision making. Unfreezing the organization improves decision making by avoiding hierarchical blockages to upward communication of information. Supplementing the authority of role and status with the authority of information means that decisions are made by persons with more information or specialized knowledge.

OD critics point out that the process has a dark side as well. OD is often threatening to individuals and can lead to manipulation by leaders or group members. OD is a widely used process that is still a controversial device.

Although OD isn't usually thought of as a tool to improve decision making, that is the practical effect. The goals of making organizations more effective, improving trust among members, and developing problem-solving climates all support an improved decision-making system.

These goals may not improve any specific decision, but they will improve decision making in general and will increase member satisfaction with the decision making system. Many organizations have used OD effectively, as the following cases show.

MARTA (Metropolitan Atlanta Regional Transit Authority) is a major transit system in Atlanta that operated under an OD management system to speed the building of its rail and transit system. In the first year, executives spent approximately 40 hours a year in off-site learning experiences for decision making, openness, and giving and receiving feedback. Two or three times a year for five years, executives held retreats to build and repair relationships and ventilate concerns. An opponent of team-building OD approaches admitted that:

> "I preferred a set of one-on-one relationships. But I came to see that we just could not have done it my way. So I changed, perhaps grudgingly, but enough so that I am now a different and better me."[30]

Governor James Hunt of North Carolina adopted an OD approach upon taking office in 1977 to implement his gubernatorial strategy. He hoped that a team-building system would motivate senior managers to implement his policies more effectively. Apparently OD helped build relationships between new cabinet members and strengthened existing relationships between cabinet members. A veteran state careerist noted:

> In previous administrations, I saw the following transition problems: The governor had no mechanism to communicate his program to the administration, and no way to deal with the personality dynamics generated within the top group. . . . I think that by having these retreats we did have the opportunity to bring to a head relationship problems between the governor and cabinet level people. . . . We avoided also a lot of undercutting through ignorance of the governor's program or what each other was doing. It also gave the governor a chance to share his way of working and objectives.[31]

Some attempts fail. One such example reported was in the Louisville School of Denistry from 1971 to 1974, where professional and academic jealousy prevented a new dean from changing the organization, and led to his resignation.[32] But successful applications increase the quality and quantity of usable information for decisionmakers in addition to increasing trust and support.

Management by Objectives (MBO)

MBO is a management system and a way of implementing decisions or programs rather than an aid to making the decisions. It is a process whereby superiors and subordinates jointly agree upon the goals that the employee or lower-level manager will accomplish. These goals, such as 30 permits issued per year, are guides to operating the organizational unit or activity and for assessing subordinate performance. The employee is not to be judged on personality traits or other subjective factors, but on goal accomplishment in specified periods. MBO is a psychological contract between the subordinate and manager. The subordinate commits himself to specified goals while the superior binds herself to judge his effectiveness only on accomplishment of the goals. This process usually involves determining overall and individual unit goals and objectives, a series of periodic checks to measure accomplishment (during which time goals can be modified), and a final review. Drucker describes MBO as ". . . the process in which decisions are made, goals are identified, priorities are set, and organization structure designed for the specific purposes of the institution."[33]

MBO also has side benefits. It increases organizational commitment of both parties and strengthens the willingness of subordinates to act. In the Public Health Service, one manager lauded an MBO system, saying:

> The Assistant Secretary of Health is out of town more than two weeks per month, giving speeches and meeting with groups. So an administrator can't just pick up a phone and get a decision from him. But administrators all know they have regular meetings with him to work out any problems. And in between their MBO meetings, the deadlines give the higher administrators leverage to get actions and decisions out of the lower ones. They can say, "I have to report all this is completed to the Assistant Secretary by our meeting next week."[34]

MBO, in theory, is an idyllic picture of all executives pulling together in perfect harmony like a team of well-trained horses, with all personal goals neatly linked to organizational goals. Sometimes MBO works like this. However, in public agencies where multiple goals create difficulties in establishing clear objectives, it is the exception rather than the rule. Police departments, for example, are expected to reduce crime, respond quickly to calls for service, and solve crimes quickly. No single criterion meets all these objectives. Furthermore, these objectives are not only potentially contradictory, but they are difficult to describe clearly. Reducing the crime rate is difficult to measure, especially in one unit, and credit may be due to forces outside the department. As a result, it's not easy to apply MBO to police departments or the public sector in general except in ways such as "30 training sessions for officers will be held each year," or "75 percent of all traffic citations will result in court convictions." Even so, these statements help develop a formal basis for judging subordinate behavior and focusing attention on performance-related issues.[35]

How does a system that emphasizes agreement in implementing or managing programs contribute to better decisions? Basically, by forcing top-level managers to focus on how decisions are implemented, MBO requires that decisions be grounded firmly in the subordinate's working situation (managers often refer to this level as "where the rubber meets the road"). In a true MBO system, subordinates resist being held accountable for objectives that cannot be met. This forces managers to account for the real problems of implementation that plague subordinates. Havens notes that ". . . the principal value of the formal MBO process lies in forcing people to think about the objectives of their activities in a more clear and precise way."[36]

Quality Circles

Quality circles (QC) are popular in private and many public agencies. The most frequent public sector examples are in Defense Department facilities.[37] QCs are associated with Japanese management and their reputation for quality control. U.S. industry use began in 1974 with the Lockheed Missile System decision, where a six-to-one return on investment was reported.

QCs are small groups of individuals from the same work site who meet regularly to identify, analyze, and solve work-related problems. QCs improve the decision-making process, but it is more accurate to say that they result in different decisions. QC decisions are made at the shop or production line level, where bottlenecks can be eliminated or working conditions improved. These are micro rather than macro level decisions dealing with specific task or production matters. They improve the decision-making process by requiring persons closest to the issue to make operational changes.

QC decisions deal with small issues only in the sense that they have little policy impact. The actual savings can involve large sums of money. One group at the Norfolk Navy Shipyard saved over $200,000 the first year by reducing tool distribution waiting lines.[38]

Quality circles are governed by strict procedures including formal top management support, a steering committee, a systemwide QC facilitator, circle leadership by the work unit supervisor, training of circle members, and so on. QCs are considered a productivity improvement device. However, by considering a wider range of issues ranging from scheduling to maintenance, they improve the decision-making process by allowing the authority of knowledge and ideas to dominate decisions at lower levels. They operate to unfreeze the organization at lower levels in ways similar to the OD process.

The Delphi Technique

The Delphi technique, developed at the Rand corporation, is used primarily for futures research. It is also applicable to the development of preferences among groups of individuals. Delphi solicits the opinions of expert panels on given issues, and through successive sets of survey questionnaires to each expert, it informs them of previous group opinions compared to their opinions and solicits further information. As individuals see the views of other experts, their opinions usually change, and over a number of questionnaire iterations, certain opinions move to the forefront. Panelists are anonymous to avoid dominance by stronger personalities. Probability estimates of events occurring are given (e.g., 45 percent of all experts on the panel believe there is at least a 20 percent probability that a cancer cure can be found by 1995). The purpose of the exercise is to gain consensus among the panel of experts without subjecting members to pressures to conform other than through the weight of expert opinion as shown on each questionnaire round.

A nonexpert panel use for the Delphi is to elicit citizen opinion and participation, as in cases such as developing long-range urban plans. In 1977, Norman, Oklahoma, extensively revised its city master plan with a Delphi exercise involving a group of civic elites selected by the mayor and city council (in this case, a group of elites ranking preferences is similar to a panel of experts making predictions). The 63 members responded to a set of questions about a range of civic issues. In the first wave of responses, housing, energy conservation, and rehabilitation of older homes ranked first, second, and third, respectively, but after four sets of questionnaires providing feedback to the panelists, rehabilitation of homes was first while energy conservation dropped to sixth. A growth guidance system and development patterns reducing transportation demands ranked 16 and 11, respectively, on the first iteration were eventually ranked third and fourth in the final outcome. This shows how the Delphi feedback technique can change priorities.

The results of this civic elite Delphi were compared to a mass citizen survey, with similar results, and the council later adopted a new general plan incorporating these results.[39] The Delphi and community survey were originally used by the council to elicit both elite and mass citizen participation. They provided useful information for decision makers, proving that the Delphi is useful in the decision-making process. Where feasible, the Delphi is an excellent way to elicit expert or elite information for decision makers.

The nominal group method (NGM), discussed in Chapter 8 in connection with a budget cutback, is another process similar in some ways to the Delphi, although the NGM is used to reach decisions rather than to provide information to the decision maker.

Citizen Participation

Citizen participation is, in a limited but rather important sense, a qualitative approach to decision making. It gathers information about citizen opinion and applies that knowledge to modify, choose, and eliminate programs. There are many devices to elicit citizen views, all of which involve gathering information from citizens directly.

Citizen participation is much more than one trick in a manager's bag of administrative techniques. It's a basic part of the broader political tradition in the United States.[40]

Citizen participation is also a means of improving decision making by increasing the amount of information, and a means of making choices more acceptable. Decisions are more readily accepted if the persons involved helped make them. The catch is that citizen views are elusive, at best. It is much easier to respond to the voice of special interests than to find out what the general public wants. Does the long-standing Friends of the Library organization, for example, represent the public interest more than 100 citizens who storm a council chamber demanding additional police protection? Public officials, from elected politicians to career managers, spend much of their time wondering whether a given group represents the public interest or only a partial interest.

"General broad-interest citizen participation is difficult to find, or even muster, in this community. Only when a government decision directly affects a person or group is interest (resulting in participation) shown," reported one Massachusetts town.[41] This view is shared by many local officials, particularly about the results of budget hearings that were mandated by federal general revenue sharing requirements. One Alabama city official reported that:

> Citizen participation could be a useful guide in formulating programs. However, it is usually the case that only minorities or special interest groups attend hearings for such programs. We, therefore, do not know what the majority of the citizens desire.[42]

These comments show that meaningful citizen participation cannot be evoked at the convenience of officials. Rather, it emerges out of a long and concerted effort. Revenue sharing requirements can mandate hearings but they cannot make participation meaningful. Fortunately, budget hearings are not the only way to elicit citizen views. A Scottsdale, Arizona city official reported that:

> Our city makes use of citizen participation throughout the year—in workshops, seminars and forums. This increases their (citizen) awareness of the budgeting process, provides elected officials with needed information. It may be that our year round program has a direct result in the low attendance at budget hearings.[43]

As in Scottsdale, there are many other devices to elicit citizen participation. At the federal level, in the late 1970s, there were nearly 1,000 advisory committees or boards ranging from the President's Council on Energy Research to the Agriculture Department's committee on Hog Cholera Eradication.[44] However, advisory committees don't rate highly as a form of citizen participation because members, at least at the federal level, don't participate in publicized meetings and are often co-opted by the agencies they advise into supporting existing programs or plans (see Chapter 5 for a discussion of cooptation). The federal government has been more successful in furthering citizen participation through its grant programs, which require recipients to develop forms of participation. For example, state bilingual education programs must have their application for federal support developed "in consultation with parents of children of limited English speaking ability, teachers and secondary students." Less specifically, urban mass transit capital improvement grants must merely "involve the public."[45]

Managers seek forms of participation that help them evaluate and modify specific government programs. One such way is the opinion survey. Kirkwood, Missouri has used a mailed public opinion questionnaire, receiving up to a 25 percent response rate. Communities as diverse as Winnetka, Illinois; Tallahassee, Florida; and Pembroke, Massachusetts use mailed questionnaires to elicit citizen comments or to advise them of what has occurred.[46] These surveys are increasingly common. Municipalities use them to assess citizen satisfaction with existing programs, and to identify service delivery problems. An official from Wichita, Kansas reports that:

> In the 1970s, citizen participation has increased geometrically to a point where every major policy decision is subject to extensive citizen input or review prior to final government action. The major reason for the increase has been an aggressive governing body which has promoted and encouraged citizen participation.[47]

Public officials are aware that substantial citizen participation in government decision making increases support for the final decision. A Fort Worth, Texas official bragged that:

> Our recently passed bond program made extensive use of citizen participation. This was the first time so much effort was taken to secure the input of the general public on a capital improvement program. . . . The result was the passage of all propositions by the widest margin in our city's history. The citizen contact was divided into two parts. First, a series of neighborhood meetings were conducted to determine what the citizens wanted to see in the program. These ideas were combined with the analysis of professional staff and the input from council members to develop a well-rounded program. Next, after the program was finalized, another round of neighborhood meetings was held to inform citizens of what actually was contained in the proposed program.[48]

For many managers, accurately assessing public opinion is a major accomplishment. The opinion survey is the best way, even though there are difficulties. Surveys are expensive, usually require trained specialists to guarantee their accuracy, and can embarrass officials if the responses demand items the unit can't or doesn't want to provide. Granted, mass opinion may not be as important as the opinion of important groups of clients, taxpayers, or others who feel intensely about issues. But no other way provides such direct, simply information from persons whose views are ultimately the only ones that count.

Citizen participation is not always a carefully planned set of surveys or public hearings. Particularly at the local level, direct confrontations can occur. In such cases, managers may get more direct public participation than they really want. Yet, troublesome as they are, demonstrations are a form of citizen participation which show the intensity of feelings that some groups have. The late Gordon Chase, once New York City's health service administrator, pointed out the strengths of this form of citizen participation as well as its difficulties:

> It is difficult to convey the emotional and professional pressures that confrontation tactics place on public managers. Examples are countless; ten constituents barging into your office to protest a rumored program cutback; fifteen more in your outer office ready to tear you limb from limb for having too few doctors in their local clinic; a drug program administrator barricaded in an office by irate addicts. . . . The really frustrating things about these encounters . . . is that community groups are usually right or at least partially right in their complaints.
>
> Why do community groups tend to be generally right on the merits? Unlike most other groups that may affect health care (or any other government service)—such as unions, overhead agencies, press—which are motivated primarily by things other than making people healthy. . . . a community group involved in health is primarily motivated by a desire to make people healthy.[49]

Few managers seek confrontations, even though, as Chase points out, this is one way to get direct client feedback about public services. As Chase points out, it's hard to mistake what these clients want and how they feel about services. The problem is that confrontations usually involve one geographical area, one service, or one client group, while the manager may have responsibility for several hospitals, many different type of services, and more than one client group. Managers are never sure that the enraged group they confront represents the opinions of a cross section of clients. This is a good reason for using citizen surveys whenever possible (before the confrontation, of course).

Continued efforts to elicit public opinion and citizen participation help the manager obtain additional information about program decisions. It's a rather difficult and time-consuming way of gathering information, but it pays large dividends compared to other techniques mentioned in this chapter. The experience of Metropolitan Atlanta Regional Transit Authority (MARTA) illustrates this idea. Each MARTA rail station had local planning committees, composed mostly of residents with some MARTA staff. These committees developed and reviewed each individual station to assure that it conformed to neighborhood individuality. Most MARTA executives attribute great success to this type of citizen participation. One commented; "Why do we have a system without graffiti?" Answering himself, he said,

> In large part, the system looks the way it does because we involved neighborhoods in designing their stations. In many ways MARTA became everyone's system—poor as well as rich, black and white. And almost everybody helps take care of the system, in their many ways.[50]

SUMMARY

This decision-making chapter dealt with the techniques executives use both to obtain higher quality information for decisions and to actually help them make decisions. Decision making is a social process carried on in a political setting, but it is also an intellectual process that is improved by more and better information. This chapter covered some of the devices managers employ to obtain such information.

The use of computers for information storage and analysis is exploding, and executives can now usually get direct access to a mainframe computer from their desk or even have a microcomputer for their use. The use of program evaluation is also increasing, as political leaders and top managers increasingly demand program reviews (there is little evidence that program managers are equally anxious to have their programs reviewed). With computers and program evaluations, the major managerial issue is obtaining and using information. Computers can provide a wealth of information, if managers are careful to assure that the information is usable—otherwise, a computerized system will not provide the information for management decisions. Likewise, much information from careful program evaluations can be developed only if top management insists on evaluations and if the fears of operating managers are overcome.

There are two broad categories of techniques for obtaining better decision-making information. Quantitative techniques involve management science, or technical and highly mathematical techniques. They include linear programming, queuing theories, network analysis, cost benefit analysis, inventory models, and mathematical simulations. Some of these techniques, such as cost benefit analysis and network analysis through PERT and CPM, are common. The other techniques, highly useful when applicable, are not common in most public management situations.

Qualitative methods are softer than management science. They include the Delphi technique, quality circles, management by objectives, organizational development and citizen participation. The Delphi is best used to obtain future predictions from a panel of experts. Quality circles are a formal work group effort to suggest operational changes. The three methods, management by objectives, citizen participation, and organizational development are not only used to garner information but also to improve the decision-making system. Generally, the latter techniques seek to bind people and groups, both inside and outside the organization, to a shared sense of values, which results in improved or new information to guide decision makers.

Effective and innovative managers make use of these methods whenever they are feasible. The methods are primarily exercises in organizational maintenance, as managers search for more effective ways to manage the organization. However, some of the qualitative methods such as OD, involve basic changes in the internal makeup of the organization. When this occurs, these methods involve strategic plans for the organization, its clients, and the representational activity involved in such plans.

NOTES

1. This list is taken largely from James Danziger, "Computers, Local Government, and the Litany of EDP," *Public Administration Review*, January–February 1977, pp. 28–37.
2. Over 40 states use computer systems for state budgeting. See Frank Kelly, "Computerization of Budgeting Processes in the States," *Public Administration Review*, July–August 1978, pp. 381–86.
3. David Garson, "Minicomputer Application in Public Administration," *Public Administration Review*, September–October 1983, pp. 543–48.
4. *Productivity Management* (Stillwater, OK: Oklahoma Productivity Center, Oklahoma State University, Winter 1984), p. 3.
5. Alana Northrup, William Dutton, and Kenneth Kraemer, "The Management of Computer Applications in Local Government," *Public Administration Review*, May–June 1982, pp. 234–43.
6. Danziger, "Computers, Local Government, and the Litany of EDP," p. 34.
7. The literature on computer and management information systems is expanding enormously. In addition to the works already cited, see the special "Mini-Symposium on Microcomputers in Local Government," *Public Administration Review*, January–February 1984. Also see Kenneth Kraemer and James Danziger, "Computers and Control in the Work Environment," *Public Administration Review*, January–February 1984, pp. 32–42; Lyle Thompson, "Manager's Perceptions of Microcomputers Impacts," a paper presented to the Annual Conference of the American Society for Public Administration, Denver, April 1984; and John Moore and Whitfield Ayres, "Computer Users among Local Governments in South Carolina," a paper presented to the American Society for Public Administration, Denver, April 1984.

8. Urban Institute and International City Management Association, *Measuring the Effectiveness of Municipal Services* (Washington, D.C., 1976).
9. Robert Pursley and Neil Snortland, *Managing Public Organizations* (New York: Duxbury, 1980), pp. 389–90.
10. Harry Hatry, Richard Winnie, and Donald Fisk, *Practical Program Evaluation for State and Local Governments*, 2nd ed., (Washington, D.C.: The Urban Institute Press, 1981), p. 43.
11. See Grover Starling, *Managing the Public Sector* (Chicago: Dorsey Press, 1982), p. 293.
12. Edwin Hargrove, "The Bureaucratic Politics of Evaluation: A Case Study of the Department of Labor," *Public Administration Review*, March–April 1980, p. 152.
13. Ibid., p. 155.
14. Thomas and Joanne Greer, "Problems in Evaluating Costs and Benefits of Social Programs," *Public Administration Review*, March–April 1982, p. 151.
15. Martin Strasberg and Joseph Wholey, "Evaluability Assessment: From Theory to Practice in the Department of Health and Human Services," *Public Administration Review*, January–February 1983, p. 69. Reprinted with permission from *Public Administration Review*, © 1983 by the American Society for Public Administration, Washington, D.C.
16 Peter Drucker, "The Seven Deadly Sins in Public Administration," *Public Administration Review*, March–April 1980, pp. 103–7, savages public agencies that do not focus on a single, clear objective. Unfortunately, legislative mandates with multiple goals often make it impossible for agencies to focus their attention on a single goal.
17. For further information on program evaluation, see Harry Havens, "Program Evaluation and Program Management," *Public Administration Review*, July–August 1981, pp. 480–85; Michael White et al., *Managing Public Systems; Analytic Techniques for Public Administration* (New York: Duxbury, 1980), pp. 86–107.; Joseph Wholey, *Evaluation and Effective Public Management* (Boston: Little, Brown, 1983); Hatry, Winnie, and Fisk, *Practical Program Evaluation for State and Local Governments*; and Aaron Wildavsky, "The Self-Evaluating Organization," *Public Administration Review*, September–October 1972, pp. 509–20.
18. For a more complete discussion of these techniques with public sector applications, see White et al., *Managing Public Systems*, pp. 360–70. Most basic textbooks have simplified explanations of this technique, for example, Thomas Murphy, ed., *Contemporary Public Management* (Itasca, Ill.: F. E. Peacock Publishers, 1981), pp. 249–51.
19. Harvey Sapolsky, *The Polaris System Development* (Cambridge, Mass.: Harvard University Press, 1972).
20. Pursley and Snortland, *Managing Public Organizations*, pp. 426–33.
21. Cost benefit analysis has a range of articles for those interested in further information. See Robert Haveman and Julius Margolis, eds., *Public Expenditures and Policy Analysis*, 2nd ed., (Skokie, Ill.: Rand-McNally, 1977); Edith Stokey and Richard Zeckhauser, *A Primer for Policy Analysis* (New York: Norton, 1978); White et al., *Managing Public Systems*, pp. 292–318; and

Richard Bingham and Marcus Eldridge, eds., *Reaching Decisions in Public Policy and Administration* (New York: Longman, 1983), pp. 196–263.

22. Starling, *Managing the Public Sector*, p. 231.
23. Ibid., p. 249. White et al., *Managing Public Systems*, pp. 209–16 provides more details, including a real-life case study of the U.S. Coast Guard's goal programming.
24. White et al., *Managing Public Systems*, pp. 224–44.
25. Starling, *Managing the Public Sector*, p. 226.
26. White et al., *Managing Public Systems*, pp. 245–66.
27. Bingham and Eldridge, *Researching Decisions in Public Policy and Administration*, pp. 124–34.
28. Peter Drucker, *An Introductory View of Management* (New York: Harper & Row, 1977), p. 453.
29. Bingham and Eldridge, *Researching Decisions in Public Policy and Administration*, classify OD and MBO as a means for organizing decision making rather than a decision-making system. Also, see Richard Pattenaude and Roy Park, "Organizational Development," in Thomas Vocino and Jack Rabin, eds., *Contemporary Public Administration* (New York: Harcourt Brace Jovanovich, 1981), pp. 97–119.
30. Robert Golembiewski and Robert Kiepper, "Lessons from a Fast-Paced Public Project: Perspectives on Doing Better the Next Time," *Public Administration Review*, November–December 1983, p. 548.
31. David Kiel, "An Organizational Development Strategy for Policy Implementation: The Case of North Carolina State Government," *Public Administration Review*, July–August 1982, p. 379.
32. Mervyn Landay, "Organizational Development in a School of Dentistry," in Bingham and Eldridge, *Researching Decisions in Public Policy and Administration*, pp. 339–52.
33. Peter Drucker, "What Results Should You Expect? A User's Guide to MBO," *Public Administration Review*, January–February 1976, p. 19.
34. James Swiss, "Establishing a Management System: The Interaction of Power Shifts and Personality under Federal MBO," *Public Administration Review*, May–June 1983, p. 243.
35. For further information on MBO in the public sector, see M. K. Badawy, "Applying MBO to the Public Sector," *The Bureaucrat*, 6, (Fall 1977), pp. 2–18; Frank Sherwood and William Page, Jr., "MBO and Public Management," *Public Administration Review*, January–February 1976, pp. 5–12; Jon Jun, ed., "Symposium on Management by Objectives in the Public Sector," *Public Administration Review*, January–February 1976, pp. 1–45; and Bingham and Eldridge, *Researching Decisions in Public Policy and Administration*, pp. 35–72.
36. Harry Havens, "MBO and Program Evaluation, or Whatever Happened to PPBS," *Public Administration Review*, January–February 1976, p. 43.
37. Stephen Bryant and Joseph Kearns, "Worker's Brains as Well as Their Bodies," *Public Administration Review*, March–April 1982, pp. 144–51.
38. Ibid., p. 147.
39. David Morgan, John Pelissero, and Robert England, "Urban Planning: Us-

ing a Delphi as a Decision-Making Aid," *Public Administration Review*, July–August 1979, pp. 144–51.

40. Carole Pateman, *Participation and Democratic Theory* (Cambridge, Mass.: Harvard University Press, 1970).
41. John Rehfuss, "Citizen Participation in Urban Fiscal Decisions," *Urban Data Reports*, 10, no. 8, (Washington, D.C.: International City Management Association, 1978), p. 5.
42. Ibid., p. 5.
43. Ibid., p. 7.
44. Advisory Commission on Intergovernmental Relations, *Citizen Participation in the American Federal System* (Washington, D.C.; Report A–73, 1979), p. 184.
45. Ibid., p. 197.
46. Rehfuss, "Citizen Participation in Urban Fiscal Decisions," p. 13.
47. Ibid., p. 13.
48. Ibid., p. 13.
49. Gordon Chase and Elizabeth Reveal, *How To Manage in the Public Sector* (New York: Random House, 1983), pp. 125–27.
50. Golembiewski and Kiepper, "Lessons from a Fast-Paced Public Project," p. 551.

CHAPTER 5

Politics and Management

Dealing effectively with political situations is a real test of management. It also demonstrates the interrelatedness of organizational maintenance, representation, and planning.

Program politics—the bureaucratic struggle for position, resources, and power to accomplish organizational and personal goals—is a staple of bureaucratic life. Programs don't advance, services don't improve, and resources don't accumulate by a sanitized form of merit established by some god-like judge.

Instead, managers struggle for their programs in a tussle called bureaucratic (program) politics. It is a game with unwritten, rapidly changing rules that all top managers engage in by necessity if not by preference. Success in this game strengthens the manager's hand in organizational maintenance by attracting new resources or keeping old ones. Success in the game manifests effective organizational representation because the struggle places a premium on effective public and private contacts and personal persuasiveness. Likewise, success occurs more often when the manager has a viable long-range strategy for her agency.

Managers who aren't effective at bureaucratic politics are generally ranked as less-effective managers in an overall rating. In most cases, their organizations will do poorly vis-à-vis other organizations, and managers may be forced from their positions. The reason will usually be "ineffective representation" of the agency. This is not incorrect, even though success in bureaucratic politics is more than effective representation.

Political success is often related to a long-term organizational vision or plan. Such a vision is the task of leadership and strategic planning. A long-term plan places focus on the endless series of spats and political struggles—directing efforts toward a long-term objective. When, where, and how to battle depend on one's goals (or lack thereof). The manager with a long-term strategy will not necessarily win more battles than other managers, but he will be fighting in the right war.

POLITICS

There are three types of politics. One is partisan, or elective, politics. It is a struggle for elective office such as mayor or senator for personal reasons or for the right to pursue policies ratified by the election.

Bureaucratic or program politics, on the other hand, is the struggle among agencies and programs for resources and authority. As Chapter 3 indicated, these organizational goals often contain the personal goals of managers. Program politics also describes how agencies adjust and try to manipulate outside forces. Conceptually, there is little difference between partisan and bureaucratic politics, for both may involve struggles between alternative policies or programs. Practically, the difference is that: (1) program politics usually occurs behind the scenes, and (2) administrators shun partisan politics because taking part endangers their programs if the wrong candidate wins. In addition, partisan politics violates norms of managerial neutrality (and it is also often illegal). Because both policy and partisan politics are linked, however, it is often hard to separate them.

A third category, office politics, involves the universal search for personal advantage, position, or power, which occurs everywhere in public and private organizations. Office politics usually affects only primarily bureaucratic issues, although it can affect the choice of programs. In addition, it may consume so much executive attention that organizational needs are neglected.

Program politics permeates the higher levels of public management—involving decisions about what program gets resources and authority to provide which services at what level. By this definition, public managers make several political calculations every day. At the same time, they almost universally deny that these calculations affect their judgment.

In the United States, it is usually improper to admit that either partisanship or program or office politics affected your actions—unless you are a politician or actively engaged in partisan politics. Even then, many people consider political activity a necessary evil at best. At the administrative level, managers are considered unprofessional if they confess that political considerations affect their behavior. On the other hand, if they ignore political realities, they are at best ineffective and at worst jobless. Why don't we admit the reality of managerial lives?

Part of the reason is a cultural distaste for all politics; another part is the natural managerial dislike for actions necessitated by outside or irrational (partisan political) forces. Perhaps part can be traced to early writings in the public administration field that advocated a rigid dividing line between politics and administration. In the same way that econ-

omist John Maynard Keynes claimed that business leaders uncon-
sciously mouth the words of defunct economists, managers similarly
mouth the teachings of deceased public administration scholars.

The Gulf (or Short Step) between Politics and Administration

A century ago, Woodrow Wilson and Frank Goodnow drew a line
between politics and administration—referring to partisan politics.
Wilson wrote in 1887 that:

> The field of administration is a field of business. It is removed from the
> hurry and strife of politics . . . It is a part of political life only as the
> methods of the counting house are a part of the life of society . . . If I see a
> murderous fellow sharpening a knife cleverly, I can borrow his way of
> sharpening the knife without borrowing his probable intention to commit
> murder with it.[1]

In other words, knife sharpening was an administrative technique neutral toward the political question of murder. Goodnow agreed, arguing:

> There are in all governmental systems two primary or ultimate functions of
> government. . . . the expression of the will of the state and the execution
> of that will. . . . these functions are, respectively, Politics and Administra-
> tion.[2]

Goodnow and Wilson tried to establish public administration on
solid ground by finding a scientific basis for it. This was necessary for
public managers claiming professional status. Trying to establish the
importance of high-level administrative action, these authors may have
drawn an overly rigid line between politics and administration. This line
is now known as the politics-administration dichotomy.

In the late nineteenth century, Wilson and Goodnow created a division between politics and administration to allow for stronger and more
creative management. Since that day, public managers have been responsible for more complex and widespread activities—from space travel to public housing. This increased range and complexity of programs
in the twentieth century gives rise to program politics. Program politics
is distinguished from partisan politics in that Goodnow and Wilson used
the latter term, but most onlookers do not make this distinction. While
the argument that managers should avoid politics is disingenuous and
pernicious, it is dangerous for managers to admit considering political
pressures—whether from partisan or program politics.

Program versus Partisan Politics

Program politics deeply enmeshes managers in issues linked to partisan politics. Career officials should not make final decisions. But managers frame the options, propose alternatives, explain the difficulties of

existing policies, and set the technical and programmatic outlines of what policies are considered. In addition, they contend for resources for existing and proposed programs. These responsibilities cannot be avoided. From the humblest city manager explaining how much a new street painting program costs to the head of NASA outlining the limits of space flight, all managers become involved in policy, if not politics.

Managers cannot avoid politics, even by refusing to initiate programs. They must manage programs and implement policies even if they had no part in initiating them. Implementation has become almost as involved in policy as the actual policy initiation. Maintenance of the organization, presumably a routine managerial function, involves policy decisions. Technical questions of how streets should be paved suddenly become arguments over whether they should be paved. Questions of paving raise the question of who pays—the driving public, the general public, or the property owner.

Patients of mental health facilities used to be warehoused in gloomy facilities, with control of their lives in the hands of psychiatrists and their helpers. Now, patients sue to obtain better treatment, and mental health clients have been released to often inhospitable communities. Not surprisingly, institution management raises major political issues. The superintendent in charge cannot treat patient care as a purely administrative issue.

Administrative issues such as patient care and road maintenance cannot avoid politics for at least two reasons. First, legislatures frequently agree on a solution to a problem without knowing what the problem is. If the problem is road maintenance, the legislature may authorize more money and instruct the administration to develop ways to spend the money effectively. Often, the administrative agency holds extensive hearings on proposed regulations. Establishing regulations often becomes as important as the legislation.

A 1972 regulation revealed by the Food and Drug Administration provides a hair-raising example of administrative regulation. The regulation specified tolerable defects constituting no health hazards in foods for human use, as shown in Exhibit 5–1. Administrators developed this regulation, presumably operating from public health standards, public opinion, and industry pressure. It is difficult for Congress to prescribe such detail for hundreds of food products—and the burden is placed on administrators.

Secondly, managing the program often uncovers policy issues that must be settled by the legislature. Should administrative hearings be held before committing a patient or closing a street? If there is a charge for certain patients, can it be collected? Should administrative officials have the power to deny access to private driveways to prevent unsafe turns? These issues should be settled by the legislature, but even the

EXHIBIT 5–1   Extract from Federal Trade Commission Regulation Specifying
Allowable Natural or Unavoidable Defects in Food That
Present No Health Hazard

Chocolate and chocolate liquor	Average of 150 insect fragments per subdivisions of 225 grams of 250 insect fragments in any one subdivision of 225 grams. Average of 4 rodent hairs per subdivision of 225 grams or 8 rodent hairs in any one subdivision of 225 grams. Shell in excess of 2 percent alkali-free nibs.

SOURCE: David Rosenbloom, *Public Administration* (New York: Random House, 1986), p. 369.

legislature will not foresee all issues. Since issues like this arise out of
program management, managers cannot avoid policy questions.

"Staying out of politics" means, in the 1980s and 1990s, that public
managers should content themselves with suggesting alternatives,
pointing out consequences, noting when programs require legislative
direction, and dutifully carrying out the decisions made by elected or
appointed leaders. This means avoiding partisan politics, which is more
than being labeled a Democrat or Republican. It means not becoming
labeled as a partisan of certain policies associated with a legislative majority or a specific executive. While implementing policy, effective managers recognize that policies and majorities change; they try not to become so committed to any one policy or majority that they cannot
adjust. This is not to say that managers should not be committed to a
long-time programmatic issue such as quality care for mental health
clients, for they must be effective in program politics. Administrators
cannot be effective over the long haul if they are committed to a single
way of caring for mental health clients, particularly if that approach is
associated with a party or an executive or legislative majority. Managers
with this view must commit to that party or interest and leave the career
service.

Office Politics

Office politics are as pervasive as other kinds of politics. Whose
secretary gets promoted? Who gets the new desk? In larger organizations, status symbols such as rugs or office locations become important
since they represent top-side recognition of incumbents. Small issues
like these are important, and managers ignore them at their peril. Being
perceived as fair in these matters is no small accomplishment, for office
politics pervades every organization to some degree. In the public sector, it revolves around the location of desks next to the top individual,

the job title change from "assistant to the director" to "assistant director," or control of another program.

Office politics is just as common in the private sector. Webber refers to the career problems of young managers who are insensitive to their political environment and the subjective criteria by which they are judged.[3] Madison et al., point out the pervasiveness of politics in a group of Southern California electronics firms. Here, politics was primarily internal, but the volatile marketing system of the firms increased the frequency and payoff of office politics to clever managers.[4] Dalton pointed out a similar tooth-and-nail struggle for control and power in a real but unnamed private firm in the 1950s. There, the head of industrial relations became the de facto head of the firm because others thought he was an headquarters agent.[5]

Office politics will always be part of organizational life as long as people have individual goals. However, the struggles for power and control that are important for agencies and public managers are usually program issues. The rest of this chapter deals with program politics.

Program Politics

Consider the decision within a municipality over whether to expand street sweeping services instead of adding another planning staff member. This may appear trivial, however, it often represents a struggle between developers and homeowners, with the public works director and the city planner as surrogate warriors even if they do not recognize the issue. This sub rosa struggle may mean that the homeowners association, for example, will regard failure to add a planner as a setback for proper zoning control and the provision of urban amenities, which means that they may worry about the city becoming too developer-oriented.

Effective public managers have learned that they cannot avoid program politics. They try to harness it to their goals. Often the difference between ordinary and effective managers is the degree to which they can link program politics to accomplishment of program goals.

This doesn't mean that life in public agencies is a naked power struggle with interest pitted against interest. It does mean that politics is a constant factor in administrative life. The manager has a key role. He isn't merely an onlooker in the struggle between interests, or even a referee whose role is simply to announce the victor.[6] Sometimes the manager manipulates or controls the struggle. Sometimes the manager represents certain interests, or sometimes she opposes them. Sometimes there is no struggle because the program is largely apolitical or political issues have been settled for a long time.

So while managing a program is not an exercise in power politics.

politics do affect programs. At the minimum, the manager must choose between alternatives or recommend a choice. These choices mean a great deal to specific interests, which is why program politics are inevitable.

THE GAME OF BUREAUCRATIC POWER

The best way to understand the job of the public executive is to view it as a game within an ultimately political process. It is political because administrative action affects social, political, and economic interests and individuals. It is a game because administrative action occurs in a game-like setting.[7]

Games include sets of roles associated with some activity. The activity is organizational or bureaucratic behavior and the roles are associated with occupations and positions within administrative hierarchies. All of us are familiar with this concept, since phrases such as "play the game" or "stay on the team" are common to both organizational and private life. Games are organized forms of competition in which all parties agree to abide by the rules that determine winners and losers. Mutual dependence is required so that the victory (a promotion or budget increase) is not hollow.

Many regulatory activities of government agencies are gamelike. A local health department, enforcing federal, state, and sometimes local laws, inspects restaurants for health violations. There are rules with fines or closures for violating these rules. The rules also limit when inspections can be made and for what reasons. There are rewards to the restaurant in avoiding fines and to the inspector in the number of good violations levied (those that hold up in court). The contest is not friendly, but both parties enjoy playing it, or at least they are willing to endure it. If either party tires of the game, they can withdraw by quitting (the inspector) or by bringing the restaurant up to code or selling it (the owner). If the actions of the inspector seem heavy-handed, and thus outside the rules of the game, the restaurateur can appeal to the legislature, the chief executive, or the media.

At times, the conflict level increases too severely, the nature of the game changes. An ideological struggle ceases to be a game. The federal government activity in the 1950s in rooting out subversives was more an inquisition than a game. The losers were branded traitors. In a present-day example, the war between law enforcement officers and drug peddlers is no longer a game. The stakes are too high for agreement on rules. Some enforcement agents have lost their lives in this high-risk war.

However, most regulatory activity is gamelike, requiring mutual role-playing, symbols, and cues that evoke similar behavior in other actors. A good example is the budget officer in any large agency. She has to be a nay-sayer within the agency to the requests that can't be granted, cutting requests to fit a budget that must be approved by the agency head and the central budget office. Appearing before the budget office, she becomes a departmental budget advocate who shows that programs can serve more people and who refers to clientele demands for the agencies' programs (which the department may have generated). When the president's budget goes before Congress, the budget officer plays a double role. She is both a team member advocating the administration's budget proposal, which may be less than the agency wants, and also a potential supporter for an increase if Congress is inclined.[8] Successful agencies gain larger appropriations, and skilled individual managers advance their careers, gaining personal and psychic income. Less-skilled managers will not advance their careers.

At times, the game degenerates into cynical attempts to aggrandize personal influence, elevate friends to positions of power, and seek status by increasing the number of subordinates or currying favor from persons in power. This behavior happens in all organizations, due to human nature. If carried too far, it will weaken the agency.

In most cases, the attempt to increase bureaucratic power is rooted in attempts to expand or strengthen one's program. Strengthening one's program generally involves using the two basic elements of bureaucratic power. The first, mobilization of support, largely arises from outside the agency. It is rooted in the willingness of powerful outside groups to support the agency to achieve their goals. The second, expertise, is based within the agency and is made up of the skills, training, education, and specializations of agency members.

Mobilizing Support

Agencies mobilize support for their program by allying with natural supporters and program clients. This indicates to legislators and political executives that the agency's programs have supporters and beneficiaries who will oppose reductions and support increases in programs. Almost every agency has some natural support, either inside or outside the government. Libraries have Friends of the Library. The Public Health Service has supportive medical and health-related groups. The Fish and Game Commission can mobilize sports enthusiasts for many issues. Other agencies, not closely associated with specific clients nonetheless have supporters. Police have widespread public support. Mental health facilities have a network of concerned civic groups. Even the Agency for International Development, seemingly without U.S. allies, receives some support from international bankers and sometimes from the State Department. An agency without allies will not exist long because of the tremendous competition for funds. If that agency cannot call on clients or internal allies such as the central budget office, the agency will wither away.

Mobilizing support is mostly seen among large agencies serving active or potentially powerful clients. Here, the agency and a dominant interest group seem to walk hand-in-hand. The Pentagon and defense contractors have close, symbiotic relations; so do the Agriculture Department and thousands of farmers. The 1985 farm bankruptcies have weakened the latter relationship, and revelation of penalties for rigged contracts have weakened the former. These strains are temporary, for both parties need each other.

An important permutation of this client-agency relationship occurs when a legislative committee, in sympathy with agency goals and interest group purposes, links hands with them and the triad forms an Iron Triangle. Agency requests receive favorable support from the committee, whose members are predisposed to the agency because they support the private interest that lobbies for the agency and often support committee members in various ways. Heclo cites one political executive who reported:

> When we tried to downgrade the . . . bureau, its head was opposed, and he had a friend in a lobby group. After they got together rumblings were heard from an appropriations committee. I asked [the committee chairman] if he had a problem with this reorganization, and he said, "No, you have the problem because if you touch that bureau I'll cut your job out of the budget."[9]

The Iron Triangle relationship exists outside of Washington, D.C. In California, there is a special relationship between the concrete and heavy construction industry, the State Transportation Commission, and the legislative transportation committee, which has favored highway construction over mass-transit facilities. States licensing boards contain industry representatives far more often than consumer representatives. Dentistry boards, for example, have more dentists than people with dentures as members. The agency mobilizes support for further dentistry regulations from dentists on the board and their professional associations. Dentists on the board often vote controls over future competition through the licensing board.

The Iron Triangle has weakened in recent years as federal spending has come under increased pressure, but it is still alive. In its heyday, it represented a classic case of support mobilization, although it was never clear who mobilized who. The Iron Triangle, in some cases, is more like soft lead as it faces deregulation and cuts in spending during the 1980s. As interests weaken, the agencies regulating them face corresponding reductions in influence. Consumer groups, once the champion of these agencies, are now ambivalent about regulation or actively support deregulation.

Regulatory agencies oppose deregulation because it reduces their influence over the industry. The industry often opposes deregulation because it disturbs existing relationships and some informal control over members of the industry. Airlines opposed federal deregulation. California realtors opposed Governor Brown's 1981 attempt to reduce state requirements for real estate salespersons. In these cases, the Civil Aeronautics Board and the California Real Estate Commission were both lukewarm about the proposals.

A nonregulatory example is the Friends of the Library. They may have raised money for the local library and led the fight for a special district to gain a share of local property taxes for library purposes. They will fight fiercely for the library, but they insist on approving library plans. Thus, the quid pro quo for their support is partial control of library policies. Without their support, a librarian is unlikely to get a new branch or an additional collection of children's stories. A powerful interest group is a mixed blessing—indispensable for support but unwelcome in program management.

Cooptation is another mobilization technique. Cooptation makes opponents or potential opponents part of the agency decision-making process, in the hope that they will defend the program they are partially responsible for. Appointments to the governing body can be formal, such as board membership, or informal, as a federal undersecretary of labor position designated for a representative of organized labor. Formal cooptation often occurs when the interest group member has a place on the governing body but must defend the policy it is partially responsible for. The position may seem powerful, but it may simply legitimize the agency's position held by a majority of the board. Informal cooptation, which is privately consulting power groups before acting, provides more recognition of the group's influence.[10]

A potential opponent of "wasting money on books" may be coopted by appointing him to the city library board, where his consciousness about the value of books will be raised, and his presence also legitimizes the use of city funds by indicating that the library budget has broad public support. Informal cooptation may involve consulting with taxpayer groups about the proposed budget so that they will see the value of higher appropriations for books.

The general public, when mobilized, is a powerful force. Usually, the general public is handled as individuals. Managers try to return phone calls promptly, take expressions of view into account, or meet with citizens upon request. This strategy, often called public relations, is organizational representation. It is important in direct proportion to: (1) the public visibility of a specific service, and (2) the accessibility of the providing agency. A local public works director is more solicitous of citizen views than the secretary of the Army. Both agencies, however, are ultimately dependent on public opinion. The 1985 revelations of severe overcharges by defense contractors, such as $500 hammers, hurt the Pentagon's case for a higher budget appropriation.

Occasionally, a specific group actually appears to represent the general public, or at least the attentive public. They can have enormous influence over agency policy. The influence of PTAs is well-known, and some school principals pray that the local president will not call that day. Generally, widespread group support, even if no dominant group exists, is evidence that agency policies are acceptable. This is why attempts to sell proposed bond issues at the local level, and at the state level, involve directed appeals to as many groups as possible—ranging from the Veterans of Foreign Affairs, the homeowners association, the AFL-CIO, and the chamber of commerce. These groups bestow legitimacy on bond proposals and other projects, and group support leads to individual votes.

Mobilizing support is a complex task involving organizational maintenance, effective and convincing organizational representation, and some strategic planning. Client groups are not always easily identified. Their strength is not always predictable nor is their support always easily won. Often, interests are divided and the unwary agency may find itself in a dispute. Environmental groups, for example, contain both wilderness and camping groups. Sometimes, the agency may be pitted against its supporters, such as when a fish and game agency tries to establish new hunting and fishing rules opposed by sports enthusiasts. Maintaining support requires a compromise between agency professionals and sports enthusiasts. Even if the commission pushed through its rules against the opposition, it would be a pyrrhic victory because sports enthusiasts' support is needed for future battles.

Interest group support is more complex than it appears. There is no longer an automatic appeal to an agency's interest group supporters in the face of budget or legislative difficulties. With Reagan administration domestic cutbacks, departments did not seek more money or outside support. Interests had to deal with Congress without administration support. Some agencies survived the cutbacks better than others. Some, particularly regulatory agencies, had made enemies and got little support. The medical society, for example, disliked the health planning program. The Urban Mass Transit Administration, supported by its interests, was cut back less.

In these cases, the affected interests did not wait for agencies to contact them, but they immediately formed alliances with Congress and other groups. These new coalitions operated independently from agency administrators. For example, business groups and representatives of the poor worked to keep Community Development Block Grants alive. This was an odd coalition created in how Congress packaged the proposed grant cutbacks. The administrative branch was ignored, and the Iron Triangle lost one leg.[11]

Support may come from inside the government. Legislative support comes from the specialized committees at the state and federal levels and from the whole legislature in smaller jurisdictions. Sometimes, a specific legislative supporter will sway the larger committee or the entire legislature. Legislative support means increased appropriations, authority, and/or involves fending off reductions in authority. Legislative support usually comes as a result of widespread support or lack of hostility in the community. Occasionally key legislative support may protect the agency against adverse action even when most legislators do not support the agency. This kind of legislative support, like the economists' lunch, is not free. Legislators exact their pound of flesh; they expect to have considerable influence over agency actions.

Other than legislative support, the executive, her aides, and her control agencies, such as the budget and personnel offices, are the other chief sources of inside support. The chief executive can be convinced that the agency deserves additional funds. Budget examiners may be impressed with the management of the agency. The personnel department sometimes quickly approves proposed reclassifications for new programs; conversely, any or all of these groups may line up in opposition to an agency. Another support is the chief executive's grant of latitude in operating a program. This strengthens the hand of managers in the agency to act decisively and to plunge ahead—secure in knowing that they will be supported by the chief. Chief executives are not always sympathetic. In many cases, as in the Reagan administration, the chief executive is committed to reductions in agency staff and appropriations.

Expertise

In addition to mobilizing support, expertise is the second major basis for agency power. The increasing specialization of knowledge and the resulting complexity of issues results in managers gaining power through command of the facts. No matter how much support is mobilized, agencies are undermined if they don't have the expertise to perform effectively.

Expertise has several aspects. The first aspect is full-time attention to the issue or program. Rarely will any other group devote as much time to any matter as the administrative agency intimately involved in it. Legislatures, unless they have large and extensive staffs, will give sporadic attention to issues. Subpart specialization also develops expertise. Each part of a matter is divided to gain high levels of familiarity with all aspects. Take, for example, a simple function such as street sweeping. Operators may be semiskilled, but they are highly trained and experienced. Persons who maintain the sweepers become experts on parts and emergency repairs. For large fleets, someone may be responsible for acquisition of spare parts on short notice. Even city managers familiar with street sweeping defer to a well-informed director of public works, who defers to a street-maintenance supervisor.

Monopolization of information is a third aspect of expertise. The information may be routine, unclassified, and readily accessible, but it's in agency files. If the agency provides the only service, few can challenge their interpretation of the facts. If a public works director notes that once rather than twice a month street sweeping is adequate, based on a comparison with other cities, who can say otherwise?

Agencies and individuals also gain influence by becoming a source of advice to policymakers. Sometimes, policymakers have no alternative source of information—a situation they try to avoid. This source of influence is limited by the weight that legislatures or executives give to agency advice. Some agencies have good track records, some do not. Executives from staff agencies, such as the budget or personnel office and the federal comptroller general or state auditor, are listened to because they are perceived as having less at stake than a specific agency. Controversial agencies have less influence. Staff of the state commission on solar energy in a damp, wintry state rarely are persuasive.

Variations in Agency Power

Bureaucrats gain power by mobilizing support and demonstrating expertise. But some agencies and bureaucrats are more influential and stronger than others. Why?

A common distinction is the strength and activity of the constituency. At one extreme, a local building department has little general support. It doesn't provide a visible function and may be at odds with its client group, building contractors. At the other extreme, a popular university system enjoys general support plus the work of specific interest groups such as alumni, student, and faculty groups. Most agencies fall between these two examples.

Divisions within constituencies have reverse effects. Universities were torn apart by student uprisings in the 1960s. Alumni and the general public withdrew support partly due to the attacks. As a result, many universities lost public funding.

The level of expertise affects agency strength. Expertise is often determined by the dominant occupation in the agency. College professors, doctors, and engineers have high status. Therefore, other things being equal, universities, public works departments, and public health departments should have more success than competing agencies if their performance is judged by the status of their professional elite. The prestige of these occupations, at times, allows the agency to escape close legislative scrutiny of top managers. Unfortunately, other things are not always equal, and these agencies get their share of legislative or executive scrutiny.

Agencies vary among internal matters such as drive for power and the quality of leadership. Some agencies seem more aggressive than others. They try to organize their clients, they push harder for additional funding, or they curry favor from legislators or the executive. Usually, this is due to a series of able and aggressive leaders rather than a vague agency drive for power. Often, it involves the provision of a popular service, such as law enforcement in a time of high crime, which makes aggressive behavior a workable strategy. The extent to which the agency produces aggressive leaders, however, is partly a function of the organizational culture. Some aggressive behavior is attributed to organizational expectations. Effective organizational leadership usually manifests itself in more effective client linkages, greater commitment to the quality of service, and better organizational planning. This is usually a function of top leadership.

The 1960s success of NASA was due to public support for the space race with Russia and to the leadership of James Webb. Another example was the early Peace Corps. It was imbued with enormous zeal and employee commitment, characteristics credited to the leadership of Sargent Shriver. A final example was the success of William Ruckleshaus in guiding the Environmental Protection Agency (EPA) through its first critical years in 1970–73. Ruckleshaus restored confidence in the EPA in 1983 after President Reagan appointed him to replace administrator Anne Burford, whose leadership had mired the EPA in severe scandals. While the latter examples involved political executive examples, there are similar examples of city managers, bureau chiefs, and department heads breathing life into sickly units. Leadership is not limited to politicians. It is often found among career managers, who quietly rebuild or strengthen their agencies, usually without the press or public notice that political executives seek and need.

CONTROLS OVER MANAGERS

Most public managers work in large agencies and are directly or indirectly responsive to elected and appointed political leaders. These career managers spend considerable time dealing directly with elected or politically appointed executives and the legislature. Most of their time and energy in presenting their agency interests and in defending it against attacks is spent with political or hierarchical heads. This is where managerial political effectiveness is displayed most frequently. Effectiveness in dealing with executives, legislators, aides to legislators, control agencies such as the budget office, the personnel office, and the courts is key to management success. In this section, the term *control agencies* describes the power centers that have some constitutional and legal authority over the agency and its managers. Chapters 6 and 7 describe more specifically the roles of personnel and finance agencies, which are referred to administratively as control agencies.

The Chief Executive

Chief executives have the ultimate administrative authority in the organization. Presidents, governors, city managers, and strong mayors are classic examples at each level of government. Their legitimacy comes from election, with the exception of city managers who are appointed legislatively. In larger units of government with many agencies or departments, the president or governor appoints agency heads.

If chief executives wish, they can become the major factor in any important agency decision or policy. In fact, they can be involved in all agency decisions, although this has its consequences. This power is limited by the energy of the chief executive and his trust in the ability of subordinate managers. It becomes destructive if the chief tries to control all agency actions down to minor decisions. It also eventually destroys the chief, for few persons have the energy to spread themselves so thin. However, chiefs must be able to affect organizational policy directly; otherwise, how else are public mandates to be translated into policy?

Agencies are perceived as resistant to new initiatives by chiefs. They have seen chiefs come and go, and current organizational policies were legitimately approved by previous administrations. In addition, there is the natural dislike of rapid change. So, as a result, agencies often present muffled and covert resistance to change initially. Senior managers usually pledge fealty to the new chief, but their subordinates remain wary. The new chief must prove herself. Proving one's self involves a period in which proposed new changes are digested by the agency and run the gauntlet of political debate. Agencies wish to ensure that new changes will stay if they are implemented. However, some agency managers prefer the status quo, although this is less an issue than most observers believe.

Waiting out the new chief executive is a time-honored strategy. It doesn't work if the chief persists and has political support for her position. The constitutional legitimacy of the chief is a powerful weapon, and over time, most opposition dissipates. It's probable that most reported resistance is a time for the agency to adjust to new leadership plus a desire to ensure that the executive is still committed to the new programs after she is familiar with agency operations and the reason for old policies. Sometimes agency resistance exists because there is support from other political leaders in the legislature or the administration.

Waiting out the new chief works if she does not care much about agency programs. She may not have any new policies that she cares about. She may wish only to preside, not to make changes. Sometimes the chief only wishes to change a policy or two, and after the change is completed, she is only sporadically interested in the agency.

On occasions, agencies greet an incoming chief with open opposition. This is a high-risk game, sometimes initiated when the chief has been openly critical of the agency's basic thrust. The chief usually wins. The chief controls the budget of the agency, transfers or removes top careerists if they resist, and generates unfavorable agency publicity. Open conflict threatens both parties. The agency almost always loses the struggle, but the chief is also scarred. He can't afford to dissipate his authority on small issues. If the agency has legislative and public support, the issue may not be worth the battle.

Cooperation between the new chief and the agency is more common. The chief cannot initiate new programs without agency support. The agency is linked to independent power bases, whose support is necessary for new initiatives. In addition, agency expertise is necessary for any program's implementation. In most cases, the chief's new policy initiatives are put in place easily unless they are controversial.

In a majority of cases, managers hope for strong policy leadership from the chief executive. They are comfortable with vigorous action from the chief, particularly when he expects career executives to help him move in that direction. Referring to a proposed New Jersey reorganization launched by Governor Kean called the Governor's Policy Management Improvement Program (PMIP), a career executive stated:

> Policy coming out of the executive office really does make a difference. It helps good managers do what they need to do. Prior to PMIP, we were operating by the old rule of "don't rock the bureaucracy." When he announced PMIP, Governor Kean gave us the impetus we needed to take charge and make change.[12]

As you can see, agency career managers have differing opinions about chief executives. Some managers are reluctant to cooperate. Many managers look forward to new leadership. The latter group wants changes in agency policies as much as the chief. They are anxious to support the initiatives because they believe in them, because they believe that the chief has constitutional legitimacy to implement them, or because this is the way to get other changes made that careerists want. Political support is gained by giving up something to get something. Managers often try to change programs or policies by moving the agency rapidly in directing changes the chief wants. In doing so, agency managers attempt to gain chief executive support so that the chief executive will be their clerk on other matters.[13] Agencies and individuals want the chief to support their budget request, defer to their policies, support them publicly, and extend operating autonomy to them. In short, they try to get the chief to advance their interests. Wise executives who agree to this "clerkship" role usually demand certain policy and operating changes that they want from the agency.

Chief Executive Aides.   Most interaction between the chief and the department or agency is done by the chief's aides, who are members of his staff. In the case of a major political figure like a governor or president, an aide or even the assistant to an aide is normally the contact for career agency heads. Relatively few direct contacts with the chief occur unless the agency is in serious trouble or has a major policy issue developing.

Aides and staffers are the chief executive's ears and eyes. They filter most of the information she gets. Top agency managers must get their story to the chief through her aides. One study of 20 federal bureau chiefs indicated that they had met with a president an average of only once every other year, or 77 times during the 170 years of service they represented. Since 25 of these meetings involved the commissioner of the Internal Revenue Service, the other bureau directors averaged a meeting every three years.[14] Technically, the bureaus reported to cabinet officers in most cases, but often they were presidential appointees or required presidential signatures for appointment. The article implied that the president's programs might be advanced by sharing concerns directly with them rather than through aides. After all, when bureaus deal with underlings, they feel less commitment to presidential initiatives. Excitement about a new administration is not reflected to interest groups or members of Congress when information comes second-hand. All in all, however, limits on the chief executive's time and the number of agencies supervised make heavy reliance on aides inevitable.

The chief executive's staff may become highly visible. Gray Davis, California Governor Jerry Brown's right-hand assistant spoke directly for Brown and acted directly on his behalf. When Gray left to run for the Assembly, his replacement, B. T. Collins, also became a major political figure. Staffers have become crucial figures with views often as important as the chief executive's views. At the federal level, a criticism of president-cabinet member relations is that a relationship between team players often becomes competition.

One Kennedy-Johnson cabinet member noted with some bitterness:

Recent Presidents have let their White House political and personal aides go much too far in pressing administrators to do things they shouldn't. Too many of them are trying to make administrators squirm. There are too many aides at the White House who are just looking for a headline for the President. You have to guard against those types. There is just too much of it and Presidents are guilty of letting it continue—they don't sufficiently realize that you have to have confidence in your departmental administrators. Perhaps, it is due to the fact that they have never been administrators—they spent all their time in the Senate.[15]

The problem has not improved. Bob Haldeman and John Ehrlichmann were much better known than any of President Nixon's cabinet officers, particularly after Watergate. Jody Powell was as well-known as many cabinet officers under President Carter. James Baker and Edwin Meese were highly visible during President Reagan's first term—before becoming cabinet officers.

Lower-level staff members are the contact for agency officials, and they normally receive less publicity. There are fewer staff members than in past years, when President Lyndon Johnson had a dozen special assistants and three or four dozen assistant's assistants.[16] Richard Nixon had a White House staff of nearly 600.[17] Actually, lower-level staff frequently get more involved in agency matters than higher-level staffers who concentrate on top-level presidential matters.

Case Study 5–1, the successful reorganization of the Department of Transportation (DOT), illustrates the importance of staff aides to the chief executive, as well as the relationship between top executive leadership and the need for agency support. It also shows the give and take in the game of high-level bureaucratic politics.

In this case, bureaus and agencies were headed by political appointees. However, the negotiation process would have been similar if the directors were careerists.

The case is also notable for an ironic turn of events. This happened in 1979, when President Carter ousted Joseph Califano from his cabinet post as secretary of Health, Education, and Welfare (HEW). In the DOT case, Califano played a key role as an aide to President Johnson.

As HEW secretary, Califano ran afoul of presidential aides. In asking for Califano's resignation, Carter said, "The problem is the friction with the White House staff. The same qualities and drive and managerial abilities that make you such a superb secretary create problems with the White House staff."[18]

The reversal of Califano's role as a presidential aide and a cabinet secretary brings to life Miles' Law, "where you stand depends on where you sit."

Case Study 5–1

CREATING THE DEPARTMENT OF TRANSPORTATION

There was no agency to coordinate or consider overall transportation policy as late as 1966, despite federal expenditures of billions of dollars each year on transportation programs. Agencies such as the Interstate Commerce Commission (ICC), the Maritime Administration, the Civil Aeronautics Board (CAB), the Bureau of Public Roads, the Army Corps of Engineers, the Coast Guard, and the Federal Aviation Agency (FAA) subsidized, regulated, and managed transportation programs. Logic called for a unified DOT, but opposition from three areas blocked its creation for years. The concerned agencies preferred autonomous status rather than merger in a large agency. Congress was lukewarm, since members looked to the agencies for pork-barrel projects such as dams, waterways, and roads, and they were not sure that a unified agency would be amenable to congressional demands. Finally, the interests were opposed. For years, airlines, railroads, and truckers dominated the agencies created to regulate them and didn't want to change the cozy relationship.

More than interbureaucratic negotiations were required to create DOT, but recounting these negotiations explains how essential departmental support was gained for the president's plan. Joseph Califano, Johnson's assistant in charge of the plan, found the FAA opposed to the plan because its administrator was afraid that his salary and control of the supersonic transport plane were jeopardized. Reassured, he supported FAA inclusion in DOT. The CAB struggled against the proposal, even though it faced only a loss of power to investigate safety accidents, not its rate-fixing or airline-subsidy powers. The CAB agreed only after President Johnson publicly committed himself to the creation of DOT. Both FAA and CAB support were necessary because their opposition, even in closed hearings, weakened DOT support in Congress.

Treasury Secretary Henry Fowler resisted placing the Coast Guard in DOT. Califano got a memorandum from Defense Secretary McNamara saying that the reorganization would enhance national security and President Johnson talked Fowler out of opposition at a cabinet meeting. Housing and Urban Development Secretary Robert Weaver resisted losing the $130 million urban mass transit program he had been given to DOT. It took a high-level task force to award it to DOT after the bill was passed.

Once President Johnson committed himself publicly to the bill, executive branch agencies fell into line. There still was tremendous legislative and interest group opposition, however. Once it became reasonably clear that reorganization would pass with compromises, Califano used his power to bind the president to make concessions to assuage powerful senators. These concessions included: (1) additional autonomy to the major internal administrative units of DOT, and (2) delegation of DOT's safety authority to a five-member, virtually autonomous National Transportation Board. This latter concession was to prevent expert safety decisions being overruled by the DOT secretary.

Within eight months of the ini-

tial presidential request, DOT was established, which united most federal transportation agencies in a $6 billion, 90,000-employee department. While the original proposal was weakened, passage was attributed to the Johnson magic. However, without the effective work of Califano, it would not have happened. The president, working through a staff aide with the department's support, prevailed. The final picture was of a president, acting as an equal, working through aides to convince other actors such as departments and Congress to assent.

SOURCE: *The Presidents' Men* by Patrick Anderson. Copyright © 1969 by Patrick Anderson. Reprinted by permission of International Creative Management.

The Legislature

The legislature is the other major control agency that senior managers deal with. Legislative relations are so crucial and sensitive that many large agencies at state and federal levels maintain specialized offices to oversee and direct legislative contacts. The reason legislative contacts are important is simple—only the legislature votes funds for the agency or approves legislation that agencies want.

Purse-string controls are all pervasive. They are a factor across government levels, for all agencies need funding. Agency managers spend considerable time testifying on the budget and on routine legislative hearings. Political executives are primarily involved, but careerists are also involved. A federal official noted that:

> Many officials complain that they must spend so much time in preparing for appearing at Congressional hearings and in presenting their programs before the Bureau of the Budget and other bodies that it leaves little time for directing the operations of their agencies. Also, the necessity for checking proposed actions and for keeping complete records of the activities in case they must defend themselves absorbs a great deal of time which otherwise might be devoted to more constructive efforts.[19]

An example of budgetary interaction is shown by a California senior manager:

> With the state budget situation that exists this year (1981), there were some political deals made which would allow a 9.2% grant to be given to various welfare recipients. In order to achieve that, because of the deal that was struck, it was necessary to find ways of saving money in other welfare and social services areas so it would become a zero sum game. As soon as the deal had been struck with the political actors in the legislature, the people in this department, including my boss and me, got involved in the process of deciding where the cuts were going to occur. Basically, this has culminated in a bill, SB 633.[20]

Occasionally, the chief executive has such extensive budgetary powers or influence over the legislature that appropriations are determined at the formulation rather than at the enactment. Then, executives spend less time with the legislature. This is common at the local level. The city council or county supervisors often have confidence in the chief executive and there is little money for expanded programs. The chief's budgetary decision is, for practical reasons, the final word.

The budget, however, is only one type of agency-legislative interaction.[21] There are nonfinancial legislative controls over bureaucratic programs. Legislative bodies, particularly Congress, often require that certain programs be reauthorized annually. This may mean that agency representatives must appear annually before committees in each congressional chamber. Agencies avoid this if possible. In addition, a legislative veto is used; Congress requires that agencies give the committee advance information about their actions, "come into agreement" with the committee about their plans, or have the plans formally approved by some congressional body. This occurs at all levels of government. For example, a state highway department may have to clear all changes in their highway master plan with a legislative transportation committee, although this is an administrative matter. While the legislative veto is formally unconstitutional, the threat of withholding appropriations if the legislature is unsatisfied usually brings agencies into compliance.

The threat of budgetary reprisals if the agency does not keep Congress informed or otherwise meet congressional expectations is common. One congressional action—specified when the Department of Housing and Urban Development was created—was that one authorized assistant secretary position was to be filled by the federal housing (FH) commissioner. This assured the preexisting FH program a visible role in the new department because Congress did not want the visible tax and other benefits given to middle-class citizens submerged in the new agency.[22] In the DOT case study, the concessions made by Califano to senators were similar in nature.

Sometimes, top executives are selected for their presumed acceptability to the legislature. In California, Governor Jerry Brown appointed exlegislators to high positions in the corrections agency and the Health Service Department. Their contacts and familiarity with the legislature gave their sketchy administrative credentials more weight, and this may have eased agency-legislative relations. With the corrections agency, selection of an acceptable head was necessary to assure creation of the agency. An unintended effect of this action is the heavier management burden on lower-level executives when the top manager is not experienced or interested in management issues. Often, this pushes policy issues down to the careerist manager, particularly if policy issues have managerial aspects.

Legislative investigations are another way that the legislative body can bring administrative agencies into compliance or otherwise embarrass them. This tactic is most effective when the legislature has adequate staff to investigate the agency. In the past, the U.S. Forest Service was investigated when it attempted to initiate regulations and policies opposed by livestock owners and grazing interests. Investigations such as this one generate unfavorable publicity for the agency and occasionally result in specific legislation eliminating certain practices.[23] When the Federal Trade Commission adopted a 1964 regulation requiring a warning on cigarette packages, an immediate investigation by the Senate-House Commerce Committee resulted in legislation amending the commission's rule and prohibiting it from further consideration of a health rule for three years. Only when the tobacco interests weakened did the warning labels become stronger.[24] Even in the 1980s, when a linkage between smoking and cancer is routinely accepted (except by tobacco interests), the government still performs a balancing act. Warnings on cigarette packages are balanced by farm price supports for tobacco growers. Concentration of tobacco interests in a few states maximizes their representation through those senators.

Legislative oversight is common between agencies and legislative committees. The committees, or their staffs, closely monitor selected agencies to assure that the bureaucracy administers programs in keeping with legislative intent. Should the committee conclude that the agency is not following its intent, the most obvious threat is to the agency's budget, but unfavorable publicity can also occur. Criticism from the legislature, while crucial to focusing public opinion on agency shortcomings, can also occur because programs are implemented in ways that the legislature dislikes but should have specified in the legislation. Hale Champion, once undersecretary of Health, Education, and Welfare notes:

> Congress does not want to resolve the question (over equal spending for athletics) between the women's organizations on Title IX and the big uni-

versities, for example. They don't want us to send those regulations back up to the Hill because there are two powerful political forces at work. They want HEW to formulate a policy and to take the heat from both sides. And it's not that we're not willing to do that, but Congress won't support us. They don't even say "You go ahead and live with the heat," they say, "you go ahead and do it and we're also going to give you heat."[25]

Legislators may use budget power to correct administrative actions they disapprove of. In 1968, HEW tried to decentralize educational programs of the Elementary and Secondary Education Act of 1965. The education lobby opposed this action because it diminished the influence of Office of Education officials in Washington. HEW Secretary Wilbur Cohen relates how the policy was changed:

> When we went up to Senate Appropriations, the committee reduced the Office of Education's budget by about $2.4 million. So I paid a visit to Senator (Lister) Hill (D–Ala), and I said, "What goes?" And he replied, "The National Education Association doesn't want that program decentralized." I said, "If I rescind that order, will you give me that money back?" And he said, "Yeah." So I rescinded that order and I doubt whether to this day it's been reissued.[26]

The oversight process can become so involved with administrative details that it sometimes prevents legislators from concentrating on legislative duties. This is a problem at local levels, as any city manager can attest to. Robert Noe, county executive of Prince William County, Virginia notes:

> I think everybody has an inclination to get mired in details. Maybe it's because that's what becomes pressing. Supervisors get calls about dogs or potholes or things that are really minute in the overall operation of the county. . . . Supervisors have to respond to calls about stray dogs and potholes or they're not reelected. I have to take care of stray dogs and potholes or I don't survive. But these are completely unrelated to where we are going, how we're going to handle the issues.[27]

Legislative oversight has advantages. It also offers the administrator the chance to do a good turn for the legislator, and often good deeds are later rewarded, as a California senior executive explains:

> Right now, the legislator has a problem in his district. A law was changed a year or so ago which has created some heartburn for some people in his district. It is not a biological problem, it's a conflict in social issues. One group like to fish, the other doesn't want anything touched. While there is no biological reason for the conflict for not harvesting surpluses, there is a social problem. . . . So I have members from his district contact me to do something about it. So we try to find some middle group to satisfy both parties.[28]

In many cases, contact with the legislature comes through the staff aides to a committee or legislator. In California, many contacts are through specialized staff consultants, who have authority to speak for a committee or a legislator.

There are other controls that the legislature uses. At the national level, the General Accounting Office (GAO), under a comptroller general appointed to a fifteen-year nonrenewable term by Congress, acts as a staff arm of Congress.

. The GAO originally was designed to track down illegal expenditures, but it now conducts audits that focus on whether or not agency program management is effective. In 1962, the GAO told the secretary of HEW that drug product testing procedures were inconsistent between the Food and Drug Administration and the National Institutes of Health (both HEW units) and reported the findings to Congress.[29] In 1983, the GAO told the Office of Personnel Administration (OPM) that many agencies were not effectively using employee appraisal systems. Recommending more OPM activity, the GAO reported its findings to Congress.[30]

In California, the analogue to the GAO is the legislative auditor. The auditor lacks some of the GAO's independence and is limited to reviewing accounting and fiscal practices under the direction of a legislative committee. California's other chief legislative control is the legislative analyst, who provides the legislature with an extensive formal report about the proposed governor's budget, which includes detailed analyses of specific programs. The analyst has a large staff working on budget issues similar to the governor's Department of Finance, but from a legislative staff perspective. The analyst's report has an important impact on the governor's budget. In 1985, for example, the analyst criticized the governor's proposal to contract out work as cost ineffective. In 1986, the analyst criticized the governor's revenue estimates.

At the local level, there are few examples of legislative control agencies other than personal staff. In large cities, such as Los Angeles, personal staffs are large.

Courts

Court actions, until recently, didn't threaten agencies.[31] Officials could be held responsible for criminal negligence, and some agency actions could be enjoined in court for exceeding authorized powers or for exercising illegal or unconstitutional grants of power. These were limited in application, however. Generally, courts weren't a major consideration in administrative operations.

Courts and judges are now asked to restrain administrative actions that interfere with private parties. Sometimes, agency members sue to protect themselves from adverse agency actions. Once courts were reluctant to intrude in administrative affairs, heeding the claim that administrators know their area best. Thus, courts were limited to assessing whether established requirements were followed. This argument receives less attention now, and courts often look into substantive questions. If the plaintiff has suffered harm, the courts are less likely to allow a presumption of administrative competency to hold.

The Administrative Procedures Act of 1946 restrains "excessive administrative authority" and is now enforced more frequently. The 1966 Freedom of Information Act provides more access of potential litigants into agency records. As a result, more agency actions are challenged. Court calendars are filled with suits raising administrative actions. Many cases challenge administrative action in complex areas such as regulation of effluent, pesticide regulation, and approval of dyes and drugs. Many simpler matters, such as municipal zoning or growth-control ordinances are attacked. New bodies of legal doctrines such as environmental protection and welfare rights have grown. The influence of judicial decisions is shown by the *Griggs* v. *Duke Power* case, which has mandated extensive validation of tests for employee recruitment and promotion (see Chapter 8).

In some cases, courts administer public programs after they have found that agency actions violate constitutional provisions. Frank Johnson, an Alabama district judge, supervised operation of the prisons, mental hospitals, and highway patrol during the early 1980s.

In the Boston school district, District Judge Garrity intervened directly to assure desegregation. Superintendent of Schools Wood recalls:

> The scope of the court's intervention . . . was simply staggering . . . During the first 18 months I was Superintendent, the court held 30 hearings and considered 109 items to assure compliance with more than 200 orders outstanding. Virtually every administrative appointment, and even decisions about curriculum, had to be approved in court ordered proceedings. The court even held hearings about whether a particular school's auditorium needed roofing.[32]

One expert suggests three reasons that courts no longer try to uphold administrative expertise. All involve administrative failings. First, administrative agencies are often captured by their clients so that the agency eventually protects the industry more than the public. Second, clients are not always treated equally, since agencies must accommodate differing philosophies of mission, and agency employees resolve issues based on different philosophies. Third, legislative bodies leave discretion to agencies who do not always use it wisely.[33]

A good example of how agencies sometimes misuse their authority occurred in Nevada from 1951 to 1963. The Atomic Energy Commission

(AEC) conducted atomic energy tests despite knowledge by scientists, engineers, and policymakers that there was danger to humans and animals. What's worse, the AEC lied and covered up its actions when responding to a federal suit involving thousands of Utah sheep killed by radioactive fallout. According to the AEC, "unprecedented cold weather" killed the sheep.[34] Examples such as this destroy arguments for court tolerance of administrative discretion.

Several court cases show how far administrative liability has been extended by the courts. In *Griffin* v. *United States*, Griffin claimed she had become a quadriplegic because she had been given polio vaccine from a faulty lot, inspected and approved by HEW's division of biological sciences. Settling out of court with the manufacturer, she then sued the government for negligence. When tests showed that the vaccine lot should not have been released to the public, she was awarded damages exceeding two million dollars. The court said,

> Where the conduct of Government employees in implementing agency regulations required only performance of scientific evaluation and not the formulation of public policy, we do not believe that the conduct is immunized from judicial review as a "discretionary function."[35]

In another case, the California Youth Authority placed a minor with a violent background in the Johnson home, but they did not inform the Johnsons. Mrs. Johnson was later assaulted and injured. She then sued the state for negligence. On appeal, the California Supreme Court held the Youth Authority liable stating:

> In sum, the instant fact situation presents no reason for sovereign immunity; not only does the officer's decision as to warning fail to rise to the level of governments decisions calling for judicial restraint, but also the state failed to prove that the officer consciously considered the risks to plaintiffs and determined that other policies justified them.[36]

A final decision is the infamous 1961 case of *Mapp* v. *Ohio*.[37] The case involved a heavy-handed search of Mapp's premises by officers pretending they had a search warrant. The Supreme Court ultimately ruled that state courts could not use evidence obtained in violation of the Fourth Amendment's guarantee of freedom from unreasonable searches and seizures. This forced police to observe the Fourth Amendment and, if police behavior did not change, it forbid lower courts from collaborating with police illegally. Horowitz claims that this has hardly deterred police behavior.[38] However, its influence on police operations is substantial if one believes the complaints of police organizations and the ensuing legislative struggles to override the case.

Constitutional lawyers claim that bad cases make bad law. The previous cases involved faulty inspection of vaccine, which results in permanent personal damage; deliberately misinforming citizens of a minor's violent history; and lying to a homeowner to conduct an illegal search. In all cases, the citizen was damaged and to deny judicial redress would have been reprehensible. But the fact that these cases involved clear administrative errors does not entirely explain the explosion of litigation, judicial activism, and increased liability on administrative agencies. The real answer is both an increase in client litigation and broadening of administrative activity. If the government certifies polio vaccine, for example, how can it avoid responsibility for errors that damage consumers?

Courts have limited ability to assess facts or consequences when reviewing administrative actions. They have been inept in judicially supervising programs, such as in prison-crowding cases in several states. Judicial assumption of authority does not reduce the influx of prisoners, for example. Nevertheless, judicial intervention is a fact of life. It will increase in coming years in many areas. A recent example was the action of South Tucson, Arizona, which declared municipal bankruptcy, unable to pay the $6 million judgment levied against the city for a police officer who accidentally but negligently shot a fellow officer in an adjoining jurisdiction.

SUMMARY

There are three kinds of politics: partisan (elective), program, and office. Managers avoid partisan politics, engage in program politics, and try to reduce office politics. Unfortunately, the blurring of any distinction between partisan and program politics has erased any line between politics and administration in the eyes of observers. Hence, managers cannot stay out of politics because they manage programs that deal with public policy issues.

Managers have always mobilized support from clients and always will do so. They have always applied expertise and application of it always gives them political influence. If they did not mobilize power and wield expertise, managers would not be faithful to public sentiment, legislative intent, the wishes of elected and appointed officials, and court rulings. However, this program political activity is not easily admitted because of prevailing public views that criticize all types of politics. Dealing with political issues is both difficult and time-consuming, particularly when managers must appear to publicly avoid politics. Officially, they are hired to maintain the organization, represent it publicly, and develop long-term plans for the organization. However, politics is the backdrop of these managerial functions, and managers must play program politics shrewdly.

Managers do not usually choose the political battleground or issue in political struggles. They respond to challenges by control groups and outside forces as they mobilize supporters or fight off challenges to their expertise. Chief executives, their aides and appointees, legislators and legislatures, and courts all limit managerial discretion and authority to some degree. But managers must organize the political response to a given issue, articulate or lead the political response, and gauge how a long-term political struggle should be waged. These are crucial administrative tasks that cannot be avoided or delegated. These tasks, as you may have guessed, are part of the organizational maintenance, organizational representation, and organizational strategic-planning process—using political analogies.

Another way to stress the role of politics is to note that managers are judged on how well the organization operates, a way to describe effective maintenance, representation, and planning. Political acumen underlies their ability to perform these tasks in a variety of ways.

NOTES

1. Woodrow Wilson, "The Study of Politics," *Political Science Quarterly*, June 1887, pp. 197–222.
2. Frank Goodnow, *Politics and Administration* (New York: Macmillan, 1900), p. 22.
3. Ross Webber, "Career Problems of Young Managers," *California Management Review*, Summer 1976, pp. 19–34.
4. Dan Madison et al., "Organizational Politics: An Exploration of Manager's Perceptions," *Human Relations*, February 1980, pp. 70–100.
5. Melville Dalton, *Men Who Manage* (New York: John Wiley & Sons, 1959).
6. Glendon Schubert, "The Public Interest in Administrative Decisionmaking: Theorem, Theosophy, or Theory?" *American Political Science Review*, June 1957, pp. 346–68.
7. The section on program politics and the individual parts such as mobilizing support and expertise are based on modifications of Francis Rourke, *Bureaucracy, Politics and Public Policy*, 2nd ed., (Boston: Little, Brown, 1976). For more information on how managers who possess expertise also develop political power, see Guy Benveniste, *The Politics of Expertise* (Berkeley, Calif.: Glendessary Press, 1972).
8. For elaboration of these roles, see Aaron Wildavsky, *The Politics of the Budgetary Process*, 4th ed., (Boston: Little, Brown, 1983).
9. Hugh Heclo, *A Government of Strangers* (Washington, D.C.: Brookings Institution, 1977), p. 155. The term Iron Triangle is credited to Douglas Cater, *Power in Washington* (New York: Vintage Books, 1964).
10. Philip Selznick, *TVA and the Grass Roots* (University of California Press, 1949).
11. Irene Rubin, *Shrinking the Federal Government* (New York: Longman, 1984), pp. 198–99.
12. James Conant, "Reorganization and the Bottom Line," *Public Administration Review*, January–February 1986, p. 55.

13. Richard Neustadt, *Presidential Power* (New York: John Wiley & Sons, 1964), coined the phrase.

14. David Brown, "The President and the Bureaus: Time for a Renewal of Relationship?" *Public Administration Review*, September 1966, pp. 174–82.

15. Interview with a Kennedy-Johnson cabinet-level administrator in Thomas Cronin, "A Cabinet of Unequals," in Francis Rourke, ed., *Bureaucratic Power in National Politics*, 3rd ed., (Boston: Little, Brown, 1978), pp. 305–6.

16. Patrick Anderson, *The Presidents' Men* (New York: Doubleday Anchor, 1969).

17. This includes White House staff and special assistants. When the total is outrageously high, executive branch agencies will be asked to put presidential or gubernatorial staffers on their own payroll.

18. James Fesler, "Politics, Policy and Bureaucracy at The Top," in Frederick Lane, ed., *Current Issues in Public Administration*. 3rd ed., (New York: St. Martin's Press, 1986), p. 94.

19. Marver Bernstein, *The Job of the Federal Executive* (Washington D.C.: Brookings Institution, 1958), p. 30.

20. John Rehfuss, CEA Interviews, 1981 (unpublished data).

21. The account of nonbudgetary interactions is largely from Randall Ripley, "Congress and the Bureaucracy," in Francis Rourke, ed., *Bureaucratic Power in National Politics*, 3rd ed., (Boston: Little, Brown, 1978), pp. 270–88.

22. Ibid., p. 275.

23. Francis Rouke, *Bureaucracy, Politics, and Public Policy*, p. 57.

24. Lee Fritschler, *Smoking and Politics* (New York: Appleton-Century Crofts, 1969).

25. Interview with Hale Champion, "The Rewards and Frustrations of the Federal Bureaucracy," *National Journal*, June 16, 1979, pp. 50–51.

26. "New Federalism V: The Bureaucracy." *National Journal*, December 16, 1972, pp. 932–33.

27. "Profile of a Professional," *Public Management*, April, 1980.

28. Rehfuss, CEA interviews.

29. Joseph Harris, *Congressional Control of Administration* (New York: Doubleday Anchor, 1964), pp. 166–67.

30. General Accounting Office, "New Performance Appraisals Beneficial but Refinements Needed," (Washington, D.C.: report to the director, office of personnel management, report 83–72, September, 1983).

31. This section is based on Donald Horowitz, "The Courts as Guardians of the Public Interest," *Public Administration Review*, March–April 1977, pp. 148–54, and *The Courts and Social Policy* (Washington, D.C.: Brookings Institution, 1977).

32. Grover Starling, *Managing the Public Sector*, 3rd ed., (Chicago: Dorsey Press, 1986), p. 138.

33. Leif Carter, *Administrative Law and Politics* (Boston: Little, Brown, 1983), pp. 212–13.

34. David Rosenbloom, *Public Administration* (New York: Random House, 1986), p. 459.

35. 500 F. 2nd 1059 (1974). This case is summarized in Carter, *Administrative Law and Politics*, pp. 278–80.
36. 447 P. 2nd 352 (1968). This case is summarized in Carter, *Administrative Law and Politics*, pp. 280–83.
37. 367 U.S. 643 (1961). This account is from Horowitz, *The Courts and Social Policy*, pp. 220–54.
38. Ibid., p. 243.

CHAPTER 6

The Intergovernmental System

This chapter is about intergovernmental relations (IGR). It is not about what the manager does, but the environment in which he performs his job. Other chapters in the book deal with decision making, budgeting, personnel, and politics. While certain techniques and knowledge allow the manager to maintain, represent, and plan for his organization, IGR, in contrast, is simply part of the management environment. Other than hiring a grants official to apply for grants, there are no techniques or secrets to IGR management. There is much to understand about IGR, however, and effective managers learn how to operate in the IGR system and learn about other actors in the system.

The simplest way to outline IGR is to use a hypothetical example of a manager's workday, emphasizing how many routine and nonroutine activities involve IGR. Her workday follows in Exhibit 6–1.

If you asked the manager what she did that day, she wouldn't mention IGR. The rally discussion or the luncheon would not stand out in her memory as an IGR event. Yet, in one typical day, she dealt with state and federal government, with organizations at the same level, and with private not-for-profit groups. Discussions ranged from state and national policy (taxes and closing air bases) to technical questions of accounting and street easements. It was a full day of IGR topics.

If one assigns the manager's IGR activities to specific functions, one might say that the letter about Central City planning, the discussion about the Central City rally and the discussion of garbage collection involved organizational maintenance. The discussions with the library board and future sales tax collections involved strategic planning. The remaining topics involved organizational representation. However, these three functions blend, and it is hard to identify precisely when the manager maintained the organization or did strategic planning. These activities occurred in an intergovernmental setting, and some familiarity with this setting is crucial to effective managerial performance.

This chapter emphasizes: (1) the complexity of governments in the manager's environment, and (2) the importance placed by many governments on obtaining grants from higher-level governments. These emphases highlight the continuing responsibility of managers to maintain,

EXHIBIT 6–1   A City Manager's Intergovernmental Contacts during a
Typical Day

7:30 A.M.	Phone call to congressional representative's office about closing of the local air force base that indicates city opposition due to loss of local jobs. The call also supports a proposed regional reservoir and discusses requirements for local financial support, suggesting some language benefitting the city.
8:30	Short chat with her former administrative assistant now employed as a budget officer in a state agency.
8:50	Phone call to general manager of the suburban sanitary district about the easement across a city street for a sewer line.
9:40	Dictate letter to Central City planning department about the impact of its master plan on the city.
10:30	Half-hour discussion with police and fire chief about protection for a rally terminating in the city after beginning in Central City. Arrangements must be coordinated between the county sheriff, Central City police and fire chiefs, four other suburbs, and the state highway patrol.
Noon	Lunch with mayor and another council member about the proposed new shopping center in an adjoining suburb and its impact on traffic patterns and the city's downtown. Some casual debate about trying to get the state legislature to allocate sales tax revenues on a county-wide population basis rather than point of origin, so that the city will share in the revenues generated by the new center.
2:15 P.M.	Preliminary discussion with the owner of a garbage collection system, who offers to improve service if two adjoining cities and the city give him a franchise.
2:30	Phone call from the executive director of the United Way to see if the manager will become a board member. Her expertise is needed since the United Way is trying to support social service groups such as the Hunger Task Force, which the city no longer can fund from revenue-sharing money.
4:10	Chat with her administrative assistant who serves as the de facto city grantsman. Topic is whether more space and overhead can be pledged to a proposed grant. She talks with the finance director to find out from the Municipal Finance Officers Association in Washington, D.C., whether the city's accounting allocations of overhead is used in other cities.
7:30	Meeting of the library board to discuss a cooperative interlibrary loan program with Central City.

represent, and plan for their organization, and the fact that these responsibilities occur in an IGR setting.

THE INTERGOVERNMENTAL SYSTEM

IGR is complex. Crucial to understanding public management, it is impossible to describe simply. IGR is so much a part of the work environment that public managers do not formally account for it as such, and it is so complex that scholars cannot easily describe it. Constantly changing, it is a permanent fixture of our government system. IGR is based on crucial constitutional arrangements, yet we speak of managing it as though it were but another administrative task. IGR has enormous fiscal consequences, but these consequences are distributed so unevenly that some government units are affected enormously while others are unaffected.

This chapter is about managing in the IGR system. To grasp the context of IGR management, however, it's first necessary to understand what the IGR system is. This system contains, from the manager's perspective, two basic parts: organizational/constitutional and fiscal.

The United States is a federal system, and each governmental level has certain prerogatives. The federal government occupies the central position with states having independent sovereign powers, including control over local governments in their boundaries. This is a constitutional division of power between the state and the federal government, and both units deal directly and concurrently with the same citizens. This fact gives rise to many issues involving federalism, such as taxation, provision of services, and political representation. Elaborate political arrangements exist to check the federal government's power. These arrangements limit the number of services, which partly explains why the federal government has to rely on grants to get states to provide these services.

These legal arrangements are one aspect of IGR. Political and fiscal interdependence among officials at all levels often changes formal relationships. There are administrative and regulatory relationships as well, as when a federal regulatory agency authorizes its state counterpart to regulate private parties within that state. These political, regulatory, and administrative relationships revolve around money. Money, together with institutional arrangements, determines the fiscal independence of many units. In even more cases, it explains the fiscal interdependence of other units.

Government Profusion

There are many governments in the United States, and they employ many employees providing a profusion of services. In 1982, there was one federal government, 50 state governments, and over 82,000 local governments. These local units were made up of 19,000 municipalities, 3,000 counties, and 17,000 townships (mostly Midwest county subdivisions). School districts, mostly the one-room schools in rural areas, have declined from 50,000 to under 15,000 in a quarter century, while special districts—local park, fire, and water districts—have doubled to 28,500 in the same period. (See Table 6–1.)

Special districts are the most interesting aspect of federalism. Created to tailor services to a specific region, they total a third of all government units. Hardly a spot in the 50 states doesn't have some kind of district. One can be born in a hospital district, play as a teenager in a recreation district, have one's adult home protected by a rural fire protection district, and find a final resting place in a cemetery district.

Since states have constitutional power to create, control, and abolish local units within their boundaries, the complexity of local government structure is an individual state political choice. Illinois, for example, has over 6,000 local units of government.

While local government units comprise over 99 percent of total government units, most are tiny with one or even a part-time employee. When gargantuan employers, such as New York City, are included, local governments employ half of all government employees. (See Table 6–2.) Local employment levels have increased rapidly, although not as rapidly as state governments. At the other extreme, federal civilian employment has declined to 18 percent of total government employment. Since the largest block of state and federal employees are public school teachers, the typical public employee grades papers somewhere in Wyoming or Wisconsin rather than shuffling them in Washington, D.C.

TABLE 6–1 Governmental Units in the United States

	1957	*1967*	*1977*	*1982*
National	1	1	1	1
State	48	50	50	50
Counties	3,042	3,049	3,042	3,041
Municipalities	17,183	18,048	18,862	19,076
Townships	17,198	17,105	16,822	16,734
Special districts	14,405	21,264	25,962	28,588
School districts	50,446	21,782	15,174	14,851
Total	102,328	81,299	79,913	82,341

SOURCE: U.S. Bureau of the Census, *1982 Census of Governments* (Washington, D.C.: U.S. Government Printing Office, 1984).

TABLE 6–2   Government Employment by Level (000)

	1964	1973	1985
Federal (civilian)	2,528	2,783	3,021
State	1,873	3,013	3,984
Local	5,663	8,339	9,685
Total	10,064	14,139	16,690

SOURCE: U.S. Department of Commerce, *Statistical Abstract of the United States, 1987* (Washington, D.C.: U.S. Government Printing Office), p. 280.

Interdependence of Governments

Since each government unit has sovereign powers in some area, they must yield to the authority of other units in other areas while sharing power in most areas. For example, a state may compel its counties to offer welfare programs. How those programs are operated, however, depends on: (1) the county's legal status in the state, (2) the degree to which state and federal funds for welfare are used by that county, (3) the county's political strength in the state (individually or as a member of a group of counties), (4) the historical role of county welfare programs in a state, and, (5) the relationship of the county to large cities in that county and whether the city has a welfare program. Exhibit 6–2 indicates how units of government, in this case cities and park districts, interact with each other.

State power to compel performance is limited. It is matched by: (1) local ability to set informal standards, (2) the perceived legitimacy of local services, (3) the local orientation of legislators who have local electoral districts, and (4) the psychological attachment of most people to their local government. The result is that state and local governments negotiate with each other—whether the negotiations are carried on in state legislative chambers, between legislators and citizens in election campaigns, or between agency managers at each level.

Local units often resent state mandates such as a required city master plan—feeling that they burden local discretion. They also may resent state educational requirements for health inspectors because they raise payroll costs that the state does not pay for. Much political struggle during each legislative session involves regulations such as these.

The opposite events occur when local government units seek state authority for local activities such as zoning beyond city boundaries, requiring a foreign language in high school, or eminent domain powers for cemetery districts. Then local lobbyists descend like locusts on the legislature to convince it to act favorably on the local request.

EXHIBIT 6–2   Chicago Park Districts

In 1975, the Chicago metropolitan area contained approximately 175 independent part districts, ranging from a tiny unit with a budget of $14,000 to the huge Chicago Park District with a $100 million budget.

Some districts overlapped city and county lines, some were coterminous with them, and some were completely inside a city. Districts had police power, could acquire open space, and could conduct recreational services, as could cities. For police protection, districts could hire their own park rangers, contract with cities for patrol, or beg cities to provide free patrol in parks. Cities needed district approval if their sewer extension crossed park boundaries. Cities could require districts to annex to the city for water or sewer services. Cities had zoning powers, so park districts had to ask them to require potential developers to dedicate park sites as a condition of development. Park districts had to meet city building code standards for park buildings or swimming pools. These overlapping boundaries and functions periodically caused conflicts.

On the other hand, cooperation was the most common reaction. Many park districts and cities shared equipment. The larger unit allowed others to share in joint purchasing agreements. Most managers were cooperative and tried to maintain friendly relations with other managers, whether in cities or park districts.

SOURCE: John Rehfuss, "Intergovernmental Conflict—The Case of Illinois Park Districts and Municipalities," *CFS Notebook* (Philadelphia: Center for the Study of Federalism, Temple University), Winter 1977, pp. 2–11.

Because no single level of government, regardless of its constitutional power, can develop and implement policies alone, all parties must cooperate to solve a serious issue. This applies to any program—from AIDS funding to Indian tribe economic development to acid rain. Political leaders and program specialists at all levels—as well as local, state, and federal governments, must join hands. Even services such as local police or elementary education are funded by both federal and state governments through grants-in-aid or shared revenues. In some cases, the state police force may provide local patrol. No function is too great or humble to share. Even states keep National Guard units and share in national defense. At the other extreme, the federal government has become involved in local zoning through grants for local master plans.

FINANCING THE INTERGOVERNMENTAL SYSTEM

IGR is driven by money. While there are many nonfinancial IGR interactions, even these are rooted in fiscal relationships. The federal government sends money to states and localities through grants-in-aid. States also give grants-in-aid to local government, but shared taxes and revenues are more common, as when sales-tax collections are divided among both parties.

Federal Grants-in-Aid Totals

The struggles over grant formulas and the level of federal participation in the grant process has taken a new turn now that grants are being cut back. Federal categorical grants (specific purpose) were cut 27 percent from 534 to 392 between 1981 and 1984, although some categorical grants were folded into block grants for general purposes, which increased from 4 to 12 in the same period.[1] Table 6–3 shows that federal grants have risen in total dollars from 1978, a high-water mark for federal activity, but they have declined when inflation is considered.

From 1960 to 1978, when grants grew rapidly, federal grants increased elevenfold in dollars, doubling from 7.6 to 17 percent of all federal budget outlays, and they increased from 1.4 to 3.7 percent of the gross national product (GNP). However, by 1984, federal grants declined as a share of GNP, of total federal expenditures, and of state and local receipts. The latter three indexes fell below 1972 levels. The 1990 projections call for further declines.

The largest federal grants were for transportation; education, training, and employment; health; and income security. These four categories totaled over $93 billion in 1986, about 80 percent of all federal grants, as Table 6–4 shows.

Some of the major aides to state and local governments are not grants, but tax expenditures. Tax expenditures subsidize state and local governments through tax incentives or tax breaks rather than grants. Some tax expenditures are constitutional, since the federal government cannot tax the instrumentalities of other units of government. Thus, interest on state and local debt is exempt from federal taxation. This reduces the cost of state and local borrowing because bond purchasers

TABLE 6–3   Federal Grants-in-Aid for Selected Years

	1960	*1972*	*1978*	*1984*	*1990*
Total federal dollars (billions)	7.0	34.4	77.9	97.6	107.9
Percent of federal outlays	7.6	14.9	17.0	11.5	9.7
Percent state/local own source receipts	16.8	26.1	31.7	23.7	n.a.
Percent gross national product (GNP)	1.4	3.0	3.7	2.7	2.0

SOURCE: Advisory Commission on Intergovernmental Relations, *Significant Features of Fiscal Federalism, 1984 ed.* (Washington, D.C.: March 1985), p. 21, table 8, and The Budget for Fiscal Year 1988, Special Analyses (Washington, D.C.: Government Printing Office), Table H-22.

TABLE 6–4 Federal Grants by Function ($ billions)

				Estimate			
Function	Actual 1986	1987	1988	1989	1990	1991	1992
National defense	$ 0.2	$ 0.2	$ 0.2	$ 0.2	$ 0.2	$ 0.2	$ 0.2
Energy	0.5	0.4	0.3	0.3	0.2	0.3	0.3
Natural resources and environment	4.3	3.8	3.4	3.2	3.2	3.2	3.0
Agriculture	1.9	2.0	1.9	1.5	1.2	1.0	1.0
Transportation	18.4	17.5	17.2	18.3	17.7	17.0	17.3
Community and regional development	4.9	4.9	4.2	3.5	3.2	3.0	2.9
Education, training, employment, and social services	19.0	18.6	19.2	19.9	20.1	20.1	19.5
Health	26.8	28.7	28.7	29.9	31.4	32.9	34.4
Income security	29.1	31.0	29.2	27.6	28.8	29.4	30.0
Veterans benefits and services	0.1	0.1	0.1	0.1	0.1	0.2	0.2
Administration of justice	0.1	0.3	0.3	0.2	0.1	0.1	0.1
General government	0.2	0.2	0.1	0.1	0.1	0.1	0.1
General purpose fiscal assistance	7.0	2.2	1.5	1.6	1.6	1.7	1.7
Total outlays	$112.4	$109.9	$106.3	$106.5	$107.9	$109.2	$110.6

SOURCE: *The Budget for Fiscal Year 1988,* Special Analyses (Washington, D.C.: Government Printing Office), Table H–3.

lower their bids by the amount of the tax exemption. Other tax expenditures include allowing taxpayers to deduct state and local taxes from federal income tax liability, which reduces the impact of state and local taxes. Exclusion of industrial development bond (IDB) interest from federal taxes is a recent tax expenditure that has grown so much in recent years that Congress cut the amount that each state can use for 1987. Tax expenditures benefiting states and localities (Table 6–5) now total about one third of actual grants-in-aid.

At the state level, much state-collected money is shared directly with local units. In 1983, states chipped in $56 for every $100 raised by local units, a total of $99.5 billion, much in a form of state-local revenue sharing. This substantial total was lower in percentage terms than the high-water year for state aid, 1980, when $64 for each $100 was made available.[2] This can be most of a local unit's income. The local unit may not feel particularly dependent on the state because these revenues are automatically received and not subject to negotiation. But the locality is dependent on the state's policies about local revenue. Consider Loomis, a small California hamlet that considered incorporation in 1982. Loomis's estimated city revenue, if it incorporated, was as follows in Table 6–6.

TABLE 6–5   Federal Tax Expenditures Aiding State and Local Governments ($ billions)

	Fiscal Year		
Description	1986	1987	1988
Deductibility of:			
Property taxes on owner-occupied homes	$ 8,595	$ 7,955	$ 7,205
Nonbusiness state and local taxes other than on owner-occupied homes	23,965	18,235	14,485
Exclusion of interest on:			
Public purpose state and local debt	9,170	10,110	10,370
IDBs for certain energy facilities	180	200	205
IDBs for pollution control and sewage and waste disposal facilities	1,455	1,660	1,930
Small-issue IDBs	2,470	2,635	2,805
Owner-occupied mortgage revenue bonds	1,900	2,010	2,035
State and local debt for rental housing	1,275	1,335	1,320
Mass commuting vehicle IDBs	20	20	55
IDBs for airports, docks and sports and convention facilities	595	685	785
State and local student loan bonds	285	310	315
State and local debt for private nonprofit educational facilities	260	280	285
State and local debt for private nonprofit health facilities	2,105	2,250	2,250
State and local debt for veterans housing	290	295	305
Total (after interactions)	$42,710	$38,970	$36,075

SOURCE: *The Budget for Fiscal Year 1988*, Special Analyses (Washington, D.C.: Government Printing Office), Table H–3.

This is not an isolated example.[3] States across the nation have become a major actor in local finance. They have the power to regulate local activities, and they have chosen to help finance them.

MANAGING IN AN INTERGOVERNMENTAL SYSTEM

So far, IGR is complex, interdependent, revolves around money, and can be highly politicized. There are, however, specific implications for managers; most involve grants.

Since most of the system revolves around grants-in-aid, the administrative issues about grants should be reviewed. While most discussion is about federal grants, the problems that exist often affect state grants

TABLE 6–6 Loomis, California: Estimated Revenues, 1982 (summarized)

Property tax (maximum set by state, collected by county)	$ 78,500
Sales tax (state established share, state collected)	150,000
Specific state subventions (cigarette tax, gas tax, etc.)	204,000
Vehicle code violations (controlled largely by state)	17,000
Total state shared or controlled revenues	449,500
Franchises, business licenses, transient lodging taxes, etc.	25,500
Use of money	7,500
Fees, charges, permits	95,000
Miscellaneous	20,000
Total controlled by Loomis	148,000
Total budget (± 75 percent shared with or controlled by state)	$587,500

and localities. Generally, state and local officials blast federal grant management, while they busy themselves in manipulating grants to fit their own needs.

Grant Problems

Grants, particularly federal grants, are designed to advance national purposes. In so doing, they often ignore local purposes. Thus, problems arise, which grant system critics are quick to point out. There are four major problems or complaints, federal grants: (1) lack coordination, (2) ignore local purposes, (3) promote narrow program goals, and (4) encourage grant mongering.[4] Here are the detailed objections:

1. Federal Programs Are Disjointed, Overlapping and Duplicative. A folk story, often repeated but never identified, alleges that one federal agency granted urban renewal money for a neighborhood targeted for removal with new freeway construction funded by another federal agency. Each federal program makes its own arrangements with local officials. The federal grant process involves a group of large bureaucracies and their allied interests that make their own deals with state and local governments. These bureaucracies are interested in their programs, not overall coordination with other programs. A Virginia county administrator commented about grant coordination:

> The non-system of Federal grants as it presently exists is economically dysfunctional. Grants have overlapping functions, contradictory regulations and confused policies. The Federal bureaucracy administering the

grants, usually but not always well intentioned, is legalistic rather than performance oriented.[5]

2. Federal Programs Favor National Rather than Local Priorities. Should federal priorities prevail over local desires, if Uncle Sam foots all or part of the bill? After all, both parties know that granting agencies use aid to advance certain priorities—national, in the case of federal grants. Localities or states accept grants because their priorities coincide with national interests. An issue arises if localities use limited discretionary funds for a federal grant merely because the grant is available. This denies other local functions the money used for a federal match. There's no doubt that if localities starve nonfunded activities in favor of less-valued funded activities, such as fire departments in favor of libraries, there may be some substitution of books for fire hoses. This is a local choice to distort its own budget.

Washington is tilting toward local priorities. In 1981, Congress, at the urging of the president, consolidated more than 50 categorical grants into miniblock grants, most of which are controlled by state agencies.[6] The quid pro quo for giving states more control via the block grant route was a substantial reduction in total money available. This means that recipients traded funding for flexibility.

3. Grants Are Controlled by Narrow Program Specialists. This issue describes picket-fence federalism, where lines of authority go vertically from federal specialists down to corresponding specialists at state and local levels. The pickets of this fence have no horizontal bars because political leaders cannot or choose not to control these specialist linkages. The Oakland case study demonstrated this linkage in action.

Specialist control of a program often results in one of two ineffective situations. On one hand, the program may move in narrow categorical paths dealing with a few clients alongside similar programs. Conversely, an ambitious program that tries to accomplish several objectives, such as the Oakland project, is torn to shreds by other jealous agency programs.

A New Jersey township manager complained:

> In my opinion the federal grant system exists only to keep thousands of Federal employees employed. It is a complete waste. All funding should be done as in revenue sharing (with no strings attached).[7]

4. Federal Discretionary Grants Promote Excessive Applications for Grants. Having a grants official to obtain federal funds is much like having a good tax accountant help complete a complex tax return. In the mid-1970s, every large city had one or more employees responsible for tapping federal revenues when possible. Since many recipients, such as large central cities, were so dependent on federal funds, a grants official to maximize their receipts was a good investment. Governor Bryant of Florida once lamented:

> The next to last year I was in office, I sent the Executive Director of our State Board of Health to Washington on a years leave of absence, badly as we needed him, just so he could learn how to operate with federal people. He has been a great help to us since that time. But you ought not to have to do that kind of thing to learn just how to get along and through this morass.[8]

Some local officials would like to see the states bypassed to simplify the grant process—allowing localities to deal directly with Washington:

> Much of the problem exists between the state and local government. Often the local will learn of a Federal program, but the state fails to react until the time limit is nearly expired. I've found this true in many states. Federal-local or Federal-metropolitan programs are more efficient.[9]

Finally, some local officials are satisifed with the grant system and with federal grants. A Florida city manager notes:

> There are a great deal of disgruntled local jurisdictions throughout the country who perpetually damn Federal grant in aid programs. . . . We have not found these regulations difficult to comply with and have received every grant that we have applied for . . . A great deal of the so-called red tape has been instituted due to non-compliance by the local jurisdiction in addition to [the need for] meeting Congressional intent.[10]

A skeptic would suspect that the difference between the New Jersey and the Florida manager was primarily success in obtaining grants.

MANIPULATING THE GRANT SYSTEM FROM BELOW

Clearly, the grant process is far from perfect. However, it is often the only outside money game in town. Federal and state aid specialists and policymakers try to pay local units to accept federal programs or expand local programs in concert with federal programs. Local officials try to use federal and state money for local purposes. From the state and local perspective, how does the top manager try to manipulate the system for local purposes?

Modify the Formula

First, recipients try to change grant formulas to their advantage. The more flexibility retained or less money committed, the better. For these reasons, top officials of recipient agencies tend to favor shared revenue, which can be used anywhere or for broad purposes in a functional area (such as highways) rather than categorical grants, which are limited to narrow areas (such as driver education). Next to shared revenue, block grants are favored most by recipients, for block grants combine several categorical grants into broader blocks, which promote flexibility among related areas. For example, the Partnership for Health Act of 1966, an early block grant, replaced 17 categorical disease grants for heart ailments, tuberculosis, and cancer into one block grant.[11]

The top-down approach of federal and some state officials favors the narrower use of categorical grants to assure that funds go to specific purposes. Since the bottom-up perspective of local officials favors broader grants, the type and formula of the grant (e.g., block versus categorical and discretional versus specific formula) are often as important as the functional area the grant serves. Robert Greenblatt, coordinator and chief, Federal Relations Unit of the Budget Division of the State of New York, while explaining how he tried to maximize total grant revenue, also sheds light on the importance of the grant formula itself:

> We try to assist both the budget examiners and the state agencies in maximizing the federal aid that comes into the state and it's usually done by formula manipulation rather than merely applying for federal grants. The place to get in is on the ground floor when Congress is reviewing the program or initiaing a program and deciding how it's going to allocate the funds. . . . We've had some successes in recent months working with various Congressional committees to alter formulas which had been proposed that would have hurt New York.[12]

Every state or large city or county with a professional staff tries to influence the establishment of formulas through organizations such as the National Association of Counties, which lobbies to increase county shares of formulas. If lobbying fails, these units try to influence how regulations are written, because the regulations are often as important as the legislation.

By the mid-1970s, local units won most formula skirmishes in federal aid battles, for the federal share of grants was increasing. While total grants tripled from 135 in 1960 to 442 in 1976, the number of grants in which the federal government paid over half increased eightfold. Those grants in which the federal government paid half or less increased only about 40 percent.[13]

Interpret the Formulas Favorably

Another way of manipulating the system is to interpret grant formulas favorably. This is as effective as setting the formula. If the formula cannot be changed, it is interpreted in the recipient's interest. The story of how California and then Illinois ransacked the federal government's social services grant programs through ingenious and brazen interpretations is told in Case Study 6–1.

On a lesser scale, one California state official responsible for managing the state food stamp program noted that:

> My job was to insure that federal regulations which were given to the State were translated into State requirements and that in the area of policy option, the state opted into a direction that was to our best interest.[14]

Presumably, federal officials vigilantly watch their grants to keep them from being manipulated. If so, the sort of "well within the rules of the game" interpretations that were made by the California food stamp official are counterbalanced by federal concern that the regulations not be bent more than necessary (although federal watchfulness did not prevent serious leakage in social service programs for states; see Case Study 6–1 at the end of this chapter).

However, zealous local officials often go beyond the stretched state interpretations in Case Study 6–1. Trying to minimize their resource commitments, they cross the narrow line between interpretation and illegal activity. In 1975, North Carolina cut back state paid employees and replaced them with federally funded temporary employees for state highway work. Comprehensive Employment Training Act (CETA) rules call for the creation of new jobs with its funding, but the reverse happened. Field personnel officers didn't realize that state employee levels weren't to decline. "Whenever it has been possible for me to hire somebody as a CETA employee rather than a state employee, I have done it," claimed one area personnel officer. "It has cut down considerably the number of state employees that we have had out here."[15]

Engage in Grantsmanship

Being an effective grants official is another way of manipulating the IGR system; some would say that one must engage in grantsmanship to survive, if your agency needs federal funding. *Grantsmanship* is a term encompassing lobbying for favorable grant formulas, making advantageous rule interpretations, and avid grant seeking. it also includes mastery of the funding opportunities and mastery of rapid preparation of specific grant proposals. Grantsmanship places heavy emphasis on obtaining every possible dollar of aid that recipients can wrangle, wheedle, or pry out of granting agencies, particularly the federal government. Formulas are changed by appealing to administrative discretion or by lobbying higher levels of government directly. Local expenditures are authorized under a different budget category. Local expenses are stretched to masquerade as legitimate overhead charges to become part of the recipient match for the grant. Everything that can be done to maximize outside aid is done by recipients. Actually, grantors aid and abet grantsmanship because they have a vested interest in continuing the program. This maintains a federal or state presence in the program area.

Grantsmanship feeds upon itself. It creates the belief that someone else's money is always available for a worthy project, and that obtaining the money is a matter of clearly portraying need. No problem exists that a more clever application won't solve. Money is always available for better proposals to tap. The federal or state treasury is there to be raided, and higher-level officials give funds away. As an unidentified southern official supposedly once said, "Federal aid is tainted. Tain't enough of it."

The range of grant options puzzles many participants seeking an honest and reasonable solution to a real problem. Governor John Chafee of Rhode Island pointed out the ranges of federal participation to the House of Representatives:

> Let us take the case of a 1-year-old boy on aid to dependent children who has a hearing problem that can be corrected. My natural response, as I am sure yours is too, would be 'correct his hearing.' However, confusion arises when one considers whether he should be referred to the public assistance program administered by the Department of Social Welfare, the Division of Vocational Rehabilitation administered by the Department of Education, or to the crippled children's program administered by the Department of Health. Under such conditions there is the temptation—and I must say this is a very real one—to refer such a patient, not to the program which is best organized to meet his particular need, but to the program in which the State obtains the best financial advantage. The Federal government will pay 50 percent of the cost when the care is provided by the Crippled Children's Division; it will pay 56 percent under title XIX since he is on aid to dependent children; and, if he is cared for by vocational rehabilitation, the Federal government will soon pay 75 percent of the bill. Each of these programs has some variation in standards for eligibility but nonetheless the differences in Federal reimbursement seem extremely puzzling.[16]

If Governor Chafee took the expected course of action, the child would be assigned to the Division of Vocational Education, since it paid 75 percent of the total costs.

Rules of the Game

Grants officials, politicians, and managers operate under a series of rules that maximize state or local independence, flexibility, and resources. Most of them are simple extensions of the grant formula application methods already discussed. They put into print the way that grant recipients operate. These rules, adapted from a list developed by

Deil Wright after years of observing grant recipient behavior, are as follows:

1. Spend higher-level dollars and to the extent possible, save your own.
2. Protect your agency's discretion and avoid control by other governments.
3. Emphasize public participation if it doesn't threaten program management; if it does, emphasize participation only enough to meet the grantor's requirements.
4. Maintain responsibility for actual delivery of services at the lowest possible level, normally local government.
5. Commit as few resources to meet financing requirements as possible. This means, for example, that a soft match of overhead is better than a hard match of actual dollars.
6. Cultivate friends and constituents, neutralize opposing interests, and use political contacts to improve your grant prospects.[17]

This may seem cynical, but it is no more so than other administrative behaviors. Grantsmanship is a game played under certain rules, with each player trying to outperform the other. In more formal terms, it is an attempt to maximize local discretion, money, and authority. These are goals that managers are paid to pursue.

FOUR INTERGOVERNMENTAL ACTORS

Let's look at four different actors in their IGR setting to examine the range of IGR activities.

An Earlier Era Sanitarian

Morton Grodins gives an account of an early sanitarian (health inspector), providing a classic statement of how intertwined all levels of government were in the 1950s:

> The sanitarian is appointed by the state under merit standards established by the federal government. His base salary comes jointly from state and federal funds, the county provides him with an office and office amenities and pays a portion of his expense, and the largest city in the county also contributes to this salary and office by virtue of his appointment as a city plumbing inspector . . .
> His work of inspecting the purity of food is carried out under federal standards, but he is enforcing state laws when inspecting commodities that have not been in interstate commerce, and somewhat perversely he also acts under state authority when inspecting milk coming into the county from producing areas across the state border. He is a federal officer when

impounding impure drugs shipped from a neighboring state, a federal-state officer when inspecting typhoid immunization serum, a state officer when enforcing standards of industrial hygiene, a state-local officer when inspecting the city water supply, and (to complete the cycle) a local officer when insisting that the city butchers adopt more hygienic methods of handling their garbage.[18]

California Transportation Planner

The district branch manager in a state highway planning department handles all aspects of the environmental program, which include air pollution, noise, water quality, biological studies, and cultural studies. As district environmental manager, she supervises all background studies that must be approved prior to actual construction. She is responsible for seeing that every transportation project in the district meets all guidelines, regulations, and laws regarding environmental protection, and that the district office has documentation to show that they met these requirements.

Since all highway department projects involve some federal money, the planner must ensure that each project meets minimum federal environment standards of the Environmental Protection Agency and the Council for Environmental Quality. Some of the major federal laws include:

The National Environmental Protection Act

The Clean Water Act

The Clean Air Act

The Federal Noise Control Act

The Wild and Scenic Rivers Act

The Fish and Wildlife Act

The National Historic Preservation Act

The Federal Highway Act

The California Environmental Quality Act

The California Fish and Game Code

All California Cultural Resource Laws

Federal and California Native American Laws

The planner must provide the regional engineer with enough information so that the engineer can certify that all environmental acts include an environmental impact statement or a negative declaration. This information and background includes attending all public hearings on the proposed transportation project as the departmental specialist on environmental impacts. For local highway aid in the district, she ensures that local government units follow all environmental laws. After construction of the project (usually a highway or bridge), she ensures that all environmental agreements are adhered to. In brief, the district transportation planner is the person who assures that all environmental regulations are followed by the state.

Ann Michel, Syracuse Grants Official

Ann Michel, director of the Syracuse city Office of Federal and State Aid Coordination (OFSAC), is a good example of how grantmanship operates. In 1976, her office obtained $55 million from state and federal sources, 45 percent of Syracuse's budget. For all practical purposes, Syracuse was a municipal pauper living on outside money. Such a condition only strengthened her position as one of the key officials in the city. Michel described her job:

> Our first function is to manipulate the system to get as much of the money as we can into the hands of the City of Syracuse, in the first instance, at least, to be used to meet city priority needs. That included grant negotiations, most heavily in the categorical and block grant systems. . . .
>
> An additional activity related to procuring maximum outside aid is fairly active participation in federal legislative lobbying efforts . . . Finally, this effort of procuring outside aid includes city-county negotiation. As cities become less able to suport functions with their own revenue you will see increasing efforts on the part of city governments to try to get the county governments with their broader suburban-financed tax base to pay for a larger share of services . . .
>
> The second category of activity within OFSAC is fiscal management and oversight. The quickest way to lose credibility with funding sources is to have an audit exception. . . .
>
> The third category of activity of OFSAC is a function we've only recently added, a division of program evaluation. It is done for several reasons. Partly it's an attempt to stay one step ahead of the funding sources, because if we discover the problems before they do and get them corrected then we continue to have the reputation we feel we need to strengthen our negotiations.[19]

Brian May, Park Director

Brian May was manager of the tiny Arden Manor Park District from 1981 to 1985 (He moved up to a top management position in a larger park district in 1985). Arden Manor comprises one-and-a-half square miles in Sacramento, California with a population of 8,000 residents.

The district has only four full-time employees, including May and the district secretary, to operate three parks, although there are several part-time recreation directors. Hard times since Proposition 13 property tax limitations have cut the full-time staff in half.

The district budget in 1985–86 was $307,000, the same as seven years earlier. The district relies on outside funding to supplement the budget (see Exhibit 6–3). Fees and charges for recreational programs have tripled and now make up 25 percent of the budget. This means that grants and outside revenues must be sought constantly, which uses a good share of May's time. May noted that the district recently completed two new parks with the aid of several federal and state grants. Some of the outside funding is from fund raising or "scrounging" as May calls it. Some is free, such as when courts sentence drunk drivers to community service work in the parks. Some is volunteer work, such as completing the pool in a third park. Most district activities occur during the summer and revolve around the pool.

It isn't easy to act as the top-level manager and do long-term planning in Arden Manor. May, whose 1985 salary was about $28,000, wheedles volunteer help, writes grant proposals, conducts recreational programs, prepares the budget, and performs other duties that link technical and managerial work, top-district policy and nitpicking details, as well as organizational maintenance, representation, and long-range planning.

The annual budget is a major headache for May. California park districts have little basis for projecting revenues. Property tax revenues depend on state and county decisions, which usually come after the fiscal year begins. Grants are uncertain. Fees and charges are controllable, having tripled since 1978. Budgets are approved on the assumption that no money other than salaries will be spent until tax money is re-

---

EXHIBIT 6–3   Outside Funding for Arden Manor Park District, 1985–86

Sacramento Housing and Redevelopment Agency	
Senior Citizens Nutrition Program	$ 1,440
Sacramento County	
Arden Library maintenance contract	3,168
Community donations	1,400
Roberti-Z'Berg urban open space grants (state)	
Playgrounds $3,968	
Pool complex (two grants) $27,000	30,968
Land and Water Conservation Fund (federal)	3,725
Insurance refund	750
Sale of personal property	675
Total	$42,126

ceived from county. Since long-term planning is impossible, every year completed without fiscal disaster is a small victory.

Arden Manor could join with other districts to form a larger unit, gaining some financial stability, perhaps at the cost of autonomy. May favors this, noting that most residents don't care who provides services. He doesn't think any consolidation will occur, however. The district could also try to form a community services district, becoming a "junior city," which would provide several services including recreation. This would also dissolve Arden Manor into the larger unit.

Arden Park will limp along, chronically short of money, hoping that a better day for park districts will arrive; Arden Manor's goal mainly is survival. Mays ponders these strategic choices between refereeing a softball game and writing yet another grant proposal.

Four Actors

The duties of the four actors vary greatly. The sanitarian was a low-level specialist, although his views were treated with care by political officials. The transportation planner also has a narrow specialist's job, but the position is crucial to the highway department's eligibility for federal funds. Michel, a full-time grants official, was involved in all types of grant-seeking and grant-management activites. Brian May was the only top manager of an organization—even though it had only four employees. His district's dependence on outside funding highlights the manager's role when intergovernmental funding is needed. No two actors had the same job, but all the jobs are intimately connected with IGR. These positions show the depth and variety of IGR activities.

SUMMARY

The IGR system is part of the manager's environment. She lives and breathes in it, without giving much thought to it. The IGR system is something one understands, not something one manages. There are parts of the system, however, that require management.

The thousands of interactions with other governmental units that occur in a year require awareness of the American political system and effective exercise of maintenance and representation functions in the manager's organization.

The manager's abilities in maintenance and representation are tested daily in the regulatory and nonfiscal issues he faces. These issues include direct and indirect state and federal mandates such as health or welfare requirements, if he is a state or local official. They include state and local reactions to top-level mandates such as community development rules (usually enforced through grant provisions), if he is a federal official.

The most widely reported part of IGR is the federal grant chase by local and state officials. Here, the grantor seeks to further national or state requirements through payments to lower-level officials, while the recipient seeks to advance her own goals by using higher-level money. The chase goes on, even though federal grants are decreasing in relative terms. Since federal grants are still prized, the local manager finds her organizational maintenance responsibilities for funding sometimes at odds with longer strategic plans, which raise questions about dependence on outside funding when continued declines in grants are likely.

Case Study 6–1

UNCONTROLLED FEDERAL SPENDING FOR SOCIAL SERVICE, OR HOW ILLINOIS AND CALIFORNIA BROKE THE FEDERAL BANK

Federal grants to states for social services became, by 1972, a raid on the federal treasury by most states until Congress put a cap of $2.5 billion on the program. Innovative and aggressive state grantsmanship, particularly by Illinois officials building on the California precedent, "broke the bank," forcing the grant program to pay virtually on demand to any state reporting social services provided in certain ways.

Social services programs were under the public assistance part of the Social Services Act. It included supporting services for grants to the poor such as Old Age Assistance, Aid to the Blind, and Aid to Families with Dependent Children (AFDC). About 40 percent of the grants went for foster child care and day care for children. The rest

included items such as homemaker services, alcoholism and drug treatment, and special services for handicapped children. The grant was open-ended, meaning that the federal government promised to match whatever state governments spent for these programs.

Despite the open-ended nature of the grant, few states made extensive use of it. California was the major exception. Total federal grants for all states increased from $241 million in 1967 to $776 million in 1971. California's share ranged from 25 percent to 36 percent of these totals.

California exploited the program but did not force it to become uncontrollable in the way that Illinois did in 1972. However, had all states used California's system of grantsmanship, the fiscal crisis would have occurred earlier. California used federal funds to expand programs. This technique appears to be an extensive elaboration of what the law may have contemplated. California used some of the following techniques to exploit the grant. The Department of Rehabilitation was renamed the Department of Social and Rehabilitation Services and given responsibility for social service functions to maximize the use of service grants. When the Federal Bureau of Family Services instructed state agencies to help remove inmates from mental institutions, several hundred Department of Mental Hygiene workers were transferred to the Department of Social Welfare to obtain 75 percent federal matching for their salaries. Under AFDC programs, attendants were not only paid with 75 percent federal matching funds, but welfare recipients were designated attendants so the federal share of their support could go from 50 to 75 percent.

Preschool compensatory education was redefined as a social service for AFDC children, thus qualifying the state program for the 75 percent federal match. The state had financed two thirds of the cost of child care centers for working mothers. It authorized county welfare departments to pay these children for providing services to current, former, and potential welfare recipients under a provision of the social security law that would result in maximizing federal participation. Federal aid went up from zero to $12.7 million in three years.

The initiative for this grantsmanship did not come from the executive branch. It came mostly from the large professional and legislative staff built up in the 1960s. They goaded and cajoled program heads of social service agencies to apply for money in creative ways and proposed laws to maximize federal grants. Their activitiy and California's success no doubt encouraged Illinois' aggressive 1972 actions. The California example showed how individual units could obtain disproportionate sums of federal aid if they had the will and resources to emphasize grantsmanship in the early 1970s.

Illinois was not only bolder than California, but more desperate due to a looming state budget deficit. In the fall of 1970, Illinois based its 1971–72 budget on the assumption that HEW would provide an additional $75 million for new proposals. These proposals indicated that the Illinois Department of Public Aid should purchase services from other state agencies such as the Mental Health Department. The services were for treatment and prevention of drug abuse, alcoholism, mental health problems, and so on. They were being provided by the department through state funds— the proposal would expand the services while substituting federal funds for state expenditures.

Technically, the proposal was to expand state expenditures for social services, but there was no promise to do so. Illinois' proposals would have widened the loophole in the federal law by making many more recipients available for support. Expenditures for adult prison inmates were justified since their incarceration was responsible for family breakup, which caused remaining family members to go on the AFDC rolls. All persons in the correctional system or mental hospitals were potential recipients of public aid who needed preventive services before they went on the aid rolls.

These bold proposals largely came from budget officials at the state level, who took their cues and technical advice from a consultant who promoted social services, and from a federal regional commissioner who was anxious to expand child-care centers. Budget officials later noted that without the grant consultant they ". . . never would have tried anything so outlandish. . . ."

The proposal was outlandish, but it worked. After much interbureaucratic negotiation between Illinois and HEW, as well as high-level negotiation between Governor Ogilvie and President Nixon's staff, the proposal was accepted. The federal grant program for social services was reduced to shambles because of lack of control. As other states tried to get their share of the windfall, requests from all states totaled double the HEW estimates. Mississippi, for example, asked for a sum that was half the state budget. Shocked, Congress approved, as part of the general revenue-sharing act, a limit of $2.5 billion for all states. Each state was limited to its share of the national population. This was, however, more than triple the previous fiscal year's sum. As it turned out, excessive grantsmanship by Illinois and California eventually limited their share of the new federal allocation.

SOURCE: Martha Derthick, *Uncontrollable Spending for Social Service Grants* (Washington, DC.: Brookings Institution, 1975).

NOTES

Note: A good overview of the intergovernmental setting can be found in Arnold Howitt, "Managing Federalism: An Overview," in Frederick Lane, ed., *Issues in Public Administration*, 3rd ed., (New York: St. Martin's, 1986), pp. 150–80.

1. Advisory Commission on Intergovernmental Relations (ACIR), *Intergovernmental Perspective 1984* (Washington, D.C.: ACIR, Winter 1985), p. 13.
2. ACIR, *Significant Features of Fiscal Federalism, 1984* (Washington, D.C.: ACIR, 1984), table 64.

3. For a comprehensive discussion of this point, see David Walker, *Toward a Functioning Federalism* (New York: Winthrop, 1981), pp. 82, 177–82; and Deil Wright, *Understanding Intergovernmental Relations* (North Sciutate, Mass.: Duxbury, 1978), pp. 330–44.
4. This list of complaints is partially based on a summary in The Controller General, *Fundamental Changes are Needed in Federal Assistance to State and Local Governments* (Washington, D.C.: U.S. General Accounting Office, 1975), p. 9.
5. ACIR, *The Intergovernmental Grant System as Seen by State, Local, and Federal Officials* (Washington, D.C.: ACIR), Report A–54, (March 1977), p. 46.
6. ACIR, *Significant Features of Fiscal Federalism 1984* (Washington, D.C.: ACIR, 1985), table 43.
7. ACIR, *The Intergovernmental Grant System. . . ,* p. 50.
8. Hearings before the Subcommittee on Intergovernmental Relations of the House Committee on Governmental Operations, *Grant Consolidation and Intergovernmental Cooperation,* 91st Congress, First Session (part one), June 1969, p. 241.
9. ACIR, *The Intergovernmental Grant System,* p. 52.
10. Ibid., p. 53.
11. Walker, *Toward a Functioning Federalism,* p. 103.
12. Robert Greenblatt, "A Comment on Federal-State Relations," in James Carroll and Richard Campbell, eds., *Intergovernmental Administration: 1976— Eleven Academic and Practitioner Perspectives* (Syracuse, N.Y.: Maxwell School of Citizenship and Public Affairs, Syracuse University, 1976), pp. 250–52.
13. Walker, *Toward a Functioning Federalism,* p. 186.
14. John Rehfuss, Unpublished research on the California Career Executive Assignment System.
15. "Federal Job Money is Going Awry," *The News and Observer of Raleigh,* December 7, 1976, as reported in Deil Wright, *Understanding Intergovernmental Relations* (North Sciutate, Mass.: Duxbury, 1978), pp. 361–62.
16. *Investigation of HEW,* Hearings before the Special Subcommittee on Investigation of the Department of Health, Education, and Welfare of the Committee on Interstate and Foreign Commerce, House of Representatives, 89th Congress, 2nd session, April 18–22, May 27, and June 20, 1966.
17. Adapted from Deil Wright, *Understanding Intergovernmental Relations,* p. 189.
18. Morton Grodins, "The Federal System," in The American Assembly, *Goals for Americans: The Report of the President's Commission on National Goals* (New York: The American Assembly), p. 265.
19. Ann Michel, "Intergovernmental Aid: A Local Perspective," in Carroll and Campbell, eds., *Intergovernmental Administration: 1976—Eleven Academic and Practitioner Perspectives,* Maxwell School of Citizenship and Public Affairs, pp. 155–56.

CHAPTER 7

Budgeting and Finance

Compiling the budget is an exercise in number-crunching. Many managers assume the technical part of the budget process is the whole exercise, and they avoid it for this reason. Some avoid budgeting by delegating it to accountants. The manager's reward is a dry, irrelevant set of figures that meet the legal requirements for a budget. Since these managers don't care for the process, this is acceptable to them.

More sophisticated managers who dislike budgeting as much as their colleagues, rely on finance or budget directors to make budgetary decisions. These managers provide a few general policies to guide the finance director, and then retire from the budget process. These managers get a more sophisticated set of dry, irrelevant figures. These managers also think that they have a good budget, and the process is satisfactory to them.

A budget without top management involvement may be in fiscal balance but it won't be in management balance. Managers cannot avoid responsibility for the decisions that undergird budget figures. Even if they dislike figures, the policy implications of these figures must be dealt with. When this is clear, it's obvious that the budget involves important aspects of the manager's job to maintain, represent, and plan for the organization.

Budgeting, like most jobs, involves the maintenance, representation, and planning functions. Organizational maintenance concerns budgeting issues such as creating and overseeing departmental work plans, directing budget implementation and authorized programs, holding budget hearings until agreement is hammered out, and processing the mountains of paper that budgeting generates.

Organizational representation involves explaining the budget document and its work programs to potentially unsympathetic legislators, executives, and citizen groups. Effective executives sell their budget needs to a range of people—always remembering that budget or financial management needs do not speak for themselves. Good managers are enthusiastic about their programs, about their efficiencies, and knowledgeable about their clientele. If the manager is not enthusiastic about the budget, no one else will be.

Budget proposals are the yearly chance for new programs. True, they are only for one year, but each fiscal year brings a chance to initiate new programs or affirm new directions that the strategic planning process requires. The annual budget period is a yearly reminder that 10-year strategic plans often begin a fiscal year at a time.

TWO VIEWS OF THE BUDGET

There are two clashing views about budgeting in the public sector. One is that budgeting is a crucial part of management and of policymaking, the other is that it is irrelevant. Both are based as much on faith as on empirical evidence. Both are correct part of the time.

One view holds that budgeting is the basis for all long-term planning; that it is during the process when most strategic planning occurs and that it gives the best outline of how basic governmental decisions are made. This is most true of the chief executive's view. It is also more accurate during the formulation and execution stages of the budget. Since all public decisions have some budgetary impact, the budget process forces these decisions to be considered at one time when the whole financial plan is considered. In addition, when some issue arises in the middle of the fiscal year, it may be deferred until it can be considered in the budget or until other financial adjustments are made in the current budget.

These conditions exist, but an opposing argument is that the role of the budget is overrated. When the chief executive makes a choice, she rarely calls for sweeping changes in priorities. When the legislature considers the budget, sweeping changes and major modifications are rare. The budget is changed incrementally and rarely represents major departures from existing policy. This is because an equilibrium exists between major budget claimants (e.g., police versus recreation versus housing versus defense). While exceptions occur, as when defense spending rose sharply in the Reagan administration, disturbances of the status quo are troublesome and not undertaken lightly. Secondly, not only is the budget incremental, it is largely irrelevant. If a program issue must be dealt with and cannot be put off, the decision is then made by the executive and the legislature without waiting for the budget. In addition, uncontrollable items such as legal obligations, salaries for persons on the current payroll, and other long-term commitments result in the budget largely ratifying the status quo. Important issues drive the budget while the budget process drives less-important issues.

So, on one hand, the budget is a means of strategic planning. On the other hand, it is a paper chase that confirms what already has been decided. Both views are correct. Sometimes the budget process is high drama. Usually it isn't, and it could easily be delayed for long periods without requiring the work associated with it.[1]

A better case for the importance of the budget process is made without downplaying its significance. Generally, the budget process drives the innovation or change process. That's because managers must think about long-range issues when they begin budget preparation. Calculations about how much money or other resources are available forces some analysis of how the job can be done for less. This holds even if the calculations are driven only by the realization that there isn't enough money to continue in traditional ways. Any improvement in services has to run the budget gauntlet. Many worthy programs don't get funded.

Some years ago, two appointed political executives proposed and installed a management system in the Health, Education, and Welfare and Interior Departments based on using the budgetary process as the bottom line. They claim their program works because it is coordinated with the budget process, which is "The one management process taken seriously by all subordinate units."[2] To them, the budget process is of central importance.

Whether one believes that the budget process drives programs and decisions or believes that events operate independently of the budget process is not the heart of the matter. The fact is that managers take the budget process seriously, devoting much time and effort to it.

THE BUDGET CYCLE

The budget cycle is the background for all management activities in the budget process. It is a continuous process of preparation, enactment, implementation, and audit.

For small agencies, budget preparation occurs from January until late May and June for a fiscal year ending June 30. During this period, departments prepare their requests, the central office reviews them, and the chief executive prepares the proposed budget for legislative review. In large agencies, states, and the federal government, preparation begins much sooner. Federal budget preparation begins up to 30 months before the fiscal year ends on September 30. This may be the longest preparation period of any U.S. unit. It means that the 1985–86 federal budget begins with departmental preparation of estimates as early as March 1984, with final completion of the approved budget on September 30, 1986, the last day of the fiscal year. Exhibit 7–1 gives an example of a more typical budget cycle.

Budget preparation is the place where long-range, strategic issues are considered. Department heads have completed their own long-range planning (at least, whatever long-range planning they will do).

EXHIBIT 7-1 Typical Small City 1985-86 Budget Cycle

Period	Activity	Actors
	Preparation	
January–April 1, 1985	Department heads review programs, adjust to estimates of revenue and policy about expenditures, propose new service levels and prepare departmental requests. Departmental budget officers fill out forms and arrange details.	Department head, central budget officials, any department budget officers.
April 1–May 15, 1985	Central office review requests, may adjust revenue estimates, compiles requests. Chief executive holds hearings with departments prior to final budget preparation.	Central budget office, chief executive, department heads.
	Enactment	
May 15–June 30, 1985	Council reviews budget, holds public hearings, may request further information, modifies budget, adopts it by beginning of fiscal year (July 1, 1985)	Council, chief executive, department head, central budget office.
	Execution	
July 1–June 30, 1986	Central budget office allocates approved budget by months to departments. Departments carry out approved programs. This stage involves supervision by the chief executive.	Departments, central budget office, chief executive.
	Audit	
After June 30, 1986	Three to six months after the end of the fiscal year, an outside auditor reviews the accounts for legality. The central budget office may make some management reviews of departmental operation for efficiency.	Auditor, department, central budget office.
	Preparation	
February, 1986	Process begins again for 1986–87 fiscal year.	

Their budget represents the best judgments of future needs and a wish list. The chief executive must bring both program and fiscal issues together at this point. It may be the best, or even the only, time that the top manager can focus clearly on the needs of the larger unit and the immediate and long-range constraints on those needs.

In theory, long-range planning should occur more frequently. It need not correspond with the budget cycle. In practice, budget preparation is the most frequent time. First, the need to propose yet another year's budget forces attention on long-term revenue and expenditure patterns. Availability (or lack thereof) of money often causes a longer look at programs than otherwise. Second, program previews associated with the budget suggest needed changes at a time when they can most easily be made. Since budgetary resources are scarce, the chief executive has to prune agency requests severely. Thus, program reviews may lead to a form of strategic planning associated with "cutback management." Finally, the planning nature of the budget process encourages top management to think about the future even though there may be no immediate financial crisis.

Legislative enactment may take an extended time or it may be completed in a rapid or perfunctory manner. Congress has approximately nine months to review the president's proposed budget before the next fiscal year begins. This is not always enough time. In recent years, disputes between the Reagan administration and Congress have sometimes resulted in continuing resolutions—with a formal budget never adopted. In small local governments, where the legislature has confidence in the chief executive or has no capacity or inclination to challenge her figures, adoption may occur after two or three perfunctory hearings.

Execution is primarily managing the spending programs that the legislature has authorized. Most of these are continuances of last year's activities, but some are modified significantly. Particularly when a new or expanded program is reapproved, prompt initiation at the beginning of the fiscal year is the mark of effective management. This ideal is frustrated by late adoption of the budget or by contingencies, usually fiscal uncertainties, which delay action. Top management usually controls spending tightly. Tight controls, usually dividing the year into 12 monthly allotments, force departments to project exactly when they will spend money so that the cash flow is precisely estimated. Tight controls also eliminate last-minute spending in June of the fiscal year, when departments try to prevent appropriated funds from lapsing.

Auditing occurs after the fiscal year ends. It is a financial and sometimes management assessment of how appropriated funds were spent. In small units, auditing usually involves the whole unit rather than departments and is normally done by a certified public accounting firm. It assures that funds were spent legally and that books are being maintained properly. Increasingly, management audits are being used. They review the wisdom of management decisions and the effectiveness of agency operation for past years.

Normally, these four activities occur simultaneously. A manager may manage one budget, prepare another, defend another before the legislature, and have a previous one audited. When the agency has a long review process and long lead time in preparation, such as the federal government, executives spend much time preparing, evaluating, and defending the budget. In these cases, managing a budget is done by subordinates and receives less attention from the chief executive.

BUDGET ROLES, STRATEGIES, AND CALCULATIONS

Excitement in the budget process generally occurs during legislative review.[3] The public and the media focus their attention on an agency or executive program pitted against a legislative committee or a single legislator. The stake is a larger or smaller budget allocation. It's not surprising that much of the budgetary literature deals with the enactment phase of the budget process. This phase is crucial to department heads who cannot spend money for their programs without legislative approval. No matter how supportive the chief executive is, the legislature sets a maximum figure. Conversely, the legislature may support departmental activity and appropriate more than the chief executive proposes. The possibility of this sometimes tempts agencies to stray from their sworn allegiance to the chief executive's proposals.

Because budgets are approved every year, because financial decisions are often based on the needs shown by the requests, and because budget enactments occur in public view, this part of the budget cycle is highly institutionalized in large agencies. This means that the various actors in the process have specific roles to play, the actors have specific strategies, and the strategies are based on calculations about what other actors will do. In making these calculations, for example, agencies will estimate what the chief executive will recommend to the legislature when they formulate their budgets. Asking for too much more than the chief will recommend makes the agency appear greedy. In addition to the general level of support, the agency also considers whether specific programs should be advanced in view of executive and legislative attitudes. Another serious matter is the respect and support for the agency in the eyes of the chief executive and the legislature. These views have a crucial effect on department-head strategies and calculations during budget formulation.

Roles, as outlined in Chapter 3, are sets of behaviors prescribed by the organizational position of an actor. A department, for example, is expected to ask for more money. If it does not, other actors may regard this as unusual and inconsistent behavior.

Consistency in role behavior makes it possible for others to calculate what a person or agency desires from a situation. Central budget officers cut budgets that they believe departmental offices have padded, maintaining the central budget office's role as a guardian of the purse. Agency budget officers assume that their central office counterparts will cut the budget and that the legislative body, with some exceptions, will mediate between them and the central budget office.

Departmental Roles

Departments generally propose budgets only incrementally different from the present. They often adopt the view that they have a base of agreed-upon functions that encompass their appropriation. They do not expect these functions to be examined closely. Critical examination, they assume, occurs when some expansion of the budget or change in their program is proposed. Departments try to increase this base by building in quality improvements, speeding service, serving more clients, or some other means. They must show that they deserve additional or continued funding, that money is spent well, and that their service is executed well. This endeavor takes considerable effort, as a higher education example shows:

> It is of vital importance that the state legislature and the taxpaying public . . . be convinced of the soundness of university operations. Under the pressure of competition from other state institutions, a large state university is often forced to put on a dramatic show of scientific objectivity in order to justify its requests for continued support. The dramatic presentations—elaborate formulas or statistical ratios—may have little to do with the way in which decisions are actually made within the academic establishment. As one administrative vice-president remarked about the preparation of the university budget, "We simply use the displays that give us the best image."[4]

Departments, bureaus, and agencies also aim for a fair share of the budget. This means that once a program is established, agencies expect that total budget increases will be distributed over time on a roughly equal basis to all claimants. To agencies, their programs are important, and important functions deserve periodic increases.

Thus, agencies vigorously defend their base against cuts, attempt to expand their base, and use a fair share of the budget as a guide. The process is neither cynical nor the outcome preordained. It simply shows how budget roles affect calculations. After making calculations based on these roles, departments modify their estimates by adding any proposed new programs judged worthy, by self-imposed restraints due to signals from executives or legislators, and by their sense of timing. Much is left for creative budget advocacy. For example, even after the Reagan administration imposed top-down spending limits on departments, with only five days notice, Secretary of Health and Human Services Richard Schweiker improved biomedical research funding for the 1982 fiscal year.[5] Agencies at all government levels occasionally use such devices as the famous Washington Monument ploy, popularized in 1971 by the National Park Service. The service suggested that it would close the Washington Monument to tourists, deliberately ranking less popular projects higher. Since Congress was sure to rescue the monument, the service hoped that these other projects would be spared also. The idea of offering popular sacrifices like the Washington Monument, knowing that they will not be accepted, occurs quite often.[6]

Budgeting is an applied art rather than a science. Attempts to expand their base are regarded as padding by outsiders but defended as attempts to improve services by the agency. The dean of budget officers, William Jump of the Department of Agriculture, once observed in front of a Congressional Budget Committee many years ago:

> There is what amounts to a natural law that is working all the time . . . that is more of a guarantee against overstaffing and similar offenses than anything that budget experts or anybody else might do, and that is that . . . our program leaders. . . . have got so many things that they see that ought to be done within the range of authorized activity in their respective fields. . . . People who have this kind of interest in their program simply do not use 25 employees where 20 would suffice. . . . To do so makes it impossible to utilize men and money for another part of the job they have been authorized to do.[7]

What happens is not padding, using excessive numbers of employees, but an attempt to accomplish more tasks that the agency already has the authority to do. At least, that's the agency view.

Agencies and their heads vary greatly in how they pursue these strategies. This was true of the federal government until the mid-70s and, even with the Reagan cuts, it is still true.[8] Other studies suggest that at municipal levels in large cities, departmental executives take their budget cues much more directly from the chief executive (in this case, the elected mayor) in forming estimates.[9] This may be more a function of limited revenues for any expansion than lack of concern for a departmental base. In many cases, budget officials, particularly low-level operatives, even dislike the term *game* when referring to their budgetary job; they feel it trivializes their duties. Most of the gaming occurs at higher management levels.

The shortage of money at all levels of government in the 1970s has modified the general assumption that the base will expand and a fair share obtained. Changes occur over time. The struggle for a fair share doesn't explain, for example, why higher education declined substantially and welfare expanded as a percentage of the state budget in California in the 1970s or why higher education recently made a major comeback. It does not explain why federal defense expenditures rose so rapidly in the late 1970s. In the former case, it could simply be that the Brown and Deukmejian administrations in California had different priorities. It is presumed, in the latter case, that the Reagan administration also had different priorities than the Carter administration, although the defense buildup began under Carter. In both cases, one should not rely heavily on academic arguments about fair shares and a base.

One uncertainty that department executives face in the formulation and enactment process is the degree to which constituent groups should be used to support their request. At the federal level, the conventional wisdom is that these groups frequently form, with the agency and the legislative committee, an Iron Triangle supporting certain programs, regardless of presidential wishes. The triangle was notably missing during the first few years of the Reagan administration, where programs were cut back deeply.

Relations between clients, agencies, and legislatures aren't this simple. The Iron Triangle is a federal creature and doesn't necessarily explain state and local budgetary behavior. Secondly, any attempt to manipulate a constituency is rather risky for the individual executive. Outside interests may not relate budgetary policy to the program they support, they may not support the program as fully as the executive would like, or they may not be influential in legislative chambers. Third, at state and local levels, the chief executive has more budgetary power than at the federal level. Many governors have line-item vetoes, and few local legislative bodies review the chief executive's budget as carefully as Congress reviews the president's budget. State and local chief executives may resent what they perceive as outside attempts to coerce them. They and legislative bodies are as able as the department executive to gauge the strength of interest groups. Finally, in recent years, there hasn't been enough income to fund programs, even if a politically popular interest group supports them.

The Central Budget Office

The central budget office is a crucial budgetary and management instrument of the chief executive. Many budget offices are large and influential. The federal Office of Management and Budget (OMB) is so important that its director has cabinet-level rank and must be confirmed by Congress. The 300-employee California Department of Finance acts as the governor's fiscal voice. The Los Angeles city and county administrative offices have for years introduced young budget analysts to their values and then sent them to departmental administrative slots socialized to accept central budget office control.

The federal OMB is a good example of the influence wielded by these agencies. Its power traditionally was related to its work in developing the president's budget, but it now extends to development of management in the agencies and to the clearance of all agency-proposed legislation.

Legislative clearance involves OMB approval for any agency-initiated legislation, so that all concerned parties can comment. Only when legislation is "part of the president's program" will the agency be allowed to testify as a favorable witness. This prevents end runs around the president.

Any agency with this much power elicits strong reactions. Wildavsky notes that the power of the Bureau of the Budget (the OMB predecessor) was often limited by how much an antagonistic Congress would listen to them when popular issues were at stake. In referring to legislative review of the popular National Institute of Health budget, one budget analyst noted:

> Usually what happened was that the President's budget got shot to hell with major increases. The staff (of the BOB) would consider the possibility of a veto. But you can't veto a health bill politically. It makes the President in favor of cancer. But you can't just crawl under a rock. What can you do?[10]

Hale Champion, undersecretary of HEW in the Carter administration, noted:

> My experience in the old days is that you had a lot of good experienced professionals, and there are still some over there, but basically OMB is not a strong part of the government and is probably the place where I've had the most frustration.[11]

Not all federal executives feel antagonistic. Some of President Eisenhower's executives lauded the BOB, saying "Its review enables us to do a better job before the appropriations committees,"[12] and "I think the Budget Bureau has done an excellent job. We have had almost no trouble in justifying what we need throughout the budget process. . . ."[13] These comments were made 30 years earlier about a much less partisan agency in a period with more resources. Even so, opinion about the OMB runs the gamut from resentment to praise.

At the state level, some agencies are more powerful than the OMB, usually in states where the governor has stronger constitutional power versus the legislature than the president has compared to Congress. In California, as in many states, the line-item veto allows the governor to eliminate or decrease specific items from the budget without vetoing the entire budget. These vetoes are rarely overridden in California. Since the governor depends heavily on the Department of Finance (DOF), its fiscal powers are substantial. Like the OMB, the DOF reviews all proposed legislation to determine if the governor should support it.

Often, the central budget office will ask departments to develop evaluation measures for future budget presentations to convince the legislative body of the value of additional resources, or to demonstrate how efficiently services are delivered. These measures fall into two categories. Efficiency measures show how well resources are used—for example, an increase in drug interdictions per Coast Guard mile of seashore patrolled. Effectiveness measures show how well the objectives of the program are met. One example is the number of minority children supported by a grant.

The use of these measures for developing program support is mixed. One article about a recent Georgia attempt noted two opposite views. An agency budget officer said:

> . . . Office of Planning and Budget requires the forms to be filled out, but no one really used them (performance measures) to evaluate budget needs. Also, no follow up is ever done to see if goals have been met.[14]

Conversely, an office of planning and budget official stated, "I have used evaluation measures on several occasions when they were the key factors in a budget decision."[15]

These views are typical of the different perspectives toward formal attempts to measure services. Central budget offices attempt to get departments to develop these measures to justify budget increases. Agencies, on the other hand, doubt that these measures, which involve much paperwork, have much effect on the legislature. They may not. In the same Georgia study, the legislative budget analyst said, "I do not read them. . . ."[16] Even so, as long as the central budget office requires measures of services, they will be developed, if only to justify actions taken on other grounds.

Locally, a budget office's influence depends on: (1) its own competence and reputation, (2) the capacity of the legislature for independent evaluation of budget proposals, and (3) the interest the mayor or chief executive officer takes in the budget process.

Even a well-staffed and competent budget office has correspondingly less influence if the legislature makes independent budget judgments, either because they have their own staff or because the unit is small enough for legislators to know it well.

The role of the mayor or chief executive officer is crucial. The budget officer almost always holds more power when the mayor is interested in using budgetary powers. If the mayor pays little attention to the budget, the budget office still may have great influence as the de facto spokesperson for budget matters. Even if the budget office has considerable independent power, budget officials prefer to have the chief executive involved in the budget, for their position is more secure.

Despite this need for top-level support, a budget office tries to keep some distance from the executive in certain ways. This slight but significant distance between the central budget office and the chief executive arises because the central budget office is an institution that outlasts a governor, mayor, or president. Therefore, the budget office has a longer view of events than the chief executive. Individual career budget examiners care about the budget office's reputation and don't want to tie it closely to an individual chief executive. Some examiners like being considered "honest brokers" between the department, the chief executive, and the legislature. Some examiners want to strengthen the budget office independently of the chief executive. They see the central budget office as the tool to strengthen fiscal management. The long-term interests of the central budget agency may not coincide with the chief executive's interests. Hale Champion, speaking from a departmental perspective, notes:

> (At OMB) they say that they represent the President's interests, but with the exception of trying to get budget control, I think they basically represent what they think about various program operations. If they confined themselves more to their budgetary and general management concerns, rather than in effect to make small decisions, either on legislation or on program operation of departments, they'd do less damage than they do now.[17]

These differences in opinion were seen in California in the years before Proposition 13. Governor Jerry Brown allegedly pressured the DOF to reduce revenue estimates so that the burgeoning state surplus would appear smaller and reduce pressures on the governor to increase services. Whether or not the DOF hedged its forecasts, the so-called "obscene" surplus continued to mount. The surplus was a factor in voter's decisions to limit local property taxes, since the money could be used (and was used) to bail out local units that lost property tax authority. This story is disputed, since some persons claim that DOF revenue estimates were as accurate as others at the time. It shows why central budget offices try to maintain a reputation for accuracy that extends beyond the term of any one chief executive.

Central budget officers have a different view than departments, and not just a top-executive viewpoint. Their members look at issues from a staff "fiscal management" viewpoint, and they are not interested primarily in department programs. In addition, budget analysts are increasingly educated in economics, political science, and business.[18] Cost benefit analysis, management by objectives, and program evaluation are the world in which they live. Trying to rationalize the budget process, they call for increasingly complex and elaborate justifications for budget requests. Such justifications take much time and technical skill, and departments often cannot comply. The result is that often the initiation and evaluation of new programs is done centrally, and there is a power shift to the central budget office. This shift takes many forms. In California, DOF central budget analysts approve individual departmental position reclassifications. Why such detailed control over operations? To control changes in organizational structure. In large agencies such as the Defense Department, there may be a corresponding drift of power from operating units to the departmental budget office for the same reasons.

Central budget offices act as a counterbalance to any departmental fair share or traditional base argument. Such a commitment restricts the chief executive's power to shape the budget. Central budget offices cherish the cutter role as a counterbalance to the agency trend (as seen by the central budget analyst) toward padding the budget. This role is one reason that budget techniques such as zero-base budgeting (ZBB) and planning-programming-budgeting systems (PPBS) are popular. ZBB or PPBS strengthen central budget agencies in two ways: first, by giving weight to their technical budgetary expertise, and second, by strengthening the threat to cut agencies. In Georgia, where ZBB was initiated, the central budget office commented:

> The minimum is less threatening than you might think . . . the departments know that we can't intend to recommend that their programs be funded at that level. But it makes them think about the possibility of a cut rather than always expecting more.[19]

The Chief Executive

The concept of a fair share or a base is abhorrent to most chief executives. Policy objectives that the chief hopes to implement in one term call for drastic funding changes (at least, this is what executives claim). Conversely, routine agency commitment to programs is the basis of agency continuity. This commitment conflicts with the chief executive's role for innovation and change. This is the chief difference between departmental or subunit and top-level management views.

The chief executive is much less constrained by pressures or constituency groups. She represents all groups and can more easily rise above them, play them off against each other, or simply ignore them. The need to run for a second term and appeal to the general public (or in the case of a city manager, to appeal to the public as represented by the city council) frees the chief executive from all but the most powerful pressure groups. It also binds her to a set of popular public values that support a specific agency. For example, the public support for law and order means that the chief executive must fund police protection in the local city budget regardless of his preferences.

The chief executive, by virture of hierarchical position, is in a good position to balance department requests and to judge what the jurisdiction's overall needs. This is not surprising, since higher-level positions generally have a broader perspective than lower levels. A broader view gives the top executive a chance to put together a balanced and comprehensive package. This is most true of top-level career officials, since elected chief executives are usually less knowledgeable about the organization unless they rely on careerists. Elected chief executives are more likely to initiate drastic budget innovations only when they regard them as publicly acceptable.

Because of their short terms, chief executives tend to take divergent approaches to budget formulation and enactment (again, appointed chief executives such as city managers are quite different from mayors or governors). Some choose to leave almost all issues to the budget director other than making a few policy decisions or setting some broad guidelines. Some executives allow the budget officer to make presentations to the legislative body and do all the work with department heads. Even second- or third-level political executives may leave most technical issues to careerists.

> An Assistant Secretary with previous executive experience will probably concentrate more on establishing program objectives and broad cost determinations and then rely on the Bureau Chiefs for detailed estimates. As long as the Bureau officers are able to support the Secretary's program decisions, the Assistant Secretary does not get substantially involved in the budgetary decision. But if something goes wrong, he will step in quickly.[20]

On the other hand, the chief may want to get involved in a major problem and its budgetary implications, as President Lyndon Johnson did by blessing the PPBS system of Robert McNamara and by his direct leadership in the legislative battles over Great Society programs. On the other hand, Ronald Reagan contented himself with broad budgetary guidelines, which he let budget director David Stockman flesh out with little guidance.

Legislatures

The legislative body has a different view than any of the actors mentioned so far. They review budgets suspiciously because of natural competition between the legislative and executive branches. Some of their interest in the budget is a search for partisan advantage if the executive branch is controlled by the other party. However, even these reactions assure that budget proposals receive a serious review. When legislative bodies care deeply about budgetary proposals or the budgetary implications of programs, the budget process can become a major public debate. In 1980, the House of Representatives heard that the OMB had withheld positions from the Immigration and Naturalization Service by imposing personnel ceilings that were followed at the cost of thousands of temporary workers. Representative Millicent Fenwick fulminated to her colleagues:

> I do not know what is going on in this Congress and in our Government. How is it the business of OMB to decide whether or not the laws we pass are sensible? Have we no right to impeach people? I thought impoundment was ended, that it was no longer legal. How is it that we have a department of the Government that simply defies Congress? What are we doing here? Have we not the right to pass laws and expect that they shall be obeyed?[21]

However, legislative bodies in smaller units or with great confidence in the executive (city manager cities, for example) may not devote much interest to the budget. Short, perfunctory hearings are common.

Some legislatures use the budget process for agency oversight. Here, program or agency shortcomings are addressed and legislative directives are given to administrators. In theory, only the executive is responsible for implementing the budget, but legislative opinions about agency management are rarely taken lightly.

One significant element of legislative budget review is the time and effort managers often devote to legislative testimony. This time varies greatly in accordance with the interest a legislative body has in the budget. Congress cares about programs and is divided into appropriations and substantive committees. This allows for substantial testimony from federal executives. They must effectively defend their budgetary requests. Agency head testimony varies considerably among the states; it depends on gubernatorial strength, relations between the legislature and the agencies, and so on. A similar situation exists at the local level, although the huge number of local units makes it difficult to suggest any patterns. Some city managers have department heads testify, while others make their own presentations. This partially depends on council preferences.

Usually, the department head makes the presentation, covering broad policy matters and outlining the budget. If the budget proposal is complex or technical, or if the agency is large, the director will be flanked by a budget officer and other aides. Program issues determine which aides are present. When the issue is technical or the department manager lacks confidence in herself, the budget officer may present the information. Even in these cases, it is more effective for the top manager to be present, since her absence raises questions about how much she knows or cares about the budget. It is most effective for the department head to appear, to summarize the issues and the budget proposal, and to turn detailed questions over to an aide or the budget officer. This is true even if the aide or officer is much more knowledgeable than the chief executive.[22]

For an important budget presentation, top managers rehearse their presentations carefully and go over legislative questions in advance. The reason for extensive preparation is that the manager's basic task is to gain the confidence of legislators.[23] Achieving this is no different from gaining the confidence of superiors in other administrative tasks. First, managers must appear knowledgeable. They should at least know the broad parameters of what is in their budget request and demonstrate a command of details. The ability to relate budget requests to program changes or to existing programs is a bonus. Unfamiliarity with the request is embarrassing because legislators may already know the answer. Stories are told of high-level struggles between career executives and their appointed heads in which the careerist has leaked to a sympathetic legislative staffer questions that will be used to highlight policy differences and embarrass the department head. Public managers can use the budget hearing format to strengthen their personal standing through effective performances, but it also works against the manager.

Confidence is gained in other subtle ways. Having a record of accomplishment over time is important. Other things being equal, senior bureaucrats have an advantage over their juniors. In addition to a record of accomplishment, it is important to play the role of advocate and bureaucrat—the role legislators expect. Police chiefs believe in law and order. State foresters believe in conservation and wilderness. State medical directors believe in better medical care. Public executives must assume the advocate role for program expansion, since any other role raises questions about the agency head's credibility. Credible witnesses have a much easier time before legislatures:

Congressman Rooney:
Mr. Andretta (Justice Department), this is strictly a crystal ball operation, is it not?

Andretta:
That is right.

Rooney:
Matter of an expert guess?

Andretta:
An expert guess . . .

Rooney:
We have come to depend upon your guesswork and it is better than some other guesswork I have seen.[24]

Being a bureaucrat is a complex role. First, the manager must be an advocate for the program. Secondly, the manager must master budget proposal details and the program it supports—in a way that noncareer officials can't. There are other helpful behaviors. Wildavsky notes that federal bureaucrats are concise, hard-working, frank, and self-effacing individuals. They are committee-member images of themselves.[25] These qualities may not help in every setting and they are not necessarily required of every public executive. But they convey an essential truth— the bureaucrat is dependable and can be trusted. Wildavsky also notes that effective presentations include some awareness of the need to safeguard public funds. The request should be described as extremely modest—considering the real need (Wildavsky does not explain how this works for a large request). Finally, gaining confidence includes revealing all facts about the request or "laying all the cards on the table." Candor is desirable since legislators frequently check answers and rarely forgive or forget being misled.

To sum up the ideal manager's budget presentation, she must be familiar with details, appear innovative, play the role of a "bureaucrat," be hard-working, and have a highly polished presentation that does not appear canned. This explains why the few presentations departmental officials make on the budget are so important in projecting competence and inspiring confidence.

MANAGING THE BUDGET

Budget management involves execution and audit, the last two points in the budget cycle. They usually get little attention except in technical financial control manuals. They involve technical and noncontroversial matters, at least in how they are treated. At the most mundane level, execution involves controlling expenditures through monthly accounting ledger sheets or computer spread sheets. It's usually done by the finance director, who relies on accounting subordinates except in the smallest unit, where the director keeps books. Little attention is paid to auditing, since audits are made by outside accountants who report to the legislative body.

Most actions in budget execution are undertaken by the central budget office and the finance director. These include allotments, or dividing the appropriation into portions, usually twelfths, for control of expenditures; creating or maintaining budget accounts to assure that line items approved by the legislature are not exceeded; and reviewing year-to-date expenditures and revenues to determine if modifications are necessary. The public manager may leave these technical issues to financial technicians, but they are not unimportant details.

Budget execution presents larger issues of importance to the top-level manager. These issues are evaluation of the service level, program evaluation, and maintaining services in the face of fiscal limits. They are the difficult tasks of budget management.

Service-level evaluation evaluates the particular level of service and considers alternative levels and their financial implications. Work performance data plus some budgetary techniques, particularly zero-based budgeting, are used in the formulation process to direct attention to the service level. How many park rangers per 1,000 visitors to a national park are needed? More importantly, can their services be modified to require fewer rangers (or can volunteers or civilians be used for some tasks)? How often should a state inspect plants for conformance to state occupational and health standards? Are two-person police cars always necessary at night in high-crime areas, or could civilians provide police support services? Judgments about service levels are made continuously while implementing the budget, and these judgments affect future budget proposals. Most managers make a careful distinction between current and improved service levels, such as increases in residential street sweeping from once to twice a month. Exhibit 7–2 shows the analysis of street sweeping cleanliness made by New York City. When the city fell short of its 1979 goals, it modified 1980 goals, but it did not change its expected levels of cleanliness.

Program evaluation is a careful analysis of the effectiveness of specific programs, such as street cleaning or early prison releases.[26] Much of the literature deals with elegant models or formal analysis over time with a control group. Thus, for example, expanded police patrols are compared to a similar period before patrols were beefed up. Results are examined and tested for statistical significance to determine if some change had occurred. With police, when small cities have poor or nonexistent records, formal comparison is impossible and the opinions of watch commanders or the chief are substituted for statistical information.

EXHIBIT 7–2   New York City Street Cleanliness Indicators; Average Percent of Districts by Scorecard Street Cleanliness

Ratings	FY 1978 Actual	FY 1979 Planned	FY 1979 Actual	FY 1980 Planned
High	14.1	20.0	7.6	10.0
Medium	49.0	50.0	42.0	60.0
Low	36.9	20.0	50.4	30.0

SOURCE: Mayor's Management Report: Supplement (New York: August 20, 1979), Exhibit E.

Maintaining services is a difficult issue, particularly under the tight constraints of today's budgets. The executive's responsibility for organizational maintenance is to assure that services are maintained. However, the vagaries of the budget process sometimes make this difficult. Budgets are often passed late, sometimes with final decisions delayed several months into the following fiscal year. This may not affect ongoing programs, but new projects or services are delayed. In addition, it is common to receive less appropriated money than in the previous year for the same projects. Sometimes budgetary or hiring freezes, necessary to save money, cripple programs. Since public-sector budgets have been under heavy fiscal pressure since the late 1970s, these freezes continue to plague program management. Legislative oversight, involving extended appearances before committees or extensive written justifications, can slow operations by distracting the attention of the chief executive. Another example of legislative budget restrictions are the limits on using certain funds such as travel. The smallest change requires a formal request. Usually, these difficulties are due to executive-legislative conflict, but sometimes the department's slipshod past performance has resulted in legislative restrictions.

Cutbacks due to funding shortfalls, delayed time schedules, and time and effort committed to legislative oversight all reduce the likelihood that budgeted programs and services will be completed during the year. Each complication is usually minor, but if several are compounded, they result in embarrassing delays.

Transforming the Audit

Audit budgetary expenditures begin after the budget year is complete and all final expenditures are made. Traditionally, the audit was a financial review of the books to assure that all expenditures were made legally; managerial issues weren't involved. The major issue was the chief executive's willingness to make minor changes in internal procedures as suggested by the auditors, such as cash handling and deposit procedures or other changes in internal procedures. Larger financial issues rarely arose.

Currently, a major top-management issue is to transform the audit from a narrow technical matter concerning only the finance director to a broader view of the effectiveness with which departments use public money. Spending public money legally is important, but spending public money effectively is crucial. It is also much more difficult. A management audit that reviews how efficiently and timely programs were performed, whether new programs achieved their objectives, and whether agencies followed the intent of the legislature and the executive is of more use than a report indicating that all expenditures were made legally (although the latter is important in assessing accountability). Over time, management audits demonstrate where major savings in program costs can be made or where money is wasted. These audits are common at the federal level. They are performed by the General Accounting Office, an arm of Congress, and they are performed at the request of individual members or committees. The audits are a kind of program evaluation from outside the agency.

FINANCIAL MANAGEMENT

Financial management deals with the mundane aspects of organizational maintenance. These aspects are a part of the management control process dealing with accounting, purchasing, insurance, and debt management. At one time, these were described disdainfully as nuts and bolts; less worthy of attention than the drama of budget allocation decisions.

Financial management historically has been less demanding for public than private managers because income is not produced by operating agency managers. The revenue department collected taxes while the department operated without reference to the collection level. Tax shortfalls and uncollected revenues weren't the responsibility of most public executives unless those managers were in special revenue units. While the chief executive was intensely interested if tax collections slowed, operating managers merely adjusted spending plans if taxes lagged and assumed that once an appropriation was granted, it was assured for the balance of the fiscal year. Internal cost controls weren't an issue as long as the finance director kept track of expenditures and the auditor checked for illegalities.

The importance of financial management is now clearly recognized. New York City's mid-1970 collapse was due to a political decision to roll over each year's short-term debt into long-term obligations. This financial management decision had little but political expedience to justify it. New York's collapse also involved failure to observe budget management techniques such as creating allotments and maintaining control of expenditure accounts. In 1984, San Jose, California officials squandered as much as $60 million of idle city funds on risky investments before the city manager was aware of it.

In the 1980s, a new emphasis on financial management has emerged. Cities, counties, and states have been beset by adverse conditions in recent years. The cost of borrowing increases as tax-exempt bonds require higher interest rates. Tax limitations have limited government budgets. Finally, governments suffered heavily during the recession of the early 1980s, and they have not brought physical facilities up to previous standards.

Most internal financial management functions are the responsibility of a finance director in a small city or spread among specialized departments in larger units. These functions include cash management, fund investment, debt management, purchasing and inventory controls, risk management (insurance and liability issues), and maintaining an effective accounting system.

The other side of financial management involves revenue. Many local revenues are remitted by the state and only need to be recorded by the city, county, or district bookkeeper. Other revenues, such as fees and charges, are collected by each department. Property taxes are collected locally by each taxing unit or county and distributed to each unit. Most states have specialized departments for individual and corporate income taxes and for sales taxes—often combined into one department of revenue. Revenue estimates are usually done by a finance office or a central budget office as part of the annual budget process.

In California, for example, the elected state treasurer sells bonds, invests idle funds, and is the state investment expert. The controller, also an elected official, prescribes and manages the accounting system and operates the state payroll office. The Department of Finance, the governor's budget office, estimates revenues for the budget and has overall financial management responsibility, which includes information systems, budgeting systems, and the linkages between them and the accounting system. The General Service Administration is the housekeeping agency for all state agencies. It has responsibilities for inventory control, purchasing, the printing plant, the central garage, and the acquisition and management of office space. The Board of Equalization collects sales, gasoline, cigarette, and alcohol taxes, while the Franchise Tax Board collects corporate and personal income taxes.

At the local level, these jobs are usually centralized under one person. The finance director may have accountants and purchasing agents working for her, while in small cities the work may be performed by clerks. An increasingly common feature is to appoint a risk manager, who generally also has the responsibility for evaluating agency insurance requirements and obtaining the best and most favorable insurance under the circumstances. This is becoming an important job, since lawsuits are now common and insurance costs are high, if available at all. Many larger units are self-insurers, but even here a risk manager is important—since insurance for some items and a cost benefit calculation of the point at which self-insurance becomes economical is necessary. The unavailability of insurance at any price has caused many localities to go "naked," praying that they avoid lawsuits.

An example of the recent interest in financial management is increased revenues raised by fees and user charges. In departments reliant on these charges, the operating manager is responsible for aggressively pursuing these charges. In some cases, budget allocations are granted on the specific understanding that fee income will increase. To the extent that departments rely on fees rather than appropriations, they can become more interested in selling the program. Their behavior resembles private managers. Where fees are discretionary, as in recreation programs, this is true. Where fees cannot be manipulated by the manager, as in building permits, it is not true.

The whole question of fees and user charges is a recent issue. Historically, heavy uses of fees were limited to a few unique operations such as municipal electrical or water utilities. Not anymore. Many officials devote great time to this issue. Chapter 9 covers retrenchment because the use of fees and charges has been a response to revenue losses rather than conscious effort to relate services to client willingness to pay.

The issues of financial management—ranging from internal matters of cost control and inventories to external issues of adequate revenue bases (including new fees and charges), is now a major concern for most public managers.

Techniques for Financial Management

There are four major techniques for financial control now used by municipalities across the nation.[27] They are program budgeting, zero-base budgeting (ZBB), improved management information systems, and performance-monitoring systems. The first two are part of the budget formulation process. Program budgeting is primarily a rigorous concern for the programs a city provides, comparing them to each other on some cost effectiveness basis to assure that the municipal bundle of services maximizes citizen satisfaction. Ideally, each program is subject to rigorous cost-benefit analyses, although this occurs infrequently in practice. Program budgeting focuses on services rather than organizational arrangements—for example, street sweeping versus sewage disposal. Exhibit 7–3 shows the proposed FY 1986 defense budget divided into broad program categories, while Exhibit 7–4 shows a program breakdown of employees and forces in the Defense Department.

Zero-base budgeting ranks all services and operations at alternative funding levels, usually the minimum level for providing a service (say, 75 percent of current budget levels) up to and above current levels. Zero-base budgets, which are tightly constructed options usually prepared by lower-level managers, display alternative funding levels before executives or legislators. They compare how a given dollar figure can provide varying levels of service across departments. ZBB is often used for cutback purposes. Both ZBB and program budgeting (as part of the PPBS system) were used at the federal level and are presently used in some

EXHIBIT 7–3   Administration's Defense Budget as Estimated by CBO, by Components (by fiscal year, in $ billions)

Component	1985	1986	1987	1988	1989	1990	Total 1986–1990
		Budget Authority					
Military personnel	$ 68.9	$ 73.4	$ 79.6	$ 85.5	$ 90.7	$ 95.4	$ 424.6
Operation and mainte-							
nance	78.2	82.5	95.1	108.9	117.7	127.1	531.2
Procurement	97.3	107.4	122.5	141.4	155.0	166.9	693.2
Research, development,							
test, and evaluation	31.5	39.3	42.6	49.3	55.9	66.0	253.1
Other	9.3	11.8	14.4	16.8	19.5	22.3	84.7
Subtotal, DoD	285.1	314.4	354.1	401.8	438.8	477.7	1,986.8
Other national defense	7.8	8.5	9.3	9.9	10.1	10.4	48.1
Total	$293.0	$322.9	$363.4	$411.7	$448.9	$448.1	$2,034.9
		Outlays					
Military personnel	$ 67.9	$ 72.6	$ 78.7	$ 84.5	$ 89.8	$ 94.5	$ 420.1
Operation and mainte-							
nance	73.1	80.0	89.4	102.4	112.4	121.7	505.9
Procurement	70.8	83.2	94.5	107.3	121.7	135.6	542.3
Research, development,							
test, and evaluation	27.3	33.2	38.8	43.8	50.1	58.1	224.0
Other	5.9	7.1	9.0	10.7	12.5	14.5	53.8
Subtotal, DoD	245.1	276.2	310.4	348.7	386.5	424.5	1,746.2
Other national defense	7.5	8.2	8.9	9.8	10.0	10.2	47.0
Total	$252.6	$284.4	$319.2	$358.5	$396.5	$434.7	$1,793.2

SOURCE: Congressional Budget Office, *An Analysis of the President's Budgetary Proposals for Fiscal Year 1986* Washington, D.C.: Congressional Budget Office (February 1985), p. 25.

states. Most usage, however, is at the local level, where it varies considerably. Exhibit 7–5 shows a hypothetical ZBB budget proposal for a city department. Here, the department head ranked the package of services (service level) for city planning most highly in the department. (1 of 5) means that there were five planning packages and that this package was the first, or the basic minimum level at which the department can operate (base). If cutbacks to the 90 percent level were desired, only the first five of 12 packages in the department would be funded. Exhibit 7–6 depicts the ZBB process.

Management information systems are computerized linkages that capture and disseminate information about finance, personnel, programs, and operations. This information increases early detection of potential difficulties in programs or finances when corrective action can be taken. Current information about estimated revenue, cash available for investment, budget expenditures, or inventories are examples of such a system.

EXHIBIT 7–4   Summary of Major U.S. Forces and Personnel for Fiscal Years 1980, 1985, and 1986

Forces	Actual 1980	Estimated 1985	Estimated 1986
Active forces (in units)			
Strategic bomber aircraft	376	298	315
Strategic defense squadrons	7	5	4
Land-based intercontinental ballistic missiles	1,052	1,023	1,009
Sea-based intercontinental ballistic missiles	576	640	688
Army and marine corps divisions	19	20	21
Naval battle forces	473	528	537
Tactical air squadrons	164	166	169
Airlift and tactical support aircraft	567	583	609
Active personnel (in thousands)			
Active duty end strength	2,050	2,152	2,178
Civilian end strength	990	1,088	1,107
Reserve and guard forces (in units)			
Strategic defense squadrons	10	11	11
Army and marine corps divisions	9	10	11
Naval battle forces	6	14	18
Tactical air squadrons	56	60	60
Airlift and tactical support aircraft	410	336	336
Reserve Personnel (in thousands)	851	1,077	1,124

SOURCE: Congressional Budget Office, *An Analysis of the President's Budgetary Proposals for Fiscal Year 1986* Washington, D.C.: Congressional Budget Office (February 1985), p. 29.

Performance monitoring systems involve early and continuous surveillance of program accomplishment by the use of effectiveness and efficiency indicators. For example, per mile garbage collection costs or traffic tickets per officer are monitored from early in the fiscal year.

The significance of these tools is that they are used more frequently than in the past. A 1983 study of cities over 25,000 persons (which overrepresented city manager cities and the use of these management techniques) indicated that program or zero-base budgeting systems were used by 77 percent of all cities, compared to 50 percent in 1976. Comparable figures for management information systems were 67 percent, up from 42 percent in 1976; and for performance monitoring, the figure was 68 percent, compared to 28 percent in 1976. These figures involve some reservations, since the issue is not whether a city reports using a system but whether the system works effectively.[28]

As an example of these techniques, the city of Dayton, Ohio specified that the deputy director of health would contract with Mt. Sinai hospital for investigative and curative services for sexually transmitted diseases. For $75,000, services would be provided to 4,500 clients during

EXHIBIT 7–5 City Z Department of Development and Planning

Decision Package Rank/Name	FY 1976 Cost ($000)	FY 1977 Cost ($000)	Cumulative Cost ($000)	Current Level
1. City planning (1 of 5)	$ 51	$51	$ 51	23%
2. Bldg. inspection (1 of 3)	97	97	148	66
3. Economic development commission (1 of 3)	13	13	161	71
4. Bldg. inspection— current level (CL) (2 of 3)	32	32	193	86
5. Economic development commission (CL) (2 of 3)	13	13	206	91
6. City planning (2 of 5)	3	3	209	92
7. Bldg. inspection— expanded service (3 of 3)		10	219	97
8. City planning (CL) (3 of 5)	16	16	235	104
9. Economic development commission—ex- panded publicity (3 of 3)		6	241	107
10. City planning—ex- panded master plan- ning (4 of 5)		10	251	111
11. Economic base study		22	273	121
12. City planning—bike paths (5 of 5)		12	285	127
Total FY 1976 Costs		$225		

SOURCE: John Rehfuss, "Zero-Base Budgeting: An Assessment to Date and a Future Prediction," *Public Personnel Management*, May–June 1977, p. 183.

the fiscal year.[29] The performance target is stated in the budget, and variations in cost of clients served is monitored. The next step is to budget the actual per unit cost of the service ($16.67), allowing perhaps 4,000 clients to be served for $66,667. The council could then choose between the number of clients or the amount spent in the coming year.

Cost accounting systems are too rudimentary in most jurisdictions to allow budgeting on unit costs, as the previous example suggests. The budget process does, however, provide a basis for many government managers to negotiate targets with their subordinates, putting these targets in a formal document. The results of these negotiations are then shown in the budget, establishing service levels of quantity or quality.

EXHIBIT 7–6   The ZBB Process

Step One

		Program A		

Managers prepare budget
  packages for each program

Package 3	(expanded)	15% (115%)
Package 2	(current level)	15 ⎤
Package 1		15 ⎬ (100%)
Base package		70 ⎦

Step Two

	Program A	*Program B*	*Program C*
Higher-level managers rank individual packages among several programs	Package 3	Package 3	Package 3
	Package 2	Package 2	Package 2*
	Package 1	Package 1*	Package 1*
	Base package*	Base package*	Base package*

Step Three

	Program A	*Program B*	*Program C*
Chief executive creates budget with packages from all programs by final rankings of Programs A,B,C, . . . X			Package 2*
		Package 1*	Package 1*
	Base package*	Base package*	Base package*

Note: In Step Three, the base level for almost all programs is normally included, but the number of packages above the base (up to current level of 100 percent, and including programs expanding the base) will depend on the revenue outlook for the budget year. Packages in their entirety should be deleted or added to assure that changes will "fit" already approved program packages.

* Indicates packages ranked high enough for inclusion in preliminary budget.

This is a major step toward greater management control. It is also an improvement in the position of subordinates, who have a better idea of what they will be judged upon.

Most governmental units don't have anything like performance standards. Even if they do, there usually is no monitoring mechanism. And, even if the targets are monitored, there is seldom a mechanism for rewarding managers who accomplish target goals. Nevertheless, the attempt to measure productivity and monitor performance through the accounting and budgeting system is a significant step forward in public management.

SUMMARY

The budget process, freed from its one-time captivity among accountants, is a dynamic exercise. Here, service levels (five or 10 new tanks?) and program choices (more state money for higher education or for toxic waste cleanups?) are selected.

There have been some sophisticated managerial uses of the budgetary and financial administrative process to make choices, set standards, improve the efficiency and effectiveness of public services, and strengthen top-level control over performance. Unfortunately, only a small number of agencies have used them to any extent. Most public agencies are not this sophisticated, and budget questions are handled in a more general manner.

Thus, despite the brave sounds of performance monitoring or accounting/budgetary account linkages, budget making is an art, not a science. This is particularly true in large jurisdictions. That's where the roles and strategies of the various budgetary actors come into play. This is where the operating manager must take pains to present the right image and the proper budgetary proposal. His or her ability to "play the budgetary game" becomes much more important. Relationships with the legislature, with the interests that surround the agency, and with the control agencies such as the finance department, mark the effective manager. Program accomplishment is still the bottom line, but skill in the budgetary process is still an important part of the job.

The manager's job of maintenance, representation, and planning is largely linked to the budget cycle. Organizational maintenance is most often coupled with the budget execution and audit stages—in other words, managing the adopted budget.

Organizational representation is linked with the exciting enactment process, with its hearings, debates, acting out of budget roles, advocacy, and budget posturing. Here, effective representation helps, at least in marginal cases. Representation is not, however, always eloquence and rhetoric as much as it is attention to budget detail and providing or anticipating information for the chief executive or legislative body.

Organizational planning is often done during budget formulation, when a long-term plan is worked out and phrased in budgetary terms. The day is gone when budgeting was a laundry list of wishes. Now, the budget process provides a natural opportunity for strategic planning; the financial implications of such a plan are immediately apparent.

The processes of maintenance, representation, and planning are not watertight compartments in the budget cycle. They are interwoven through the budget process, as with most other management processes such as decision making or personnel.

NOTES

1. For a true parody of the municipal budget process, see Joseph Freeman and Reggie Whitley, "Budget Policy: Good Servant, Bad Master," *Public Management*, April 1980, pp. 14ff.

2. Lawrence Lynn and John Seidl, "Bottom Line Management for Public Agencies," *Harvard Business Review,* January–February 1977, pp. 144–51.
3. Aaron Wildavsky, *The Politics of the Budgetary Process,* 3rd ed., (Boston: Little, Brown, 1979), chapters 2 and 3.
4. Francis Rourke and Glen Brooks, "The Managerial Revolution in Higher Education," *Administrative Science Quarterly,* September 1964, pp. 180–81.
5. Lance LeLoup, *Budgetary Politics,* 3rd ed., (Brunswick, Ohio: Kings Court: 1986), p. 75.
6. Ibid., p. 79.
7. Wildavsky, *The Politics of the Budgetary Process,* p. 24.
8. LeLoup, *Budgetary Politics,* p. 71.
9. Arnold Meltzner, *The Politics of City Revenue* (Berkeley, Calif.: University of California Press, 1971).
10. Wildavsky, *The Politics of the Budgetary Process,* p. 45.
11. Interview with Hale Champion, "The Rewards and Frustrations of the Federal Bureaucracy," *National Journal,* June 16, 1979, pp. 50–51.
12. Marver Bernstein, *The Job of the Federal Executive* (Washington, D.C.: Brookings Institution, 1958), p. 79.
13. Ibid., p. 59.
14. Thomas Lauth, "Performance Evaluation in the Georgia Budget Process," *Public Budgeting and Finance,* Spring 1985, p. 73.
15. Ibid., p. 73.
16. Ibid., p. 73.
17. Champion, "The Rewards and Frustrations of the Federal Bureaucracy," p. 51.
18. Robert Lee and Raymond Staffeldt, "Educational Characteristics of State Budget Officers," *Public Administration Review,* July–August 1976, pp. 424–29.
19. Thomas Lauth, "Zero-Base Budgeting in Georgia State Governing—Myth or Reality?" *Public Administration Review,* July–August 1976, pp. 413–24.
20. Bernstein, *The Job of the Federal Executive,* p. 20.
21. *Congressional Record,* 96th Congress, 2nd session, July 1, 1980, 126 House 5952.
22. Congressional enactment of the budget, and to a lesser degree, legislative review, is the best studied part of the budget process. This is the entire subject of Wildavsky's works, the standard in the field. There is some attention elsewhere to presidential power and executive conflict with the legislature through the budget, largely through the president's power to impound funds. See Wildavsky, *The Politics of the Budgetary Process;* Richard Fenno, *The Power of the Purse: Appropriations Politics in Congress* (Boston: Little, Brown, 1966); Wildavsky, "Political Implication of Budgetary Reform," *Public Administration Review,* Autumn 1961, pp. 183–90; Ira Sharkansky, *The Politics of Taxing and Spending* (Bloomington, Ind.: Indiana University Press, 1969); and Louis Fisher, "Impoundment of Funds; Uses and Abuses," *University of Buffalo Law Review,* Fall 1973, pp. 141–200.
23. Wildavsky, *The Politics of the Budgetary Process,* pp. 78–79
24. Ibid., p. 74.
25. Ibid., p. 74.

26. Harry Hatry, Richard Winnie, and Donald Fisk, *Practical Program Evaluation for State and Local Governments* (Washington, D.C.: Urban Institute Press, 1981).
27. Theodore Poister and Robert McGowan, "The Use of Management Tools in Municipal Government," *Public Administration Review*, May–June 1984, pp. 215–23. For a sophisticated explanation about how some management tools can be linked in a management/financial control system, see Frederick O. R. Hayes et al., *Linkages* (Washington, D.C.: Urban Institute Press, 1982).
28. Poister and McGowan, "The Use of Management Tools in Municipal Government," pp. 215–23.
29. Hayes, *Linkages*, p. 105.

CHAPTER 8

Managing Public Personnel Systems

Personnel management is a topic central to organizational management. Few other managerial skills are more important than dealing effectively with employees, and few failures are more expensive. The manager has two related tasks; to manage workers effectively, and to manage them within government employment rules. Unfortunately, these tasks sometimes work against each other—making the manager's job difficult. To treat both aspects of the manager's job, this chapter is divided into two parts. First is the process of managing in civil service systems and second is the nature of personnel issues.

This chapter's civil service system section includes the history and development of civil service systems, management in civil service systems, and some traditional personnel functions. The second section is about broad personnel issues that affect managers directly. The current problems of unionization, maintaining organizational flexibility, and equal employment opportunity consume substantial amounts of managerial time and effort. Wise managers, however, spend equal time and effort on developing issues such as the quality of worker's lives, changing employee lifestyles, the changing work force in today's organizations, and employee counseling and career development.

Personnel management falls into two of the three basic managerial functions; organizational maintenance and planning. Most personnel tasks, such as determining compensation, staff recruitment, or employee training and development, are organizational maintenance. But maintenance and long-range planning are intertwined through accomplishing these tasks. Implementation of any organization's long-range plan depends on an effective and motivated work force. This partially depends upon how managers ensure that the maintenance tasks of recruitment, training, and compensation are done.

To some extent, organizational representation is also involved, since the public must be convinced that the organization is doing well, including the performance of its workers. This public information task is, however, less involved than organization maintenance and strategic planning.

CIVIL SERVICE SYSTEMS AND MERIT SYSTEMS

Understanding public sector management begins with understanding the civil service system in which most managers work. The traditional public personnel system is a civil service system, a term often used interchangeably with merit system, although the two terms are not the same. Civil service systems have a Civil Service Commission to hear appeals of actions that allegedly impair merit or the employment of the best employees without regard to any other criteria such as political beliefs. Merit systems, mostly found in smaller cities, rely on good management and good political intentions to accomplish the goals of the merit system.

Both systems are merit systems, but civil service systems rely on an independent commission to enforce rules assuring merit. Merit is a slippery term. Such matters as unvalidated examinations, where the best candidates are not selected; and poor management, where training, career development, and proper compensation are neglected or mishandled occur in both systems and damage merit.

A major criticism of civil service systems is that Civil Service Commission rules are so cumbersome and time-consuming that it is impossible to manage the organization. Civil service systems are marked by rules designed to prevent abuse of the merit system. These rules, adopted by the commission or the legislative body, include such matters as the requirement that appointments be made only from the three candidates who score highest on the civil service examination or that every position in the organization be assigned in a designated classification. While all organizations have operating personnel rules, in civil service organizations, only the commission or sometimes the legislature may change them, and they can be quite inflexible.

Managers complain loudly about their lack of ability to discipline, transfer, and reward employees. One business executive commented after a tour in the federal government:

> Civil service today is designed to insulate federal personnel practices from the claims of merit. You learn very rapidly in government that if you want to get, or hold onto, good people and avoid being stuck with the lemons, you must learn how to thwart the Civil Service Commission and its regulations.[1]

The corresponding charge against merit systems is that personnel actions, without a Civil Service Commission to guard against merit violations, will abuse employees and yield to political pressures. This happens even with the Civil Service Commission. Even so, most managers would rather not have a commission since they feel it ties their hands when dealing with personnel and prevents them from managing effectively. This is true even when the system is managed by a personnel director and the commission hears only appeals about the merit system. The existence of a commission usually means that a set of restrictive rules exist that bind manager and employee, and almost any action can be appealed to the commission. In cases such as the commission successfully eliminating a candidate from an employment list on some technicality (causing the best candidates on the list to be lost), commissions seem more associated with concern for technique than performance.

Development of Civil Service Systems

The outlines of the present system, at least at the federal level, were set in 1883 when the Pendleton Act established the first bipartisan Civil Service Commission and a system of competitive examinations. While the first commission responded to growing distaste for the patronage system, civil service roots go back to the founding days of the United States.

For the first 40 years of the republic, government positions were filled by a sophisticated patronage system based on merit. Members of the social elite were selected by each administration for the limited number of positions, with heavy emphasis on social standing, loyalty, and education; this passed for merit in those days.

President Andrew Jackson, triumphing over the establishment, ushered in the spoils system. It was based on the phrase "to the victor belongs the spoils" and meant that all positions changed, including clerks and janitors, when the opposing party won. Jackson felt that anyone was competent to perform public service. All presidents after Jackson used the spoils system. Abraham Lincoln used it to build support for his Civil War policies.

However, public opposition to the spoils system was growing. After a disappointed office-seeker assassinated President Garfield in 1881, a civil service reform act was passed two years later. The next quarter century saw great change in personnel practices in the federal government and in many large states. Civil service systems, fueled by moral indignation over the practice of spoils, tried to end corruption forever. To do this, it insulated the personnel function from the legislature and executive branches, creating problems of executive responsibility and leadership which continue today. Often, it was hard to appoint anyone but the best test taker, even when skills other than written proficiency were desired. This period, exalting the common man (if he did well on tests), had little interest in educational achievements or in the development of a top-level administrative class such as in Great Britain. During this period, from the 1900s to the Great Depression, the civil service reformers' view of merit was dominant. It was achieved in several ways: by insulating administration from politics through civil service commissions, and by extraordinary efforts to perfect entrance examinations, create precise job descriptions, and develop comprehensive classification plans.

The first hints of a new emphasis on executive leadership instead of the prevailing belief in neutral competence occurred in 1937. The Brownlow Report, demanding stronger presidential leadership, also called for the use of broadly trained, generalist managers.[2] The Brownlow Report proposed, for example, that the Bureau of the Budget be brought from the Treasury Department to the White House office, subtly suggesting that budget analysis was not always well done in an atmosphere dominated by an accounting mentality. In 1955, the second Hoover Commission recommended a Senior Civil Service of generalist managers for assignment to top-level positions as needed.[3] The creation of the Senior Executive Service (SES) in 1978 was in response to the Hoover Commission recommendation, although it took nearly 25 years.

By this time, the number of federal employees had grown considerably because of new social programs created in the Depression and during the mobilization of World War II. The civil service grew by a series of "blanketing in" incumbents. Originally patronage appointees, these incumbents became civil servants and their successors were appointed through competitive examinations. When President Franklin Roosevelt blanketed large numbers of employees in the 1930s and early 1940s, civil service appointees reached 90 percent of all employees at the federal level, a figure now approached in most large states.

The number of public employees at all government levels has grown dramatically from a handful of federal and state clerks in 1776 to the millions of public employees 200 years later who provide a range of duties. The number still grows, although not evenly at all levels. Table 8–1 indicates that growth is fastest at the state level, although certain local units such as special districts and counties are also growing rapidly. Table 8–2 indicates the number of employees in specific occupations. Forty percent of all employees are teachers or hold teaching-related positions.

MANAGING IN A CIVIL SERVICE SYSTEM

There are several consequences of managing in a civil service system. Some are due to the civil service system, some are the consequence of government's role in society.

The Professional State

There are many professionals in government. These professional employees include accountants, social workers, engineers, doctors,

TABLE 8–1 Change in Government Employment by Level, 1975–1985

	1975 (000)	1985 (000)	Percentage Increase
Federal (civilian)	2,890	3,021	5%
State	3,271	3,984	22
Local (total)	8,813	9,685	10
County	1,563	1,891	21
Municipal	2,506	2,467	(2)
School districts	3,969	4,416	11
Special districts	383	519	35
Townships	392	392	0
Total	14,973	16,690	11

SOURCE: U.S. Department of Commerce, *Statistical Abstract of the United States, 1987*, (Washington, D.C.: Government Printing Office), p. 280.

nurses, psychiatrists, and teachers. They exceed the number of positions in the private sector. The mark of a professional is commitment to professional norms. This rarely contradicts good management, but it creates in employees a tendency to look to the profession for guidance. A doctor or pharmacist will never change a diagnosis or prescription to suit her supervisor—and she will protest loudly about infringements on professional prerogatives. After all, these have been internalized since medical school (or engineering school or accounting classes). Managers may have broader considerations. However, their lack of specialized

TABLE 8–2 Selected Government Employment by Function, 1982 (000)

National defense and international relations (civilian)	1,101
Education	7,119
Health and hospitals	1,653
Police	760
Postal service	754
Highways	552
Natural resources	443
Financial administration	438
Public welfare	430
Fire protection	317
Sanitation and sewage	221
All other	2,902
Total	16,690

SOURCE: U.S. Department of Commerce, *Statistical Abstract of the United States, 1987* (Washington, D.C.: Government Printing Office), p. 280.

knowledge makes them vulnerable to charges of meddling in areas they know little about.

There is one advantage to outside norms. Professionals, adhering to norms, require less detailed supervision because these norms assure satisfactory performance. To a substantial degree, however, the manager must accept the engineer or forester's definition of performance. Managers, unless they come from that profession, cannot judge performance directly. Contributing to this problem is the movement toward quasiprofessions of police and fire fighters, city planners and personnel directors. These groups insist on autonomy in determining work standards and already have considerable discretion in their work.

In organizations with a dominant professional group, managers are usually promoted from professional ranks. This solves the problem of subject matter knowledge, if the supply of professionals contains persons with management skills.

Professionals present an extreme example of the establishment of work standards by outside groups, but this phenomenon is not limited to them.[4] Many civil servants work in services that touch outside individuals and groups directly. These groups can be extremely vocal, often feel a proprietary right to the services they receive, and have much influence with legislative bodies. Managers have learned to be cautious. At one extreme, the secretary of labor has to be acceptable to some elements of organized labor, which limits the president's choice (or the governor's or mayor's choice for similar positions). At the other extreme, a subordinate city planner may not be promotable to the top city planner's job because she is unacceptable to business or homeowner interests because of her attitudes toward restrictive zoning. Outside groups veto inside selections, shield insiders, and demand certain levels of service regardless of management wishes.

Punishments and Rewards

Difficulties in enforcing standards are not due to civil service systems, but the phenomenon is associated with public agencies and with civil service systems. A management difficulty directly due to civil service systems is the reduced ability of public managers to punish and reward subordinates, as compared to the private sector. However, for two reasons, the difference between public and private is often overemphasized. First, private managers have less power over subordinates than conventional wisdom assumes, and certainly less than 20 years ago. Secondly, public managers have more power than most choose to exercise. For example, more unsatisfactory employees could be discharged during their probationary periods when there are no restrictions on such removals (other than for discrimination against protected classes).

Once probationary employees become permanent, taking disciplinary actions for failure to perform becomes difficult. The primary reason for this difficulty is the civil service employee's right to appeal adverse actions all the way up to a formal Civil Service Commission hearing. The purpose is to prevent arbitrary or capricious actions, but the system also prevents some legitimate actions because managers or supervisors conclude that the paperwork necessary to document their case is not worth the trouble. Thus, nonproductive employees are frequently ignored or bypassed rather than dealt with directly.

Often, disciplinary action is not taken because good management is not rewarded in public agencies (neither is the work of good subordinates). There is less reason for managers to "bite the bullet" in disciplinary matters. Additionally, public-sector managers often lack the ability to reward good employee performance. Senator Abraham Ribicoff of Connecticut, supporting the Carter administration Civil Service Reform Act, said:

> The system's [Civil Service] rigid procedures, providing almost automatic pay increases for all employees, make it as difficult to reward the outstanding civil servant as it is to remove an incompetent employee.[5]

On the other hand, Pierce interviewed many managers about civil service impediments to good management:

> We found in over 600 interviews that in many cases the blame for the inability to make any progress programmatically was placed by management on the civil service system, when in fact the management did not know where it wanted to go, what it wanted to do, and as a result, what kind of people it wanted. So it tended to make the system a scapegoat.[6]

Inability to reward and discipline employees is one shortcoming of civil service systems, at least from the manager's point of view. Case Study 8–1 shows how this can work. But discipline and reward systems are only one way that civil service systems affect management, although they are the most obvious. The lack of a clear assessment of success in the organization is another (the "lack of profit as a bottom line"), as is the existence of multiple goals. And, the existence of many professionals in the organization adds complexity to the management of public agencies. These complexities are not all due to civil service systems, but they are all associated with government agencies and civil service.

Case Study 8–1

DISMISSAL FOR CAUSE ISN'T ALWAYS EASY

Hunter v. Ann Arbor

In 1966 Robert Hunter became a complaint investigator for the Department of Human Rights of the City of Ann Arbor, Michigan. He advanced to the position of assistant director of the agency. In May 1970 he was appointed acting director of the department. He re-mained in this post until November when a permanent director was appointed. Hunter then resumed his position as assistant director. In January 1971 a dispute arose between Hunter and the new director. The latter was displeased with Hunter's performance and on January 18 sent the following letter to him.

January 18, 1971

To: Robert H. Hunter, Assistant Director
           Human Rights Department

From: James C. Slaughter, Director [*signature*]
           Human Rights Department

Re: Attendance and Conformity to the Responsibilities of your
           Position as assistant Director

1. On Monday, January 4, 1971, you did not report for duty at 8:00 A.M.
   I was informed by the Principal Clerk Stenographer that you were
   taking the morning off and would be in in the afternoon.

   On the above date, you arrived at approximately 12:15 P.M.
   dressed in slacks, sports shirt, and jacket, but left almost immediately
   and did not return to the office that day or to my knowledge perform
   any duties connected with your position.

2. On January 5, 1971, you did not report for duty at 8:00 A.M. I was
   informed by the Principal Clerk Stenographer that you would be in in
   the afternoon. You came in at approximately 12:10 P.M. and left
   shortly thereafter. When I returned from lunch at approximately 2:00
   P.M., I was informed that you had taken the rest of the day off on sick
   leave.

   You have continued on sick leave since.

3. On Wednesday, January 13, 1971, I was informed you were seen driving your car during duty hours.

4. On Thursday, January 14, 1971, I observed you at Division and Huron Streets at approximately 12:00 noon driving your car.

5. I was informed that you were observed in the Golden Falcon during the week of January 11, 1971.

6. On Wednesday, January 13, 1971, you attended the School Board meeting at 7:30 P.M. According to an article in the *Ann Arbor News*, you participated in the meeting in a manner that is not the present policy of this Department.

7. On January 15, 1971, when at my request you came in to discuss the concerns I had about your absences, I informed you of my concerns and questioned you about your activities, especially as they related to enrollment at the University of Michigan Undergraduate School. You may remember that you had requested permission to work part-time in order to go to school full-time and I refused that request. I informed you at our meeting on January 15, 1971, that I had reason to believe that you had enrolled full-time at the University of Michigan. You stated to me that you had enrolled but not full-time.

   I also questioned you about your illness. The only explanation I received was that you are sick and are seeing a doctor. I informed you that I accepted your explanation but, that if you were not being truthful, I was going to request your resignation. You informed me at that point that I could request your resignation if I choose but that I had better be ready to fire you. I informed you that if I requested your resignation I would be able to dismiss you; permitting you to resign would be for your benefit. At this point you began to shout at me, accusing me of attempting to intimidate you. I consider your action of continuing to shout at me, even after my warning that I considered it insubordinate, an attempt to intimidate me and a serious act of insubordination.

Due to all of the above, I have come to the following conclusions:

1. Your activities in the past two weeks have not been those that are normally acceptable for an employee on sick leave.

2. Your enrollment at the University of Michigan would seem to make it difficult—if not impossible—to fulfill your full-time duties as Assistant Director.

3. Your enrollment at the University of Michigan, knowing my full view on such an eventuality, raises question as to your commitment to the present HRD.

4. You are insubordinate and such conduct is not acceptable in the HRD and will not be accepted from a staff person.

After receiving the letter, Hunter retained counsel and together they met with the director and city attorney. Subsequently, a meeting was also held with the city administrator. However, the dispute was not settled in this manner, and Hunter was terminated without a formal hearing. Hunter took his case to federal court and filed an application for a preliminary injunction barring his summary dismissal. In this action he alleged that he had been fired because of his race, in violation of the Constitution.

Although the court made no findings with regard to this claim, it did hold that the due process clause of the Fourteenth Amendment required that Hunter be afforded a hearing before an official not involved as an adversary against him.

The city argued that the power of summary dismissal was required to maintain a relationship of trust between its department heads and their immediate subordinates, as well as to maintain high levels of morale and efficiency at all levels of employment. The court, however, reasoned as follows:

Against this interest, admittedly an important one, must be weighed the interest of Hunter that is being affected by the City's action. Hunter, like any employee, has a purely economic interest in being employed. But although the immediate economic effects of his discharge are substantial, it is clear that his interest involves more than a narrow interest in a particular job. Hunter also has an interest in his future employability. This is an interest which every employee has and which can be adversely affected by any terminatiion. It is, however, particularly susceptible to damage in the case of a person who is seeking employment in high levels of city government, where employability is highly dependent upon professional reputation and past employment performance and where employers can properly demand the fullest disclosure of an applicant's personal and employment history.

When the effects of government action on the individual's interest are so wide ranging and basic, it is a constitutional requirement that the government's action not be based on certain types of motives and that it have some rational basis.

Based upon this reasoning, the court ordered that Hunter be reinstated, retroactive to the date of his termination, at full pay and that pending further dismissal proceedings, the city need not require him to engage in active duty. Although the decision did not preclude a legitimate dismissal, it did make evident the difficulty and potential expense of taking ad-

verse action against public employees, even when the need to do
so seems abundantly clear.

Mr. Hunter was eventually dis-
missed.

SOURCE: Jay Shafritz et al., *Personnel Management in Government* (New York: Marcel Dekker, 1978), pp. 165–67.

THE ORGANIZATIONAL COMPLEXITY OF PUBLIC PERSONNEL SYSTEMS

Describing public agencies as having a civil service or merit system doesn't say much. There is great variation between government units and between agencies in the same jurisdiction.

Existence of a formal Civil Service Commission proves little, for commission powers vary greatly. Some commissions hear only appeals, while others operate the entire personnel system. Most can initiate their own investigations even if they have no administrative power.

In addition to differences already mentioned, civil service systems are changing in many ways. At all levels of government, agencies are operating with fewer employees due to tax limitations and the economic slowdowns of the early 1980s. Large numbers of public employees are unionized. Many functions of government are contracted out, with the result that private employees are performing public functions. Layoffs of employees, once unheard of, are now common. All of these factors have an impact on civil service, but perhaps most profound are the reduced levels of employment. Where layoffs have not occurred, hiring freezes are common and lower employee levels are achieved through attrition. These cutbacks, required because of reduced revenues, have reduced employee ranks. They have shaken the assumption that there is job security in the public sector. True, layoffs have been conducted under civil service arrangements that usually call for seniority and other protections such as bumping rights; senior employees can insist on rights to lower-level positions if they are laid off, ultimately pushing out the newest employee. Even with these protections, however, jobs are scarcer and less secure once they are obtained.

Unionization is also changing traditional civil service patterns. All types of traditional civil service issues, such as salaries, classifications, fringe benefits, promotion policies, and layoffs are now negotiable. Unionization exists uneasily with civil service systems. Commissions have less influence as many issues are handled during collective bargaining sessions. Many employees look to their union rather than to the commission for protection.

As a counterbalance to unionization, there is increasing pressure to strengthen management. Much of this is due to demand for increased productivity, since it is often assumed that productivity requires more management discretion; although there isn't much evidence to support this supposition. Thus, the demand grows to weaken civil service limitations on disciplinary matters. A related trend toward merit pay, usually at the discretion of supervisors, is also present. Both of these trends strengthen managerial powers.

Managerial muscles are being flexed. Dismissals of federal workers for all reasons increased 15-fold from 1978 to 1985 after passage of the Civil Service Reform Act.[7] This increase was due to a combination of reasons such as management expectation of greater top-level support for disciplinary actions and the need to reduce staffing levels due to budget cutbacks. This occurred with no additional powers granted to managers. It suggests that managers are fooling themselves if they claim that civil service rules prevent stronger action.

Top Management Personnel Controls

Personnel controls are usually managed by the personnel or personnel management department. At the federal level, it is the Office of Personnel Management. For the State of California, it is the Department of Personnel Administration. These controls usually include classification, appointment, recruitment, promotion, pay, training, and discipline. Often these controls have been delegated to departments, and in these cases, the central agency sets standards and monitors performance. Some functions, such as pay, are still provided centrally because of the need for uniformity, as in a comprehensive pay schedule.

These personnel controls over the department manager are significant, but they are not necessarily top-management controls. Whereas the budget office usually operates under direct orders from the chief executive or a budget aide, the personnel functions do not always reflect top-level views. In many cases, the chief executive has no strong views.

At the federal level, the Carter administration Civil Service Reform Act of 1978 divided the old Civil Service Commission into two parts: an Office of Personnel Administration (OPM) and the Merit Service Protection Board. The Merit Service Protection Board is headed by three members appointed on a bipartisan basis for seven-year nonrenewable terms. It hears employee appeals and can order corrective and disciplinary actions against employees or agencies. This type of reform is spreading to state and local government units.

The OPM acts as an arm of the president, complementing the Office of Management and Budget (OMB) fiscal control with personnel control. The OPM has decentralized most functions such as classification and recruiting, maintaining only oversight responsibilities. The OPM is less of a force than the OMB because budget powers are more effective than personnel controls. In addition, personnel actions such as hiring freezes and personnel ceilings are managed by the OMB, not the OPM. The early Reagan administration hiring freeze required approval through the OMB.

The influence of personnel controls over operating departments varies at the local level. In small cities or counties, the personnel function may not be decentralized. In small agencies, the personnel function represents the chief executive's views unless civil service provisions have placed independent agencies in control. An exception to this are the police and fire boards of small Illinois municipalities, which control personnel policy for uniformed services. In Los Angeles, the mayor appoints commissioners for each department who review departmental operations and control top-level personnel appointments, including the department head. In California, the State Personnel Board, until recently, had major personnel powers, although the Finance Department controlled budgetary implications of personnel policy. These personnel powers were significant, as a high-ranking department official noted:

> I was brought to the department because they had a huge crisis on their hands. I had good experience in personnel management and I knew the system and how to get things done. My predecessor was a very good person but did not know the system, and the department was in the process of expanding dramatically in the mid-sixties. They needed someone who knew something about recruitment and how to get things done through the State Personnel Board.[8]

The role of the State Personnel Board is declining due to collective bargaining. Functions such as training, employee counseling, and classification are performed by the Department of Personnel Administration because that department conducts collective bargaining negotiations for the governor. However, if those functions have significant fiscal impacts, the Department of Finance would have considerable influence.

This California experience involves the decline of the State Personnel Board (a Civil Service Commission) in favor of a Personnel Department and control of personnel policy by the Finance Department when money is involved. These are typical of what is happening across the nation.

TRADITIONAL PERSONNEL MANAGEMENT FUNCTIONS

Traditional personnel functions are technical and the responsibility of a personnel manager. Line managers don't become familiar with these techniques any more than a Director of Public Works becomes familiar with accounting department ledgers. However, the effectiveness of the personnel department affects every line manager directly because of its direct relationship to personnel management in each department. Since up to 80 percent of all agency costs involve labor costs, public managers should have a healthy interest in personnel matters even if they never venture into the personnel department.

Recruitment and Selection

The initial personnel activities in the employment cycle are recruitment and selection. Examinations, historically the essence of civil service, are part of the selection process.

The initial personnel activity is recruitment. It is simple for low- and entry-level jobs such as typists, clerks, police, park rangers, and janitors. Potential employees seek these jobs and little recruitment is necessary. Key professional positions for accountants, engineers, or physicians are more difficult to fill. Special classifications or salaries above entry level are often required to attract candidates. Management positions are usually filled by promotion from a lower level or occasionally from outside the agency. Attracting managers with private experience has proven difficult. Persons who would normally be interested in higher-level positions have not usually been interested in public employment, mostly due to lower salaries. When it is necessary to recruit high-level managers or even key professional employees, government increasingly relies on management recruiters or "headhunters," which parallels the private sector practice.

Selection is the process of choosing employees from the pool of applicants recruited for a job. It is difficult to generalize about this process, which varies among agencies. Typically, selection involves a review of the applicant's work record or resume, a written test, an oral examination, and a background check. Then, a list of successful candidates is prepared and certified for the person who will make the appointment. Usually the list is prepared in order of scores. The traditional list called for appointment from the top three scores (the rule of three) no matter how small the spread of scores. Variations are increasingly used, such as the certification of all who pass the test or the top three ranks rather than scores. Appointing from the top three ranks, such as 84, 85, and 86, means that persons receiving 85 percent, (for example 84.51, 84.7, 84.8, and 85.4) have the rank of 85; the same applies to ranks 86 and 87. This gives the appointing authority the choice of many more candidates without debasing the quality of candidates—since there is little difference between a score of 84.51 and 87.49. Sometimes, additional points will be added either for seniority within the agency or for veteran's preference. The five or 10 points for veteran's preference has been a boon to applicants who are veterans ever since World War II. It is extremely distasteful to civil service reformers who insist that it discriminates against nonveterans and should be limited to one-time bonuses. Finally, local jurisdictions often require successful candidates to reside in the city or in a specific area.

Historically, merit systems have emphasized selection because it is the point where nonmerit or patronage decisions creep in. This accounts for the emphasis on written examinations designed originally to eliminate discretion by the appointing authority and to measure merit. Merit, which was presumed historically to reveal itself through pencil and paper tests, now includes items other than written scores. Performance records, oral interviews, assessment center ratings for management positions, certificates of educational accomplishment, and other modifications of the written test are now used.

Many of these changes have been caused by the need to validate tests. Validation demands that tests predict actual performance on the job. Certain minority group members doing poorly on written tests, have challenged them as biased since they do not predict job performance. One example of this is the demise of the federal Professional and Administrative Career Examination (PACE). This test allowed college graduates without specialties such as accounting or forestry to enter federal service. The test was abandoned in 1982 because minority candidates failed the test disproportionately with no evidence that test scores actually predicted job success.[9]

Top managers, if their agency does its own recruitment, must examine the candidates in terms of qualifications and geographic and demographic makeup. Particularly important is some assessment of how newly recruited employees match the mix of skills the organization will need in future years. Another important issue is the length of time between recruitment and selection, since excessive delays cause superior candidates to withdraw, and lower the image of the agency in the eyes of job seekers.

Position Classification and Compensation

Position classification is important to personnel management as it is necessary to compress thousands of individual jobs into a few groupings for pay purposes. Thus, for example, a police officer may be rated the same as a senior building inspector because the different kinds of required experience, education, and ability are valued equally. In the federal government, all jobs are combined into 18 grade levels from beginning clerk to top management. Most other governmental units have a similar system. In addition to the job's scope, classification is important because assigning people to the wrong classifications can ruin organization morale.

The advent of collective bargaining has changed classification considerably. All groups cannot be kept closely aligned to others when salary agreements may distort the classification plan. Classification plans are also distorted when it is necessary to hire key individuals at market rates above their classification. From a management view, rigid classification systems limit the ability to reassign, promote, and attract people. From a personnel point of view, if plans become more flexible, problems of equity, consistency, and employee morale multiply. The best advice to the agency manager is to hire a competent, experienced, management-oriented personnel director and turn the job over.

Compensation plans involve a number of factors. Public employees deserve wages comparable to their private counterparts, but this comment hides complex issues. Historically, public employee salaries lagged behind industry, but this is no longer true in most large public organizations, particularly for lower-paid positions. Indeed, critics allege that because of extensive fringe benefits, particularly retirement benefits, lower-level public employees are overpaid. Conversely, pay for senior managers in most jurisdictions still lags behind the private sector.

The promotion-career-training subsystem is an important part of the personnel function. Promotion policies involve the conditions under which employees will move up in the organization. Career development is a process through which employers develop or identify long-term opportunities inside and outside the organization. Finally, training is the organizational attempt to prepare individuals for promotion and for careers inside the organization. If employees perceive that the best-qualified individuals are advanced, that training is related to specific organizational or job requirements, and that true careers exist in the agency, morale and performance will be high.

Another question is how employee performance ratings can be used effectively. Most public and private organizations don't have effective performance evaluation systems. In the private sector, they are important. They are likely to become more important in the public sector because of the movement toward merit pay, which will be formally based on a rating system. In most public agencies, the employees are ranked satisfactory even when raters do not consider their performance satisfactory. The system does not distinguish between effective and noneffective performers. This becomes a problem when employees must be selected for promotion, for assignment to training activities, or for salary increases. Performance evaluation is a difficult and, to most managers, disagreeable job. That's why it is so often avoided or done in a slipshod manner. This is unfortunate, because more effort directed by public managers to performance evaluation would improve a number of other personnel matters ranging for promotion to career planning.

Public personnel systems are often underfunded compared to private counterparts. In 1977, the personnel-to-staff ratio in government agencies was 1:272, or one personnel employee for every 272 employees. This exceeded the ratio in all industry categories except manufacturing plants with over 5,000 employees and a few other industries. Most private employers such as banks or public utilities had more personnel employees per employee. Government spent about 1 percent of payrolls on personnel, while some industries were spending as much as 5 percent of payroll.[10] More management time and public money will be needed before the traditional public personnel activities such as training, selection, and career development get the attention needed to make government personnel management more effective.

CONTEMPORARY ISSUES IN PERSONNEL MANAGEMENT

The technical aspects of personnel management are significant to managers even if they do not work in personnel. However, there are three broader issues that top managers grapple with: unionization, maintaining flexibility in organizations, and equal employment opportunity. While they affect personnel techniques indirectly, they affect public employees in important ways.

Unionization

Over half of all public employees, including teachers, are represented by labor unions or professional organizations that formally bargain on behalf of members.[11] For the last quarter century, public managers have had to formally negotiate with employees over wages, hours, and working conditions. To indicate the importance of this issue, a survey of prominent members of the International City Management Association revealed that "personnel administration, including labor relations," was one of the two most important information bases for future urban administrators; the other was a knowledge of urban affairs.[12]

To traditionalists, it is unthinkable that public employees should insist on the right to organize and strike. That, however, has happened. The growth of public service unions is part of a growing power-equalization movement. Public workers are tired of being treated as second-class citizens. Employees have seen how private unions have improved working conditions and salaries, and they want the same results. This is ironic, since private-sector unionization is not increasing at all: many unions have had to give back hard-won benefits to save their jobs, and many nonunion employers freely pay union wages to keep out unions. Nevertheless, unions are here to stay, and the issue is how management deals with them.

Collective bargaining is no place for amateurs. Management must be represented by professional negotiators, preferably by those who have detailed knowledge of each labor contract. Normally, these negotiators are personnel specialists familiar with the contract, the range of employee benefits, the importance of contract interpretations, and the implications of concessions.

In general, the top manager should not be involved in negotiations, since she must ratify any agreement before sending it to the legislature for final approval. She will set the limits for the negotiator in consultation with the legislature and the chief executive.

One crucial matter is assuring that lower-level supervisors understand the contract and interpret it consistently. More bad blood between management and labor occurs during the implementation of a contract than during negotiations.

Historically, criticism of public sector unionization was partly based on the two bites of the apple issue. Public employees help elect their ultimate bosses, legislators, who are sympathetic to their case. Therefore, it is unfair for them to have the right to negotiate their benefits directly. They should have one option or the other. This argument had some validity in highly publicized cases in the late 60s and early 70s, such as in New York City. There, unions negotiated lucrative contracts after mobilizing their members behind successful candidates. However, in recent years and outside urbanized settings, the theory doesn't work. Unions don't have the clout to extract favorable contracts. Management is bargaining from a stronger position.

Now, many managers are using the collective bargaining process to link salary increases to work output. This productivity bargaining strategy is used in about 20 percent of all cities with populations over 25,000—mostly by city managers. The use of productivity bargaining doubled between 1978 and 1984.[13]

Unions are now on the defensive. Since the late 1970s, managers have argued that it was better to take a strike than give in to exorbitant demands. While the loss of services to citizens may be significant, the jurisdiction does not suffer lost revenues. It's unlikely that public agencies will face serious strikes since public support for strikers is low, and it is unlikely that strikes will result in a higher settlement. This is particularly true in light of President Reagan's 1981 mass dismissal of striking air controllers.

The long-term future of unionization is uncertain. Private-sector unionization is declining as a percentage of the work force. Many new jobs are exported to other countries; white collar jobs, less likely to unionize, are increasing, and employers pay premium wages to keep unions out. What does this mean for the public sector?

There is still a strong drive to unionize the public sector. Countering this is a weak relationship between unionization and worker benefits. Employees are not necessarily better off economically by joining a union. If there is a need or demand for unions in the future, what will their function be? Presently, at the federal level, unions bargain only for working conditions and hours. If negotiations involve a series of minor issues, perhaps unions are really only an elaborate institutional method of ventilating employee grievances. Even if this is the case, a formal means of expressing employee dissatisfaction is useful and necessary. Unions, for the foreseeable future, will represent workers on behalf of certain issues; labor management relations will still be an issue.

Maintaining Flexibility and Responsiveness in the Organization

Assuring flexibility and responsiveness in public agencies, particularly at upper management levels, is an important contemporary problem. How can agencies with civil service system protection for employees still assure flexibility and responsiveness by top careerists toward political leaders? This question has received less academic attention than issues such as labor management relations or equal opportunity employment, although it is just as important.

The flexibility and responsiveness of the bureaucracy has received plenty of attention from critics of the bureaucracy as well as from legislators and executives. This is particularly true when new administrations come into office. While many complaints are unjustified, some are well-aimed. Some studies indicate that government executives, when compared to private counterparts, perceive a weaker link between actual performance and performance incentives such as security or promotion. The same differences exist regarding organizational commitment.[14] Thus, some government executives find that their performance has little to do with the distribution of rewards. In terms of flexibility and responsiveness, this could mean that quick adjustment to a new administration will not be rewarded and slow reactions (footdragging) will not be punished. If true, this confirms the critic's conventional wisdom. In addition, the reported lower level of organizational commitment may also work against change. One California official, referring to the need for top-level flexibility, commented:

[It] seems to me management needs to have people they feel are capable of doing the job, and secondly, that they can get along with and work with. Civil service is not very flexible in that respect.[15]

This does not mean that allegations of foot dragging need to be taken at face value. Political critics tend to believe that old policies should be revoked instantly as soon as a new administration comes into power, and that new policies should take effect immediately and operate like clockwork. They don't, of course, and they really can't be expected to. First, new programs have glitches and must be debugged. Even if the plan works well, it takes time to staff offices, and hire and retrain people for the new program. Second, old habits die hard, and often it takes time for new ideas to penetrate organizations to become new habits. Often, pressure groups, foiled at higher levels, get involved at lower levels to slow operations. Finally, sometimes careerists resist change in favor of comfortable old ways of working. This happens, but not as often as alleged.

The key is to increase top-level flexibility and responsiveness, because top-level executives can assure that the whole agency responds effectively. Responsiveness is the willingness of careerists to make changes in programs and accept the initiatives of a new administration. Without such willingness, new administrations are hamstrung and there would be a loud clamor to remove all members, much as in the days of wholesale removals in Washington, D.C. whenever a new president came into office.

Flexibility is the ability of an agency or group of agencies to rotate managers, professionals, and lower-level employees among different jobs as demands change. Specific needs of new, changed, or existing programs call for managers with different backgrounds and experiences. Political leadership must make changes in top management, particularly in selecting management from government service as a whole rather than from a single agency or department. Otherwise, it would be impossible to fit men and women to jobs and obtain a comfortable mix of managers and responsibilities.

The trick is to institutionalize methods that assure top-level flexibility and responsiveness. A solution often involves some corps of top-level officials whose members can be moved around, reassigned, or removed as needed. In most cities with populations over 25,000, city managers constitute this corps. City managers are hired and removed at the pleasure of the city council, although an increasing number work under contracts. They usually have more authority than other government managers, and they exercise it throughout their term in a given city, an average of about five years. Their visibility and responsibility for results gives them power. They also have formal power—appointing and replacing top departmental officials. Managers and department heads constitute a flexible and responsive group.

In cities without managers, not extending civil service protection to department heads assures responsiveness, or it assures political leaders that they hold the control.

At the state level, by 1978, at least 10 states reported incentive programs for management performance.[16] Frequently, this involves some kind of management by objective approach, since awarding incentives usually leads political leaders to conclude that top manager or subordinate performance has been adequate and merits a bonus. Each state varies since there is no model.

At the local level, 48 percent of all cities with populations over 25,000 use incentive plans such as innovative work hours, merit pay, and bonus pay. Most of these cities are nonunionized city-manager cities. Their number has tripled since 1976.[17]

California adopted a Career Executive Assignment (CEA) System in 1963. Most high-level civil service jobs have CEA designations. Careerists are assigned to them after a review of qualifications and an oral interview. CEAs can be removed nonpunitively upon 20 days' notice and revert to their previous civil service posts. Careerists get to CEA jobs by proving themselves in management positions. The plan, conceived to beat off attempts by the legislature to create more noncareer exempt appointments, emphasizes responsiveness to political policy, but selects civil servants for promotions. There is no performance incentive other than the fact that CEA positions are higher paying than nonCEA positions and the natural desire of incumbents not to be removed from positions.[18] At the federal level, the Civil Service Reform Act of 1978 created a Senior Executive Service (SES). There are about 7,000 SES members, all at GS–16 or higher levels, of which about 90 percent are career civil servants. Accorded elite status by selection and special training, members may be transferred as political leaders desire—carrying their rank to a new assignment. Retention is based on performance measured by high appraisal ratings from review boards of peers. "Involuntary assignments" by new chiefs may only occur after 120 days of service under a new administration of a politically appointed superior. There are handsome bonuses promised for performance, up to $20,000 in some cases, although bonuses have been severely scaled back from the original provisions in the reform act. SES members have given up some security in return for SES membership, although poor ratings generally mean only a return to a grade rating of GS–15; because of salary compaction at high levels, this may not even involve a reduction in pay. So far, the experiment is not working. Many SES members, stung by cutbacks in potential bonuses, choose to quit or retire.[19] It will be years before the SES experiment is finally judged, but it is the most ambitious attempt to create an elite corps of top managers at the federal level. When the SES plan is combined with merit pay for lower-ranking managers at GS 11–15 levels, the Reform Act is a bold attempt to assure more flexibility and responsiveness in federal managers.

Equal Employment Opportunity

Equal Employment Opportunity (EEO) is the last of three contemporary issues in personnel management. The specific provisions that affect personnel practices grew out of the 1964 Civil Rights Act, the Equal Opportunity Employement Act of 1972, and a plethora of court decisions beginning with *Griggs* v. *Duke Power Company* in 1971.[20] *Griggs* held that company requirements for a high school diploma and passing a standard general intelligence test for promotion were invalid. The test and requirements were not related to job performance (e.g., possession of a diploma and/or passing the intelligence test did not predict performance on the job) and discriminated against blacks.

EEO is the attempt to end discrimination against groups such as women, minorities, and the handicapped, who historically have been underrepresented in the work force. It is a moral and legal issue. In a sense, however,—although this was not the formal reason for the Civil Rights Act—the equal opportunity movement is regarded by managers as an attempt to make the organization more representative of the community it serves. If women are 40 percent of the work force in the community, they should hold 40 percent of the jobs at all levels in the organization. This improves the organization's legitimacy in the community.

Who Is EEO For?   It is easy to identify traditional groups such as women and minorities for EEO purposes. They are well-defined in law and practice. What about marginal or developing groups. Persons who are disabled or over age 40 constitute groups liable to become more important in the future. As the population ages, more people will be in the protected over-40 group. The term *disabled* covers more groups than persons with crutches and braces. Alcoholics and drug users will argue that they suffer from a disability, as do many people suffering from stress. Obesity as a physical disability has won a few court skirmishes. Homosexuals and lesbians may become protected groups, probably by legislative or court action.

Some managers have much personal responsibility for affirmative action, the means by which equal employment opportunity is implemented. One California state executive noted:

Affirmative action hiring is something now that is very timely. The Department of Fish and Game is under a mandate right now to hire minorities in 60% of all our hirings. I try to coordinate that program to see that as people are hired at the entry level their numbers coincide with that entry level figure we are supposed to meet for hiring minorities.[21]

Comparable worth, another issue, is somewhat related to equal opportunity employment. Women are clumped in lower-paying jobs such as clerks or typists when compared to male-dominated jobs such as equipment operation. This is true even though the latter are increasingly open to women. Market-pay surveys show that equipment operators are paid more than clerks or typists. Job evaluations, however, often show that clerical jobs should be rated equally with male-dominated occupations based on skills required for the job. Should a female clerk be paid less than an equipment operator just because she can be recruited for less? Many organizations recognize the inequities but are reluctant to abandon the market as a pricing system. They argue that the anwer is hiring more women equipment operators. Some jurisdictions, under pressure from employees or unions, still rely on market surveys but deliberately pay female-dominated classes more than the survey suggests. Some argue that the issue should be settled by collective bargaining. Comparable worth was predicted to be *the* personnel issue of the 80s, but modest accommodations during the decade defused the issue.[22]

Certain personnel functions are more subject to challenges on EEO grounds than others. Selection is subject to the most legal challenges. Traditional pencil and paper tests, oral interviews, and acceptance of educational achievements are not good enough. Tests for employment must measure job performance, for example, a college degree requirement for a recreation supervisor must predict actual job effectiveness. Tests must be validated against performance or replaced. Validation is expensive and difficult, and some agencies have tests like those used in assessment centers. These centers use performance-related predictors such as in-box exercises or management games to measure interpersonal skills. These tests work well for positions requiring interpersonal skills, and to date, assessment centers have not been successfully challenged for selection or promotion purposes. In many cases, performance at an assessment center is used as a promotion test. Selection validation for lower-level positions such as clerks is still difficult.

Promotion is another area subject to considerable challenge, particularly since "promotability" is extremely judgmental. Management decisions regarding employee selection for training and performance evaluation are sometimes challenged. Evaluation presents a particular problem since ratings determine eligibility for promotion, training, or disciplinary action.

Validation of examinations and other personnel activities is an attempt to rediscover merit. It ensures that qualified persons are selected based on an evaluation of their performance, rather than an unfounded belief that education or intelligence is the basis for performance. Managers, until affirmative action became an issue, did not try to relate performance to selection in a consistent way. In effect, then, EEO pressures were useful in forcing management to do what had been overdue. Granted, the need to find measures that predict performance poses many problems. Many agencies have given up and select a sufficient percentage of minorities or other protected groups to avoid challenges.

FUTURE HUMAN RESOURCE ISSUES

Human resource issues of the 1990s are forming in the shadows of traditional personnel matters.[23] Most wise managers spend more time on future human resource problems than on personnel issues of the 1980s.

The issues of the 1990s are human resource issues rather than personnel management issues. Human resources management includes the same functions as personnel management, but the change in words is significant. The term *human resources* is almost universal. It denotes that employees are important organizational resources.

Changing Lifestyles

Societal values in the United States are in flux; rapid changes are occurring in employee job commitment. Many workers, at all levels in the organization, are finding their main interests involve activities that aren't work-centered. Employers moan that absenteeism is up and productivity is down. Most of this is an employee commitment to off-the-job interests. One can argue that employers don't own an employee's time once the quitting bell rings, but the issue is deeper. The development of a leisure rather than work-centered lifestyle has profound implications for organizations and for the nation's economy. It is seen in many ways. For example, more employees now resist geographic relocations to better jobs. Increasingly, individuals seek a location before seeking a job—partly as a statement about the primacy of their lifestyle over job demands.

Economic conditions often result in lifestyle and work ethic changes. Highly trained or educated individuals who cannot get a job using their skills can't be blamed for questioning the value of the work ethic. People forced to share work or work part-time may find that they prize the extra leisure time. The result is the same whether one chooses a lifestyle incompatible with the traditional work ethic or develops a negative work ethic because of poor economic conditions.

In the early 1980s, there was a substantial increase in part-time workers in the work force (less than 35 hours weekly). The number of part-time workers grew faster than full-time employees. Individual preferences for leisure rather than for work caused some of the increase, but most of it was due to economic difficulties. Part-time or intermittent work was the best employment that workers could obtain. The movement toward a shorter and less well-paid work week is due partly to personal preferences and to economic forces.

Since the early 1980s, the economy has grown stronger and unemployment has dropped substantially. If the economy does not stay strong over time, short weeks may continue, resulting in manager headaches. Moonlighting may increase (if workers can find extra jobs). Commitment to the organization may decrease. Finally, less work may result in less value placed on work by employees. This might mean less interest in working when on the job, presaging a long-term decline in productivity. This is arguable, for some persons maintain that competition for jobs makes persons who have them more anxious to work hard. Economic hard times, in this light, are good for worker productivity. This suggests that productivity is up when the economy is down; an unstable condition when times are good.

No one knows what 1990s lifestyles will be, but they will have a powerful impact on organizational life. Managers should pay close attention.

The Changing Work Force

The nature of the work force is changing rapidly.[24] A demographic explosion is occurring. About 20 percent of the adult population is between age 45 and 64. This "middle group" will nearly double by 1990. Balancing this trend is a shortage of younger workers due to the baby bust of the 1960s and 1970s. This may reduce teenage and youth unemployment but any reduction will be overshadowed by the fierce competition among the middle group for promotions. This struggle will be made fiercer by the entry of minorities and women into traditionally white male territory. The competition for advancement and better jobs will increase stress in the workplace. Organizations will become more involved in stress reduction programs, and the mental or physical health of employees will assume higher priority. There will still be many losers in the promotion sweepstakes in each agency, and losers may band together for support. In the public sector, veteran's preference points on examinations have shielded veterans from competition, and other groups may organize to promote their cause through collective action.

This could result in unionization, even by managers. Managerial unions already exist in Europe.[25]

Pension and retirement issues will also be critical because it is unclear what the bulge in the 45 to 64 age group will mean. If employees do not retire earlier, the squeeze for promotions and better jobs may get tighter. Retirement plans are based on assumptions about preferences for work and actuarial estimates. A changing work force may force major changes in pension systems. A small example is the new practice in some small cities of limiting the number of years a police officer can serve to less than 20 so that she cannot collect generous police pensions. Sometimes, police officers must switch to a civilian job so that they retire with lower benefits.

The middle-age bulge in the work force will be highly educated. This usually means an increase in the quality of the work force, which is a strong factor in productivity. If well-educated people are frustrated by lack of advancement, their stress may reduce productivity as much as high levels of education increase it.

Quality of Working Life

Much has already been said about the quality of working life in organizations (QWL).[26] Employee and societal demand for better working conditions will make this a major issue in the years to come. Many QWL issues have surfaced already.

Occupational health problems arising from pollution and long-term carcinogens such as cotton dust and asbestos in the workplace are visible. There are health issues directly related to employees in public agencies. Eye fatigue and back problems from sitting at a computer monitor is already an issue. In California, a new state energy-efficient building was plagued by complaints of employee dizziness and sickness. The problem resulted when pollutants emitted by resins and office equipment could not be released into outside air. Long- and short-term hazards of the workplace may crowd out traditional concerns for the reduction of workplace accidents.

The aforementioned increase in the education of the work force is related to another QWL issue. Workers will probably demand much more control over their jobs. The predominance of the professions in public agencies means that professional norms determine substantial portions of the job. Nonprofessional employees will press for more autonomy in their jobs. There could be a demand for joint labor management teams (well-managed organizations have already created these teams), particularly where employees are represented by unions. Worker representation on management committees also may occur, particularly where the issue involves some contractual responsibility to employees. An example of this is worker representation on a pension investment board. Complicating this issue is the fact that many employees do not care to be involved. Managers must deal simultaneously with employees fired with the zeal to participate and with employees who are apathetic about the work environment.

A final QWL issue is a demand for more variety in the time when work is performed. This involves the great popularity of flextime in many offices. Flextime allows workers to choose their hours of work—other than a few core working hours around midday. It is no boon to managers or top professionals, for they often wind up with longer days, as lower-level employee flextime expands the total day. If some employees are present from 6 A.M. to 7 P.M., some arrangements for supervisory and management employees are necessary. The compressed work week (for example, four 10-hour days), less popular in recent years, may return if the work week declines to 36 hours. The days in a week, if only four are worked, will be less tiring.

QWL issues may be important to workers, but productivity will be more important to managers. Managers fear that productivity will decline. Attempts to increase productivity include contracting out, or letting private parties provide the service as long as the per unit cost is lower than using public employees. San Francisco contracts with its previous management staff for budget services, with the staff operating as private consultants. The Defense Department contracts with private firms for a wide range of services, while many local governments contract for public projects. The concern for productivity could lead to more organizational alternatives, such as flextime, compressed work weeks, or work at home. Many employees now work at home, particularly with a computer. Another common suggestion for improving productivity is linking pay to performance determined by employee appraisals. A final suggestion is developing more organizational commitment through improved benefit packages, particularly devices such as the cafeteria system of flexible benefits.

Counseling and Career Planning

Counseling and career planning is another issue related to QWL. The work force will be more educated, but there may be less opportunity for advancement. Even highly educated employees will be retrained in specialized areas. Counseling will also be important because the workplace may be more frustrating to employees. The alternative to effective counseling and career planning is constant turnover and the loss of employee morale, a high price. Career planning prevents the waste of human resources in ill-planned or futile careers and also aids persons who face the promotion squeeze in the 45 to 64 age group.

Newer types of counseling will increase in importance. Preretirement counseling, already common, will increase as people face choices between retirement and their right to work longer. Substance abuse counseling is also increasing in importance. Alcoholism now costs government and industry billions of dollars in lost productivity.[27] Drug abuse is increasing rapidly although it has not reached the levels of alcoholism. Identifying, counseling, and disciplining employees who abuse substances will take an increasing amount of managerial, supervisory, and personal time in years to come.

Much counseling activity for employee problems does not involve substance abuse. Employee stress, family and relationship issues, an inability to handle finances, and legal aid are matters requiring heavy investments in counseling systems. They have already been the subject of collective negotiations in California, where formal employee assistance programs (EAPs) have been negotiated.

The 1990s Employee

It's not clear that social values new workers will bring to work in the 1990s will be productive or not. Future workers may desire challenges and work for high achievement—needing little supervision. Conversely, they may seek only security and tenure, while assuming little responsibility for the organization or for productivity. Most scholars express the hope that future workers will demand challenges, but they fear that workers will seek only security and shun responsibility.

Managing human resources in the 1990s involves motivating a new kind of worker and modifying the work force for him or her. Employees will be increasingly concerned with personal rather than organizational lifestyles. Public agency managers will have to adapt work patterns to these newer values, which will mean embracing flexible work hours and compressed work weeks. It will mean more flexible compensation packages to account for changed employee preferences—for example, when a working spouse prefers additional vacation and less medical coverage. It means less reliance on executive relocation for filling higher-level positions. And, it means less autocratic, paternalistic, or laissez-faire employee supervision.

These changes only involve work practices and employee rules; they are easy changes. It is simple to install cafeteria systems of employee benefits or to adopt flextime. The more difficult assignment is cultivating motivation, particularly when employees are driven by different values than the past. The effective 1990s manager must sense and act on the needs and values of workers. She must mesh organizational demands for productivity with employee demands for autonomy and independence. Effective managers will be diagnostic and clinical, not authoritarian or laissez-faire. They will be problem-solvers, not technicians.

Two conflicting forces will make motivation difficult, even for talented managers. The first force is that demand for productivity and high performance will increase. Countering this force, employees will be less concerned with organizational values than with personal values. A complex carrot-and-stick system will be used by effective managers and organizations. The carrot includes sophisticated and generous bonuses for high performance. These bonuses will be financial and nonfinancial; they will go to rank-and-file employees as well as managers and professionals. The carrots may include organizational incentives such as autonomy and work assignments matching lifestyle preferences, as well as financial rewards.

The stick will be stronger organizational and disciplinary tools. Examples are the power to withhold salary increases and greater ease in applying routine disciplinary actions. Merit pay at the federal level and in many state and local units is another example.

Motivating the work force and modifying organizational arrangements to meet employee needs is not far from what good managers presently do. Motivation will be more difficult in the future. This is another way to say that management will be more complex and difficult in the future. Organizational leadership, ability to motivate, and a willingness to deal with individual differences will mark the talented manager in the future, just as they mark today's talented managers.

SUMMARY

The top-level manager's responsibility for human resources is summarized in organizational maintenance, representation, and planning. Organizational maintenance, which takes a majority of time, has two primary parts. The manager must assure that: (1) the personnel director is managing personnel resources well, and (2) that the use of human resources contributes to the organizational mission. These items mean that the personnel subsystem must work well and that the organization uses its human resources well. The danger is that: (1) the manager will either turn over all responsibility for human resources to the personnel director, signaling that he doesn't care or doesn't have any ideas about what to do, or (2) he will overcontrol minutiae, frustrating the personnel department while abandoning broader responsibilities.

Looking ahead to the heady atmostphere of 1990s human resources, it's easy to forget that most managers still grapple with personnel issues of the 1980s such as unionization and equal opportunity. Sometimes they worry about mundane matters such as training or compensation because there is no personnel director or department. And, they wrestle with these matters in organizational structures designed in the 1950s—many with powerful and inflexible Civil Service Commission rules. Managers may look forward to the future, but they don't forget that they live in the present.

Human resources primarily involves issues within the organization. However, there are organizational representation jobs for top managers that affect human resources. They involve "spreading the good word." Top managers must let community organizations and key individuals know that the agency is performing well, that goals are met, and that programs are delivered (assuming these statements are true). This provides important support to the human resources subsystem. It supports recruiting efforts by creating a favorable image in the community. It also has a positive effect on employee morale, for all employees do better work when their organization is presented in a positive manner.

One should not be too idealistic. Morale and recruiting are helped by communicating the good word, but crash programs don't change an agency image overnight. The change occurs slowly, and it doesn't happen if the agency doesn't deserve support. But making it happen is part of the organizational representation function.

Organizational planning must look at human resources in terms of changes that will occur in the organization's services and how changes affect human resources. The 1990 work force will be different from the current one, marked by intense competition for top jobs among individuals with different value systems who will make powerful and nontraditional demands on the organization. The society that produces a changed work force also presents new demands on the organization, and it is the strategic job of the top-level manager to sense new demands.

NOTES

1. Robert Domce, "Coping with the Civil Service," *Fortune*, June 5, 1978, p. 132.
2. President's Committee on Administrative Management, "Report of the Committee of Administrative Management in the Federal Government" (Washington, D.C.: Government Printing Office, 1937).
3. Commission on Organization of the Executive Branch of the Government, "Personnel and Civil Service, A Report to the Congress" (Washington, D.C.: Government Printing Office, 1955).
4. For a discussion of professionalism, see Frederick Mosher, *Democracy in America* (Oxford, 1968). Also see Michael Lipsky, "Toward a Theory of Street-Level Bureaucracy," in Willis Hawley and Michael Lipsky, *Theoretical Perspectives in Urban Politics* (Englewood Cliffs, N.J.: Prentice-Hall, 1976), chapter 8.
5. *Congressional Record*, August 24, 1979, S14267–14268.

6. Neil Pierce, "State-Local Report: Proposed Reforms Spark Civil Service Debate" *National Journal*, December 6, 1975, pp. 1673–78.

7. *Washington Post*, November 11, 1980, as quoted in Grover Starling, *Managing the Public Sector* (Chicago: Dorsey Press, 1982), p. 472.

8. John Rehfuss, unpublished research on the California Career Executive Assignment (CEA), 1982.

9. "PACE Exam Abolished for Federal Employment," *Public Administration Times*, June 1, 1982, p. 1.

10. William Glueck, *Personnel: A Diagnostic Approach*, 3rd ed., (Plano, Tex.: Business Publications, 1978), p. 14.

11. Richard Kearney, "Public Employment and Public Unions in a Time of Taxpayer Revolt," in Stephen Hayes and Richard Kearney, eds., *Public Personnel Administration* (Englewood Cliffs, N.J.: Prentice-Hall, 1983), p. 195.

12. John Kerrigan and David Hinton, "Knowledge and Skills Needed for Tomorrow's Public Administrators," *Public Administration Review*, September–October 1980, pp. 469–73.

13. Theodore Poister and Robert McGowan, "The Use of Managerial Tools in Municipal Government: A National Survey," *Public Administration Review*, May–June 1984, pp. 215–23.

14. Hal Rainey, "Perceptions of Incentives in Business and Government: Implications for Civil Service Reform," *Public Administration Review*, September–October 1979, pp. 440–48. Also see Bruce Buchanan, "Government Managers, Business Executives, and Organizational Commitment," *Public Administration Review*, July–August 1979, pp. 339–47.

15. Rehfuss, CEA research.

16. James Jarrett and Dick Howard, "Incentives and Performance: Minnesota's Management Plan" (Lexington, Ky.: Council of State Governments, February 1978).

17. Poister and McGowan, "The Use of Managerial Tools in Municipal Government," pp. 215–23.

18. John Rehfuss and Debra Furtado, "Bureaucratized Management Reform— The Case of California," *State Government*, August 1982, pp. 47–55.

19. See Patricia Ingraham and Charles Barilleaux, "Motivating Government Managers for Retrenchment: Some Possible Lessons from the Senior Executive Service," *Public Administration Review*, September–October 1983, pp. 393–401; and Bernard Rosen, "Effective Continuity of U.S. Government Operations in Jeopardy," *Public Administration Review*, September–October 1983, pp. 383–92.

20. *Griggs* v. *Duke Power Company*, 401 U.S. 424 (1971).

21. Rehfuss, CEA Research.

22. At least 30 states have established mechanisms to evaluate jobs based on comparable worth. The state of Washington recently won an appeal of a lower court ruling that required expenditure of approximately half a billion dollars to equalize men and women's pay rates. However, the state had begun a program of comparable worth compensation. Minnesota, Iowa, and New Mexico also funded some comparable worth programs. Many local units are making modest adjustments that will reduce male and female salary differentials considerably. Advisory Commission on Intergovern-

mental Relations, *Intergovernmental Perspective, 1984* (Washington, D.C.: Advisory Commission on Intergovernmental Relations, 1985), p. 23.

23. This section is based on John Rehfuss, "Human Resources Management in the 1980s," a paper presented at the Master of Arts in Public Affairs program at Northern Illinois University, DeKalb, Illinois, September 1983.

24. This section is based on Clark Kerr and Jerome Rostow, eds., *Work in America* (New York: Van Nostrand Reinhold, 1979). Note the article by Daniel Yankelovich, "Work, Values, and the New Breed," pp. 3–26.

25. Russell Smith and William Lyons, "The Impact of Fire Fighter Unionization on Wages and Working Hours in American Cities," *Public Administration Review*, November–December 1980, pp. 584–89.

26. See, for example, Richard Hackett and Lloyd Suttle, *Improving Life at Work* (Santa Monica, Calif.: Goodyear Publishing, 1977).

27. Randall Schuyler, *Effective Personnel Management* (St. Paul: West Publishing, 1983), p. 305, estimates the annual cost of alcoholism among federal employees from $275 to $550 million.

CHAPTER 9

Cutback Management

There are a few issues in public management that public executives like less than cutting back the organization. Unfortunately, since the late 1970s, it has become a fact of life in most agencies.

There are personal and organizational crises involved in cutting back. Personal careers are ruined. Layoffs are common. Long-term employee commitment to the organization is rewarded by the prospects of no advancements or job loss. Employees find their organizations losing influence and declining in service to clients. The most mobile employees leave the organization. Organizations must be slimmed or closed down.

Two basic management jobs predominate. Organizational maintenance deals with the immediate management issues involved in cutting back, while strategic planning is required in making long-term assessments of what strategies will do the least harm to the organization and employees.

Organizational maintenance tasks revolve around keeping the organization together while reducing its size. The damage from hiring freezes and reduced capacity to meet client demands must be minimized. Power must be centralized so that the best decisions for the organization can be made. Outplacement services for employees must be created. The belief systems of employees must be changed—specifically, the "tooth fairy" belief that cutback is only a temporary situation must be dispelled. All these issues are basic maintenance issues, but they may not be effective long-term responses to cutbacks unless they are part of a long-term strategic plan.

An effective long-range strategic plan requires a hard look at the options for cutting back with the least long-term damage to the organization. Strategies must be selected for cutting back. These strategies, moreover, must be part of a larger plan for making the unpleasant choices required when an agency has to retrench. Choices to rely on attrition instead of layoffs are critical. New ways to finance services such as fees and charges or contracting out must be considered, even though clients may be served less effectively. Decisions such as selectively cutting or applying across-the-board cuts must be made. Another critical decision for the manager is whether to resist or cooperate as outside forces dismantle the organization.

Organizational representation is important during cutbacks, for it is necessary to cutback effectively and to convince other actors that you are doing so. Effective representation also involves articulating the strategic choices (when and if they are appropriate for public discussion). In this regard, cutback management is similar to other management activities, for it demands effective maintenance, representation, and planning by top managers; the difference is the pain that cutback management brings to the organization and its members.

CUTBACK MANAGEMENT IN PERSPECTIVE

Before 1978, this chapter would not have been written. The crunch between the cost of public services and the willingness of citizens to pay for them hadn't arrived. The cutback era of the 1980s started in 1978 with Proposition 13 in California and spread across the nation rapidly. Forty four tax or expenditure limitations were on ballots across the nation. Proposition 2½ hit Massachusetts in 1980. Both Propositions 13 and 2½ limited property tax revenues in an unprecedented manner. A number of matters contributed to the need for cutbacks in almost every agency at every level of government in the 1980s. Taxpayers closed their wallets. Double-digit inflation struck in the early 1980s. The federal deficit prevented further expansion (except for the military and social security) at the federal level and cut off grants to states and localities.

Managers of public agencies began to cut back, a new and unpleasant task. Worse, this was a long-term decline in the public sector. What was needed, although all managers didn't grasp the point, was strategic planning.

Of course, skill and psychic energy in organizational maintenance was required to cut back here or there, promise this or that, and deal with budget and personnel crises. Skill in organizational representation was needed to keep a positive public face as specific cuts were necessary. But all of this was dealing with immediate crises. The real issue was making sense out of these crises and plotting a course for the agency in the years to come.

Every manager didn't do well with strategic planning. Some couldn't break the cycle of maintenance activities. Some couldn't convince their subordinates, peers, and superiors that a broader view was necessary. Some, even with vision, couldn't resist powerful forces to cut back or retrench in the old ways. And, some never saw that the need for planning was greater than ever.

But most good managers, at all levels and in almost every agency, quickly saw that cutbacks would become a way of life, and that their organizations had to find a way of operating with fewer resources. There were many solutions, among others; (1) changing service levels, (2) becoming more efficient, or (3) attracting resources from elsewhere, such as with fees and charges. Better managers developed goals and plans for cutbacks. Weaker managers failed to do so. Cutback management, like few other tasks, demonstrated the difference between gifted and ordinary managers.

WHY CUTBACKS?

In the mid-1970s, a funny thing happened on the way to a bigger and better public sector. Suddenly, for the first time since World War II, there was less money to fund services and less expressed public demand for them. New words, *retrenchment* and *cutback management*, slipped into the vocabulary of public managers. Most managers were suffering from retrenchment and practicing cutback management. They didn't enjoy it.

Most agencies, except for the Defense Department and scattered agencies here and there, began cutting back to lower levels. In the decade since cutbacks began, many agencies have completed the cutback process and are operating at lower levels. These new levels are marked by fewer employees, lower agency budgets, hiring freezes, and less tax revenue. At the state and local levels, cutbacks are still happening because the federal government is cutting back federal aid and because of tax revolts such as Proposition 13 in California and Proposition 2 ½ in Massachusetts permanently limited revenues. Since the depths of the early 1980s recession, states and localities have recovered somewhat from financial difficulties, but many remain in a tight fiscal dilemma. At the federal level, the Reagan administration cut domestic programs other than entitlements such as Social Security. The only real growth industries in the public sector in the 1980s were federal defense spending and interest payments on state, local, and federal debt.

These downward pressures on government spending will continue in the future because of gaping federal deficits of up to $200 billion each fiscal year. These deficits became so huge that public opinion forced Congress and the president to deal with them. The method they chose was the Gramm-Rudman-Hollings budget amendment of December 1985. It called for the annual deficit to be cut to zero by 1991, at the rate of $36 billion a year. If the president's budget did not meet these goals and Congress could not modify the budget, automatic reductions were made by the General Accounting Office (GAO), based on estimates by the Congressional Budget Office and the Office of Management and Budget. These automatic cuts spare social security payments, interest on the debt, and some entitlement programs, but fall equally on defense and nondefense items. The president must apply the cuts.

The Supreme Court outlawed the role of the GAO in the Gramm-Rudman-Hollings act because as an organization of Congress, the GAO cannot dictate executive branch acts, but Congress still could make the necessary cuts in the president's budget. In 1986, the first cuts were made across the board, affecting every agency. There was considerable objection to automatic cuts, particularly on defense, and equal opposition to taxes necessary to prevent the cuts. As a result, Congress, in 1987, revised the Gramm-Rudman-Hollings act. This change delayed the date for elimination of the annual deficit until 1993, provided for an automatic spending cut in future years if the approved budget did not provide for them, set the 1987 deficit reduction at $23 billion with future deficit reduction targets (including a $10 margin of error before the automatic spending cuts are activated) at $154 billion for fiscal 1988, $146 billion for 1989, $110 billion for fiscal 1990, $74 billion for fiscal 1991, $38 billion in fiscal 1992, and a balanced budget in 1993.[1] There are doubts that Congress and the president will maintain this draconian series of cuts without raising taxes or abandoning the process. Gramm-Rudman-Hollings guarantees that federal budget policies, in the future will feature cutbacks and retrenchments.[2]

Tables 9–1 through 9–3 document the reductions. Table 9–1 shows that federal aid to state and local governments peaked in 1978 at 32 percent of all money state and local governments raised. In 1983, it totaled $93 billion, but after accounting for inflation the total was less than 1978.

During the 1957–78 growth years, state and local spending increased 4.4 percent per year, while the number of employees increased 2.7 percent per year (Table 9–2). However, the next three years saw little

TABLE 9–1   Federal Aid to States and Localities for Selected Years (constant 1972 dollars versus current dollars)

Year	Total Federal Aid (billions) 1972 Dollars	Total Federal Aid (billions) Unadjusted Dollars	Federal Grants as a Percentage of State/Local Revenues from Own Source
1954	n.a.	n.a.	11.4
1964	14.7	10.1	17.3
1974	37.9	43.4	25.8
1978	49.4	77.9	32.1
1981	46.1	94.8	28.4
1983	40.7	92.5	22.3
1986 (est.)	39.3	100.7	n.a.

SOURCE: Advisory Commission on Intergovernmental Relations, *Significant Features of Fiscal Federalism, 1984* (Washington, D.C.: 1985), table 8, p. 21; table 43, p. 63.

TABLE 9–2 Annual Percentage Growth in Total State-Local Expenditures and Employment (adjusted for inflation)

	Expenditures	Employment
1957–78	4.40	2.7
1978–81	0.54	−1.1

SOURCE: Advisory Commission on Intergovernmental Relations, *Significant Features of Fiscal Federalism, 1984* (Washington, D.C.: 1985), table 8, p. 21; table 43, p. 63.

growth, while employment declined. Between 1978 and 1983, per capita state and local government spending, adjusted for inflation, declined 6.5 percent, although after 1983 there was some increase in total spending.[3] Since this comeback occurred despite fewer federal grants, states and localities spent more of their own money.

State and local borrowers now are more willing to support bond issues than a decade ago. In November 1984, voters approved $3.8 billion in bonds, 85 percent of the total value on the ballot, and in November 1983, $3.4 billion, 90 percent of the total value on the ballot, was approved. This compares to only 10 percent of bonds approved in 1975.[4]

However, this improvement leaves most state and local governments at slightly lower levels than in 1978 (Table 9–3). Since federal civilian employment also decreased in this period, relatively few employees at all levels are providing services.

MANAGING WITH LESS

The 1978–83 cutback in public spending was severe and sudden. This growth rate since 1957 doubled a budget every 16 years without considering inflation. Such steady growth developed a frame of mind and patterns hard to break, which is a difficult part of retrenchment for managers.

TABLE 9–3 Public Employees per 10,000 Population, Selected Years

Year	Federal Civilian	State	Local	Total
1972	134	120	325	579
1978	126	136	356	618
1981	119	135	341	595
1983	117	133	332	582

SOURCE: Advisory Commission on Intergovernmental Relations, *Significant Features of Fiscal Federalism, 1984* (Washington, D.C.: 1985), pp. 133–34.

Retrenchment—Problems and Issues

Retrenchment brings problems to managers, employees, organizations, clients, and politicians. To clients, it is usually a loss of services and a decline in their political power. To legislators or an elected chief executive, it reduces their power to legislate or act on behalf of their parties and coalitions. Difficult choices must be made, and a decreasing pie has to be sliced among claimants. To the organization, the natural drive to grow and expand programs must be halted, affecting the careers of members. Employees face lost pay hikes, potential layoffs, and extra work with fewer colleagues. Managers see programs halted or slowed and face unpleasant personnel actions.

In general, public agencies expand and provide services based on the assumption of a growing budget over time. An expanding base makes it possible to promise employee A more resources and to promise employee Y a promotion. Client groups can be promised more services the next year. Losers are promised a brighter tomorrow where they become winners. This cycle is reversed with retrenchment. Every action threatens to deprive someone of resources. This calls for different management practices and policies.

Specific actions result from decreased budgets. In most cases, a hiring freeze for all positions occurs. There are always exceptions for some positions or agencies, but vacant positions usually remain unfilled. If the freeze is of significant duration, some agencies or divisions feel more damaged than others. Positions become vacant at different rates. Morale problems arise because the remaining employees must work harder and receive fewer resources. Exacerbating morale problems are the freezes that occur when promotional positions are eliminated or left vacant to save money. More jobs become temporarily or permanently dead-end, and employee morale suffers as traditional career advancement opportunities vanish.

Equally excruciating are the decisions between programs at budget time. Expansion plans cannot be kept. Committed employees become discouraged. The loss of morale is more severe and widespread than when a promotion is foregone. Most agencies have some fat here or there, but these resources vanish rapidly, and muscle follows fat. Budget making becomes an exercise in distributing misery.

No matter how hard managers, department heads, and other officials struggle, retrenchments cause specific cutbacks to clients. In the mid-1970s, for example, New York City had to repeal the City University's open tuition policy, which had assured almost any New Yorker a college admittance, and the city levied tuition for the first time.[5] In California, after Proposition 13, public schools were closed, 13,000 school teachers were laid off, class sizes increased from 20 to 25, and the average age of teachers increased from 28 to 41.[6] In addition, park and recreation staffs were decimated and library hours were cut back.

Some managers looked at Proposition 13 as a challenge and encouraged colleagues toward greater efficiency, doing as much with less. One manager exhorted other managers to maximize the opportunity as follows:

> Think back on all of those things local government has proposed to do in the past decade to improve delivery of services and somehow failed because the political climate was wrong, or we did not have adequate incentives or, indeed, courage to effect needed change. The reverse is true today. Conditions do indeed exist that will accommodate change better and quicker than we have ever witnessed in the past. As managers, it is our job to maximize that opportunity by using fewer resources given us to do the best job possible.[7]

While many managers desiring to play efficiency experts had muttered about excessive spending prior to Proposition 13, few relished the actual cutbacks. Cutback management, particularly when in effect for many years, is not a happy lifestyle. Retrenchment brings several issues to the forefront that rarely occur during better times.

Political Leadership

One issue involves political leadership in times when money is scarce. Legislative bodies often try to regulate what they can no longer do by spending. This includes states mandating local governments to provide new or expanded duties without providing the necessary resources. A California example with universal application is the legislative practice of adding responsibilities or constraints to local government to accompany subventions. After Proposition 13, the state provided additional local money from its surplus, but it forbade locals to cut police or fire services, raise local salaries, or have reserves above a certain level. This made the state legislature a local decisionmaker because it: (1) assured that certain services, such as libraries, would be cut to protect police and fire, (2) interfered with local union contracts by mandating no salary increases, (this provision was later thrown out by the courts), and (3) penalized efficient local units by negating bail-out money if local units had adequate reserves.

The same actions are taken by the federal government when it reduces money for programs by wrapping a lower funding level into a block grant. The claim is that increased efficiencies made possible by reducing grant requirements justify the lower level of support.

Increased regulation occurs when industries are required to meet standards that require private expenditures for activities previously funded publicly. Developers are asked to pay for more public improvements in their areas or streets when local governments cannot fund the project.

Another important issue in cutback management is assuring that decisionmaking is centralized. Individual departments or subunits cannot respond to any change. In good times, proposals to spend any surplus occur naturally, but the reverse doesn't occur. No one will propose much of a slash in a budget. Top management usually has to propose cuts, unless agencies are forced to offer programs for the budget sacrifice. Another reason for centralization is timing. Response to decreased funding levels may require quicker action. Consistency requires that one person allocate cuts—whether selectively or across the board. Strong, centralized management also is important because weakly-managed units undergoing cuts experience greater stress or resort to simplistic service cuts based on political or idiosyncratic grounds.[8]

Centralized management is important, but it has little effect without legislative leadership. The best priorities for cutbacks are useless unless endorsed by the legislature. Actually, the best priorities are formally adopted by the legislative body and the chief executive. This ensures that priorities will be followed, since agencies are less likely to play one party against the other.

Irene Rubin indicates what happens when the administration and legislative bodies have differing views about the need to cutback or how it should be done, as in 1981 and 1982 under President Reagan. Rubin's five case studies of federal agencies led her to the following conclusions about the results of extensive cutbacks:

1. The president controlled cutbacks and career officials did not coopt his appointed officials.
2. Federal bureaucrats did not obstruct policy objectives.
3. Some agencies did not resist cutbacks. They self destructed and were easily terminated.
4. Reagan's popularity achieved temporary suspension of interest-group politics.
5. There was little evidence of coalitions among agencies, congressional committees, and interest groups. The Iron Triangle did not appear. However, interest groups and congressional committees made it difficult for the administration to target cuts, and the administration relied on personnel cuts and internal reorganization. This damaged management.
6. The effect of cuts, reorganizations, and reductions in force reduced employee morale, productivity, and willingness to make hard decisions.

7. While it is possible to cut back the federal government, it is impossible to do so and simultaneously improve management. The goals work against each other.[9]

Above and beyond the question of formally adopting cutback priorities is the fact that little effective cutback management can occur without legislative support or acquiescence. Cutbacks in spending are as hard for legislators as they are for managers and program specialists, and the legislative body may not agree on a set of priorities. They may, however, endorse a management list of priorities, or grudgingly accept it. In these times, managers had better not look to the legislature for plaudits at their skill in making reductions. They may have to settle for public criticism, sniping at specific suggestions, and cries of outrage—followed by resigned acceptance of the budget.

When cutbacks occur, wise managers redouble their efforts to keep legislators or legislative staff aware of how retrenchment efforts are proceeding, assuming that the chief executive and staff are already well-informed. Legislative oversight of agencies can result in individual legislators giving contradictory signals to agencies, giving advice contradictory to management plans, and making a difficult time harder than necessary. Keeping the legislative body informed does not always prevent confusion or contradictory information, but it is minimized.

WHY IS IT SO HARD TO CUTBACK?

Cutting back agencies or organizations is like pulling teeth. People have a deep dislike and fear of it. The prospect of layoffs galvanizes unions, employees, legislators, and managers into alliances to avoid them. Why?

One reason is that public-sector layoffs were rare until the 1975 New York City crisis, when the city nearly went bankrupt. Public managers didn't have much experience with reducing the work force's size.

Another reason is that until recently, public-sector employment was secure, although not the quickest way to riches. Thus, employees are shocked at the possibility of any cutback involving layoffs, for many are not psychologically primed for that possibility.

Beyond psychological and historical reasons, there are specific reasons why managers find it difficult to whittle down their organizations. Levine, after studying cutbacks in many cities, suggests a number of reasons.[10] The most significant reason is the "tooth fairy" syndrome. People are optimistic. Faced with cuts, they believe that in the night (in reality, the next budget year) a good fairy will arrive and the emergency will melt away. Managers find it difficult to devise cutback plans because no one will believe them. If they are believed, people still resist because they await a miracle. People also wait for someone else to offer one of their programs as a token sacrifice to tide others over until the expected return to normalcy. Such stonewalling is made possible by the belief that the crisis will not affect one's own program.

Another difficult problem is the paradox of "irreducible wholes." This means that one simply can't cutback across the board because the agency did not grow evenly and is not even controlled by one unit of government. Programs are interdependent and critical masses of expertise are spaced randomly. An example is the criminal justice system, where law enforcement, probation, court, and corrections subsystems are intertwined. Some of these are local functions, some are state functions, and all are federally financed. No manager controls more than a tiny part of the system.

In such cases, a rule of thumb is to cut interdependent programs equally and to cut independent programs on merit. Unfortunately, no one person or unit of government can make such a decision about merit and interdependence. Cutbacks become random in such cases.

Levine claims that the "efficiency paradox" is most troublesome to public managers. There are two major reasons. First, across the board cuts hurt efficient programs more than inefficient programs because there is less fat in the better-operated program. Past frugality on an agency's part results in savings diverted to less-efficient organizations, which biases the larger system against efficiency. This increases less-productive agencies. Secondly, since most agencies are perceived as inefficient, this increases the tendency to cut all programs equally, and it increases the disincentives to be productive. In cutback times, it is usually too late to do anything about this. In good times, organizational reward systems need to be changed to show that frugality and efficiency are rewarded.

Levine mentions other dilemmas or paradoxes. The participation paradox arises when people are invited to participate in cutback decisions and use this chance to fight cutbacks more effectively. The forgotten deal paradox arises when promises to help agencies in the future if they undergo present cutbacks aren't honored because of legislative action, changes in management, and so forth.

The productivity and management science paradoxes are related. It takes money to be productive, since training and capital equipment are needed, but when cutbacks come, there is no money. Similarly, management science capacity in computers, research, and analysis is needed most when the agency faces cutbacks, but it isn't there because in abundant times, slack resources were invested in building programs—not analytic capacity.

Levine's final paradox is the free exiter problem. He refers to a tendency for the most competent and mobile people in organizations to leave when cutbacks occur—precisely at the time they are most needed.

Reward systems to keep key people in organizations must be developed. In California, for example, many top managers left local government shortly after Proposition 13 because they either felt past efforts were unappreciated or they chose to take advantage of their mobility.

Cutting back is always difficult, but often harder in the public sector because most agencies have not experienced it and because of these unique paradoxes and issues.

Managerial Strategies for Cutting Back

There are several management strategies for handling cutbacks.[11] Some involve specific techniques, such as zero base budgeting (ZBB) and the nominal group method (NGM).

Nominal Group Method. The NGM, developed in the 1960s, is designed to increase ideas, reduce the dominance of experts and specialists, and focus attention on the items most important to participants. It is a structured group process rather than a conventional brainstorming session. Most NGM settings involve 50 or 60 people divided into small groups. Each person gets a card to record their feelings about organizational difficulties or proposed solutions. After completing the cards, each person reads one solution and the leader records it. This process continues until each idea is recorded. Discussion then occurs, followed by a vote that determines the best solution or the most significant difficulty.

The process was used with the Kent, Ohio city council to reduce a proposed budget by about $2 million in 1978 when the council was in turmoil over managerial resignations and revenue shortfalls. Council members wrote a list of items in response to the question: If 1979 expenditures must be reduced, which proposed programs and activities should be reduced? The 49 items produced were ranked by each council member. A second questionnaire showed preferences and a final ranking produced the final cuts. The final ranking was done after a popular vote rejected a tax hike.[12]

Zero-Base Budgeting. ZBB is a way to select programs for elimination by comparing them with other programs across departmental or agency lines. Each department head prepares a budget request with separable packages, each at a percentage of the current year budget, as described in Chapter 7. Chief executives and legislatures can then approve any program in any department (for example, 80 percent of the present year budget level) without endless arguments about specific programs. Presently, about a third of all cities with populations over 25,000 use zero base budgeting, although not all use it for cutback reasons.[13] A variant of ZBB called *decremental budgeting* is used in Dade County, Florida to help make cutbacks.[14]

Miscellaneous Techniques. Other techniques include the use of cost benefit analysis and citizen surveys. Cost benefit analyses rank projects against others based on the greatest return to the agency for a given expenditure. Evaluating a stream of costs and returns into the future makes this method complex. Citizen surveys use the views of service recipient and/or the general public as a basis for making cuts. Citizens, as service recipients, are in a position to choose among competing programs. At a minimum, citizen preferences reflect satisfaction with programs—even though they may not distinguish among them. The difficulty is the same as with any public opinion polling—cost, accuracy, constructing a questionnaire, and so forth.

In addition to specific techniques, managers sometimes resort to simple bargaining with departments over proposed cuts. This is an attempt to agree over cuts through consensus. Here, the emphasis is on achieving a united front. Consensus makes cutbacks more acceptable, although perhaps not as rational as the NGM or ZBB systems. The test of a good cutback is agreement or cheerful resignation, in the same way that the test of a good policy is agreement. While it is hard to get people to agree to retrenchment that damages their program, this is true of a formal cutback program. Here, compromise replaces more rational techniques.

Regardless of the approach to cutbacks, it is important to involve employees when cutbacks do occur.[15] Employees must shoulder the additional work when freezes or layoffs occur. Their morale is important and their counsel should be sought as the crisis is clarified to them. After that, decisions should come quickly to avoid prolonged uncertainty and agony. A frequent but counterproductive managerial practice is retiring to a closed office to prepare a cutback plan in isolation. This practice prevents leaks but it fails to command any widespread support. Consultation, however painful and time-consuming, is the best way to gain support.

One tactic for avoiding employee and agency management opposition to a large cutback is redefining the goals. Public managers are usually deeply committed to a program even though the goal is unattainable with cutbacks. Managers should create new and more modest goals with program heads that are attainable under fiscal constraints. For example, if recreation programs heavily subsidized by the city are no longer possible for all ages, the new goal might be providing any program in which participants will fund 40 percent of the cost. Modified goals allay the fear of program managers that they will be responsible for precutback levels with reduced funds.

A final element is obtaining legislative and political executive support for the plan, which has budgetary, personnel, and political implications. This support must be developed as early as possible. Presenting a cutback plan as a fait accompli will fail. Political leaders may not like a specific proposal. They dislike plans that they were not consulted about and they often dislike plans where all affected agencies are not in agreement.

STRATEGIC CHOICES

The most significant issues facing managers during a retrenchment period are strategic choices about how the organization should operate with less funds.[16] Whatever managerial strategy for facing cuts is adopted, the agency will face lower funding levels. This requires specific cutback choices.

Layoffs versus Attrition

After early cuts in office supplies, travel, and other expendable items, managers and employees face the question of layoffs. In many cases, layoffs are inevitable. However, there is usually a choice between immediate layoffs and planned attrition programs. Attrition through hiring freezes is normally used, for agencies hate to lay off workers. However, sudden emergencies or unplanned additional revenue shortfalls sometimes make layoffs necessary.

Layoffs have costs. Good but anxiety-plagued employees quit. Productivity often declines, particularly if the most recent hires are better workers but get laid off first since they lack seniority. Layoffs raise unemployment charges. Laid off employees, if recalled, cost money to rehire.

Planned attrition may reach the lower staffing goal as well as layoffs. The only drawback to attrition is its unpredictability; it occurs unevenly among subunits and occupational classes. Planned programs of attrition, supplemented by voluntary reductions in the employee work week, may avert layoffs if management can look far enough ahead and put a plan into action.[17]

A major advantage of attrition programs is that they avoid the difficulties and controversies when women and minorities are laid off. These employees, particularly minorities, are usually the last hired due to recent affirmative action programs, and they are the first to be laid off. This LIFO system (last-in, first-out) is in litigation, with conflicting court rulings. Protected groups, particularly if hired under a consent or court-ordered ruling, have insisted they need preference to retain their share of the work force, regardless of seniority agreements. The most recent

Supreme Court ruling permits some affirmative action considerations when hiring but not during layoffs. The present confusion is an excellent argument for a well-planned attrition program undertaken with advice of counsel.

Cutting Selectively

Another issue is whether cutbacks should be distributed across the board, or whether certain programs can be slashed deeply. Many agencies, facing the "target the cut or share the pain" choice, opt for across the board cuts. These cuts are easier than selecting the program facing deep cuts. Broker governments, where the unit has been a broker between coalitions of interest groups, pursue this "defend the base" strategy. This results in across the board cutting, as explained by New York City Budget Director Melvin Lechner, who argued in 1975 that:

> There's a limit to how selective you can be in budget terms. You get to the point where it's impossible to say whether you should cut police or hospital or educational programs. So we simply went across the board.[18]

New York had more severe cutbacks to make than most units, but it's clear they chose to "share the pain." That's not surprising. Managers who make deep cuts in one program, even after consultation with affected agencies, will hear from program administrators, legislative committees, individual clients, and interest groups. The vociferous objections of the targeted program and its supporters may drown out the sighs of relief from spared programs. The slogan "share the pain" reflects the belief that everyone and every program is equally deserving and should be treated equally. Yet, in many cases, this should not be done. All programs were not created equally and do not contribute equally to the organization's mission. Treating unequals equally is as bad as treating equals unfairly. The organization is weakened, particularly by equal cuts in capital improvements or maintenance for every unit. Universities are noted for cutting supplies, travel, maintenance, and library books before touching personnel. Overstaffed academic departments avoid personnel cuts while the library may never recover, affecting the academic capacity of all departments. Conversely, localities usually cut police and fire personnel last due to the perceived public support for law and order, while libraries and parks are cut first.

Agencies can bounce back from one- or two-year cutbacks, so short-term, across the board slashes may work at first. Eventually, this type of cut weakens the stronger programs. The secret is to select the most logical programs for deeper cuts and reduce them at the right time. The right time is early enough so that across the board cuts haven't bled every program dry and also when it is politically feasible.

The timing of cuts introduces another issue for managers: the ability to forecast how long revenue shortfalls will last. One year is nothing, and usually two years are sustainable. Five years of across the board cuts, on the other hand, weakens all departments. In the latter case, cuts should have been targeted. If managers foresee extended hard times, deeper cuts should be made earlier. One option is to indicate that if revenues are short by a certain year, programs x, y, and z will be cut heavily, but that in the interim, cuts will be spread among all departments. This strategy allows time for planning, but risks the "paradox of participation" when departments x, y, and z rally to resist future cuts. This is why many managers will not tip their hand regarding potential deep cuts even if it permits advance planning.

Resistance or Cooperation

In discussing cutbacks, agencies must decide whether to resist any cutbacks or to cooperate with central management and accept them, minimizing their impact.[19] If the agency elects to accept cuts, it must decide to spread them out among subunits or cut certain programs more deeply. This is a lower-level replica of the "target the cuts" or "share the pain" issue. It assumes that the agency has some capacity to select its programs for selective cutting. Clever lower-level managers may insist on such a prerogative in return for accepting top-level targeted cuts.

However, initial decisions to resist cuts are usually made almost automatically. This is a pro forma rejection preparatory to further discussions, and it often buys time for internal agency discussions. Agency stonewalling occurs when it appears that the initial position will not succeed. Stonewalling is a high-risk strategy. If full-fledged resistance fails, with interest group alerts and calls to legislative supporters not working, there may be immediate cutbacks, layoffs, and considerable embarrassment for the agency. The stakes are high, so an agency decides to resist cuts only when it: (1) believes the cutback period will be short-lived, (2) makes an assessment that political support for the agency is available and effective, and (3) disregards the long-term consequences of resisting top management.

If the agency is strong, effective, and expects to outlast the top executive and the cutback period, resistance may work. However, top managers fight back because their retrenchment proposal will fail if too many agencies resist effectively. Thus, agencies that decide to resist cutbacks should prepare for a battle.

Contracting Out

Contracting out is often advocated as a major retrenchment option. It is the practice of having outside individuals, firms, or groups provide services previously done by agency employees. There is a dizzying assortment of work contracted out, and there are nearly as many kinds of arrangements made to do it. The federal government awards 18 million contracts a year for $160 billion. Employees of government contractors outnumber federal employees three to one.[20] A city may contract with a private service bureau to provide computer services. The state may have all its printing done privately. Highways are built through contracts with large firms. Counseling services to low-income persons may be done by a nonprofit social service agency. The County of Los Angeles provides at least 30 types of municipal services to contracting cities— ranging from police patrols to building inspections.

One Los Angeles suburban city manager asks specific questions about any proposed new service. The questions deemphasize adding staff, since added productivity rests on a small, lean work force minimizing service delivery responsibility by contracting out. The following questions are asked:

Can the service be purchased from another jurisdiction?

Can the city enter into a joint management agreement to provide the service?

Can the city participate with a special district to provide the service?

Can the city buy the service from a private individual or nonprofit agency?

Can a new service provider be created?[21]

The contracting out issue becomes heated under several conditions. First, it may run afoul of civil service provisions that city or county work be done by persons selected under merit provisions, or that no civil service job can be performed by noncivil service persons. Second, unions object to having work done by private, nonunion workers— sometimes even if the contractor is unionized. Finally, if the work is not done more cheaply or is done sloppily, the agency is charged with subsidizing private contractors at public expense.[22]

In addition to costs, there are two other reasons for contracting out in the public sector. The first is to avoid organizational red tape or civil service hiring rules. This comes close to admitting that the organization cannot manage itself efficiently. The second reason is more common than realized—to buy flexibility and remove the responsibility of supervising public employees. Management, free from supervision problems, can devote time to other pursuits. A third, not-so-sound reason is that it may be politically popular to reduce the number of agency employees by placing them on private payrolls, even if this does not reduce total costs.

The reason for contracting out, as far as cutback management goes, is to save money. In many cases, it does so.[23] When contracting saves money, it is an effective way to cut back. Unfortunately, contracting out can be expensive. Outside contract costs include the time spent in preparing, bidding, or negotiating the contract, dealing with any layoff or return rights of personnel, contract supervision, and evaluating the contractor's performance. A rule of thumb calls for outside contractors to be 10 percent below the government unit costs and to allow for these additional costs.[24] Unless the contract is carefully drafted and well-monitored, it is impossible to compare costs accurately. The net result is a lower level of service with no cost savings. Nevertheless, many jurisdictions rely heavily on contracts for service delivery—justifying them on cost savings. In some cases, outside contracts are an indirect savings of money through cutting service levels; although the agency can't admit this publicly.

Fees and User Charges

A highly successful, but somewhat controversial way that many governments raise revenue without raising taxes is by increasing current fee and user charges and by enacting new ones.[25] Fees and user charges have been a major income source for states and localities for many years, but they are now used in nontraditional ways. Previously, such charges were heavily concentrated on automobile user-based taxes such as motor fuels, fees for vehicle operation, and charges for driver's licenses. Some were used by publicly owned utility operations such as water or electricity. These traditional charges still bring in the most fee and user revenues.

Fees include items such as school lunch charges, higher education tuition fees, parks and recreation charges, sanitation fees, and transit revenues. A significant charge is for development of property, when local units require that builders contribute to them for the costs of public capital improvements. These costs range from the traditional sewers, streets, and street lights to payments for or donation of land for schools and parks. Sometimes the entire school must be paid for by the builder. These higher costs are passed onto the buyer and capitalized in a long-term loan, while previously they were paid for by taxpayers. Over the long term, there may be little difference in who ultimately pays. In the short term, particularly in California, new home prices rose because of the fee, and the buyer substitutes home interest payments for city property tax.

Tables 9–4 and 9–5 show the importance of current charges, even

TABLE 9–4   Current Service Charges as a Percent of Own Revenues

	1957	1967	1977	Percentage Increase 1957–77
U.S. cities	12.7%	15.7%	18.6%	46.5%
U.S. counties	15.1	17.5	13.8	(8.6)

SOURCE: Lloyd Mercer and Douglas Morgan, *City and County User Charges in California: Options, Performance and Criteria* (Berkeley, Calif.: University of California, Institute of Governmental Studies, 1981) p. 7. Percentages computed by author.

though motor fuel and other automotive fees are excluded. The 50 states raised 8 percent of their total revenue from these charges, while local governments raised nearly three times that much. The state/local total was about $60 billion. The use of fees has increased steadily in municipalities across the nation, although it has remained stable in counties. These fees are palatable to the general public according to a 1981 national poll.[26]

In California, since Proposition 13 froze property taxes, development charges (builders call them exactions) have risen considerably. Local units are "frontloading" onto developers the entire future cost of the development—school buildings, fire stations, and park land. If the developer balks, the project is denied with no economic repercussions, since the municipal cost of servicing the area is greater than what could be raised under the 1 percent limit on property taxes. States such as Florida are also using more charges than in the past, but California is the leader—raising nearly half of its money for capital improvements in this way.[27]

TABLE 9–5   Total City, Total State, and Local Revenue from Service Fees and Charges, 1980–81 (millions)

	Total	Percentage of Own Revenue
All states	$19,288	8.0%
All local governments	41,632	23.6
Cities only	18,084	23.9

SOURCE: William Coleman, *A Quiet Revolution in Local Government Finance* (Washington, D.C., National Academy of Public Administration, 1983), p. 4.

Since cities using their zoning power don't have to grant the project, the term *development exactions* is apt. Paul Gann, a godfather of California's Proposition 13, was quoted as saying, "We got the property taxes cut, but they immediately took the dough back in another way."[28]

Developer exactions, however, are only the most visible form of current charges. There are many others. Automobile parking is more expensive. Recreational activities have higher charges and may require a minimum of participants per event. Hunting and fishing licenses may rise. Xeroxing charges for public documents now recapture all costs—including administration and overhead.

There are excellent economic reasons for user fees. They effectively measure and modify user demand. Parking fees for park users, for example, prevent overuse of limited space by providing it to persons with a higher preference for parks, as measured by their willingness to pay. User fees prevent shifting of social costs from private individuals to the community. Police officers are assigned to plant entrances or shopping centers, who for a fee, take care of privately created traffic congestion. Finally, equity is improved between different classes of people, as in the case of residents and nonresidents of a service. Nonresidents are charged an additional fee because they don't pay local taxes. This works nicely for items such as library cards.

There are some political advantages, too. User charges are as acceptable as the taxes they replace. They avoid unpopular political decisions by turning over the costs of a service to users. One drawback is that charges or fees are not deductible from federal income taxes, as are property taxes, but this has not become an issue.

The biggest disadvantage of user fees or service charges are economic and political. Some argue that the fees are regressive, falling on the shoulders of persons least able to pay. Park and recreation facilities and sewer or water charges are used heavily by low-income persons. As fees increase, the revenue system becomes less equitable.

Others say that the poor subsidize cultural activities under any local tax system, and that utility user charges are no more regressive than the property taxes included in rent payments. In any case, it's doubtful if economic arguments have much bearing on the question. User fees will be used as revenue sources until the charges become onerous and the public objects.

There are many other implications. One is to determine how deeply governments should be involved in economic activity, particularly when the government unit is a partner in real estate activity. Fairfield, California takes a share of gross receipts from a shopping center in lieu of development fees for parks, schools, police, and fire services. The developer saved up-front cash outlays at the cost of future sales receipts, but Fairfield may have made it difficult to avoid future conflicts of interest.

Since fees or user charges represent new revenues, top managers may have to urge subordinates to discover new charges to justify their budgets. Department heads have sometimes found that top management will increase their budgets only if the increase is met by higher fees and charges. It is not always desirable to signal to department heads that their time should be used searching for higher or additional fees.

Some heads of optional services, such as libraries and parks, have developed a vigorous marketing orientation. Library displays and open houses may coax additional patrons into reading rooms, even with higher charges for library cards and each book checked out. Park departments compete with churches to increase the number of wedding receptions held in the park multipurpose building. It's open competition in some cases. So, if fees and user charges continue to increase, so will the demand that managers aggressively seek customers.

SUMMARY

Retrenchment and cutback management were words heard rarely by public managers until the mid-1970s. They have been on everyone's lips since then, despite a period of sustained growth since the early 1980s. The brutal cutbacks of the late 1970s and the early 1980s are over, but the good old days of flush budgets will probably never return. Cutbacks are still necessary in many agencies and managers have much interest in productivity.

Retrenchment brings a host of problems. Initially, organizational maintenance problems predominate. Clients lose services, agencies lose appropriations, and legislators and top managers lose power and influence. Employees see career plans in disarray. Legislatures, foiled by lack of money, sometimes rely on regulatory power to achieve public goals. This tactic has mixed results. Agency managers try to centralize power to cutback with some order.

Cutting back is not a job for the faint-hearted. Program managers refuse to believe that cuts are inevitable. Many programs, built laboriously and bit-by-bit over the years, are hard to cut because they are intertwined with other programs. Across the board cuts damage all programs, yet targeted cuts are resisted vigorously. Employee participation may slow cutback decisions. The best and most mobile employees leave when cutbacks loom.

The long-term health of the organization demands organizational planning. One aspect of planning is developing a set of management strategies for cutting back. Some strategies, such as zero base budgeting, involve rational assumption, while others primarily involving participation among agency members facing cutbacks, rely on consensus to make decisions.

Beyond specific cutback strategies, public executives also face strategic choices when retrenchment is necessary. One question involves the choice between attrition and layoffs to reduce staffing levels. Basic strategies involve two new ways of providing and financing services. Contracting out services to private or other governmental or nonprofit providers is a common response. The use of fees and charges to align public services more closely with demand and willingness to pay is growing rapidly.

Dealing with retrenchment and cutbacks involves strategic planning. It also involves organizational maintenance, a traditional concern of public managers. This is the job of providing services as economically, efficiently, and effectively as possible. In some cases, contracting out is a cost-effective means of providing services. Fees and charges may link demand to lower cost provision of services. There is tremendous pressure to reduce taxes, or at least not increase them, and managers in the public sector are adjusting.

Case Study 9–1

SHUTTING DOWN THE COMMUNITY SERVICES ADMINISTRATION

Agency closedown is perhaps the ultimate challenge in cutback management. It is a challenge few have experienced, a challenge even fewer of us seek. At the same time, as governmental cutbacks increase, the closing of an independent agency is no longer simply a theoretical concept. Therefore, it may be worth looking at the management approach through which the first independent, peacetime, federal agency in decades has been eliminated, the Community Services Administration (CSA).

Seven weeks after Congress acted, CSA doors were closed. This closedown action was largely unprecedented, but the attempt was not totally unexpected in view of earlier efforts to end the agency when it was called the Office of Economic Opportunity (OEO). Certainly, as a candidate, Ronald Reagan had campaigned vigorously both to return community decision making to state and local governments and to simplify the structure of government. Eliminating CSA and making its programs eligible for block grant funds administered by the states fit both campaign pledges.

Predictably, these actions were opposed vigorously by community action agencies throughout the nation and by most CSA employees. The typical employee had little confidence in the effectiveness of block grants and was very apprehensive about his or her own ability to find new jobs, at least jobs with comparable pay and career satisfaction. Some felt the closedown symbolized a government which had lost interest in the poor. Severe budget cuts in human resource programs coinciding with the closedown intensified these concerns.

Because of the volatility of the closedown issue, the activism of the community action agencies, the strong mission orientation and advocacy history of CSA employees, and the budget cutbacks, the iron triangle was expected to demonstrate its strength, and a highly organized and emotional nationwide campaign to block the closedown was expected. This did not occur for several reasons.

First, a stronger leadership role of the president than we have seen for some time took the starch out of the opposition.

Second, the White House and OMB wanted to approach the closedown on a professional basis with sensitivity for the CSA employees.

Third, many of those involved in community action agencies, including congressional supporters, believed that the effectiveness of CSA had declined to the point that the agency was not worth a last ditch battle.

Fourth, and most important, the career leadership submerged their personal disappointment at the demise of CSA, and demonstrated professional pride in successfully pursuing a task they did not like.

In the end, the closing of the agency, quite apart from issues related to the wisdom of the action, was generally regarded as quite successful in carrying out the president's goal and doing it on schedule and without noticeable political damage.

From the outset, we planned the agency closedown around resources represented by CSA career employees despite familiar warnings that the agency was rife with militant activists who could not be trusted and who would undercut me and the president at every turn. I was advised not to bring regional directors to Washington because they would seize upon this opportunity to lobby Congress. I was urged to abolish the regional offices because they were "hotbeds of dissension," and if this were not done, to place trusted advisors in each office with the "right viewpoint" who could provide us with a flow of private information and whose presence would discourage regional directors from straying from the fold.

These suggestions were repugnant to me and in direct conflict with the spirit of the OMB and White House guidelines. But although they were rejected out of hand, they do represent a mindset with which too many political appointees in recent years have approached their relationships with the career service.

We tried very hard to approach our unpopular task from the opposite tack; one of trust and confidence in the work force. We were repaid with an employee effort that was outstanding, despite the fact that the agency was burdened with major deficiencies in its administrative systems, and was confronted with low employee morale.

It became clear very quickly that for some time the CSA political leadership has had little interest in or tolerance of good management. Sustained laxness in contract and grant management had predictably attracted severe congressional criticism. It had also handicapped the effectiveness of CSA in working with its hundreds of grantees across the nation, and had discouraged many of the career employees from attaining the level of effectiveness of which they were capable. Ironically, the politicizing of the grant process had eroded the political support of the programs.

This may have contributed to the fact that during the difficult closing weeks of the agency, when they might have been expected to relax their efforts with a "couldn't care less" attitude, virtually all the career leadership did the precise opposite. They quickly took on the unprecedented multiple challenge of closing the agency, carrying out their share of the planning for transition from categorical to block grants, and at the same time greatly increasing their attention to stronger financial controls over the ongoing 2,000 grants they were administering. This meant tackling a peak workload during a period of peak emotional stress during which each person was facing unemployment within a few weeks.

Refunding of grantees was not permitted if required audits were delinquent or significant audit deficiencies were outstanding. Teeth were put into the negotiation of disallowed costs. Anti-lobbying controls were greatly tightened. The Inspector General had already emerged as a new factor, and the office became far more active in the closing weeks. Milestones were established for over 200 closedown actions, weekly reports turned in, and weekly status sessions held, supplemented by additional decision meetings. Extensive transition groundwork was laid with each state, and considerable leadership was provided in this respect by most CSA field offices at a time when they might have been expected to be fading fast. The value of strong regional offices, an increasingly scarce feature of federal departments and agencies, was demonstrated over and over. In late afternoon of the final day, all regional directors were involved in a conference call, working hard to close out audits, transfer records, and all the other actions required for closedown.

Thirteen task forces were established to plan the transition on closedown. Most of these were composed entirely of headquarters and field office career people and all but two were chaired by career leadership. Yet all were fully responsive to presidential and congressional policies, as most of us fully expected them to be.

A small number of people were detailed from other agencies to help meet the heavy workload and to fill in for those who had left for other jobs. Their help was of critical importance to the closedown. More widespread use of detailees, however, would have been resented by CSA employees, and considerable difficulty might have been encountered in blending their activities with the CSA work force.

Considerable attention was given to reaching out to the employees. I tried to meet every employee in the agency, including those in each regional office, and a personally signed certificate of appreciation went to each. Group meetings were held. Information flow, inadequate in the beginning, became quite current and informative later in the process. We made every effort to be candid and open in discussing conditions.

With few exceptions, the political and career leaders functioned as a team. Staff meetings always involved both. Senior career people knew what was expected of them and why. Our track record at the lower levels was less good. Some of my closedown decisions were understandably painful to many who had spent most of their careers with the agency, but none were made without first consulting with experienced careerists to find ways of minimizing the impact on employees and grantees.

Total closedown of an independent agency presents several dimensions of difficulty not confronted by those facing the more customary cutbacks, different from a base closing which at least has the assistance of a parent department. Employees in an independent agency, for example, have no personnel office around after the closedown date to help with personnel records or to straighten out gliches in final paychecks, lump sum leave, and severance payments. The personnel office on which employees rely so heavily in RIF situations is sorely tested by the more frequent 5 percent to 15 percent level of agency RIFs. With a total closedown, however, the percentage is an unyielding 100 percent and the personnel office is overwhelmed. Further, each member of the personnel office is also spending part of his/her time looking for a new job, and on any day may no longer be there to help. Supplemental help has to be obtained.

A critical mass of tension and emotion occurs when the severity of cutbacks approach dismantlement of an agency. In a total closedown, the trauma experienced by a whole office can be devastating, and requires a series of special steps just to remain operational. The literature simply does not deal with this phenomenon. No guidelines or checklists on how to manage agency dismantlements exist. Little comprehension of the magnitude of the managerial task is to be found.

One of the most v___ing problems is that of developing a program for helping employees prepare for termination and the location of new employment without financial and emotional bankruptcy. It soon became clear that government programs used in the past for limited RIFs simply were not useful for CSA. Because these programs had so little credibility, it was difficult to persuade employees to participate.

It quickly became apparent that we needed to design and execute our own outplacement effort on a crash basis. Career counseling was provided, resume training made available, and a range of special steps taken. Letters were sent to every governor, and several hundred officials in both private and public sectors. The employee union had vigorously opposed the closedown, but once Congress acted, their leadership was very forthcoming in advancing numerous constructive suggestions which we found most useful. The beginning steps were faltering and our employee credibility at first was no better than the government-wide programs. By the time the agency ended about five weeks later, the homegrown CSA outplacement activities had become quite effective. But for many we had geared up too late.

Employees at headquarters and each regional office were urged to establish clubs for the exchange of information about jobs and to provide mutual support after the agency closed on September 30.

OPM_ tain space, _ staffing to assist t_ eral months after clo_ boxscore on how many wanting new jobs have bee_ to relocate is not yet complete_

Finally, the strong supportive role of OMB leadership and the outstanding support of GSA should be highlighted. A number of OPM professionals tried to help in every way possible despite the limitations of the government-wide systems. I would suggest that the CSA closedown demonstrated:

> With very few exceptions the career leadership will respond responsibly under the most difficult circumstances if treated responsibly.
>
> A "people oriented" approach is essential to motivate employees to perform under the extreme emotional stress of agency closure.
>
> A professional public administration approach can be highly effective in an area of great political controversy.
>
> It is actually very easy to mesh the political and career leadership into an agency management team which can quickly and effectively execute Presidential policies.
>
> We have not developed adequate policies and programs for lessening the im-

pact of massive RIFs on employees who have devoted long years to public service. Government cannot guarantee employees continuing employment, but much can be done to help employees make a successful transition.

The low priority generally accorded effective management in Washington is bad politics as well as bad government.

Dwight Ink, "Agency Shipmanship: The Ultimate Challenge," PA News, December 15...

Case Study 9–2

RETRENCHMENT IN CINCINNATI AND OAKLAND

Retrenchment in Cincinnati

The fiscal crisis in Cincinnati resulted from a combination of several factors: one was a long-term economic base erosion, resulting from population decline, that was reflected in very slow growth of the assessable tax base; the second was a continuing if gradual drop in the tax rate; the third was a drop in net revenues available to the city after a period of expansion and windfall growth. All of these factors came together in 1976 to create an anticipated deficit of nearly $20 million, were the city to maintain services at 1975 levels.

The city's response to this crisis was fairly quick and determinate. Maintenance and capital expenditures were deferred. The city imposed a hiring freeze which created position vacancies through attrition. The manager shifted ex-

penditures from the general operating budget to the capital budget and to federal grants; personnel were encouraged to transfer into auxiliary enterprises.

In the second phase of the response, personnel were cut back. This cutback involved both attrition and layoffs. Some departments were affected more significantly than others, reflecting some selectivity based on prior growth and other administrative concerns but also reflecting political priorities. Major cuts occurred in the police, fire, recreation, highway maintenance, and waste collection programs. Some other proposed cuts in areas like health were overturned by the city council, but generally the city manager's decisons were implemented.

The next stage of the retrenchment process reflected political pressures against the cutbacks and problems inherent in increased reliance on federal aid. During this period the police and fire unions began a petition drive to put a referendum on the ballot to establish minimum levels of staffing in the city charter. Even though this effort was soundly defeated at the polls in 1978, the mayor and council who had opposed the referendum began to press for hirebacks and a moderation of the hiring freeze. The city's black leadership joined this effort to rehire laid off employees since many of them were recently hired blacks who had been laid off in accordance with seniority criteria.

The manager wanted to continue the freeze in order to create a substantial end-of-year "savings" which could be rolled over to balance the following year's budget. The council advocated a revised policy of rehiring two people for every three who left of their own volition but the city manager argued that the city could only afford a one-for-three hire-back policy. The manager set up an administrative board to handle requests to refill vacant positions and in effect was able to control the hireback rate through administrative delay. The city manager's policy of maintaining forced savings through attrition allowed the city to recover from its earlier policy of deferring maintenance on its capital plant. Despite the advantage of the attrition management plan, however, extensive attrition eventually began to erode the labor force in an erratic manner. To

overcome the worst inequities and work bottlenecks, the city manager established minimum staffing levels by department. Thus, the one-for-three hireback system was to be applied judiciously and not across-the-board.

While the manager maintained his year-end savings plan, the council was successful in rehiring personnel in some departments. To pay for the rehires and to restore service levels the city adopted a policy of divesting itself of some functions to other levels of government. It began by transferring the court system to Hamilton County, and later transferred its city university to the state and its hospital system to the county.

Just as forced savings solved some problems while creating new ones, the increased reliance on federal revenues produced new problems. One problem emerged when HUD changed the kinds of expenses that could be included in the Community Development Block Grant program. HUD had made it clear that for the second round of funding, general social services were not allowable unless they were targeted at a specific neighborhood or at lower and middle-income residents. The city had placed much of its Model Cities social programs under the CDBG program and now had to find alternative sources of funding or drop the services. A second problem was that Anti-Recession Fiscal Assistance (ARFA) funding ended in 1978, creating a shortfall of several million dollars. Third, the number of CETA employees available to staff city programs began to decline because of increasingly tight restrictions. As a consequence, either the city had to assume the cost to CETA employees from its general fund or initiate a second round of acute cutbacks. . . .

Retrenchment in Oakland

Oakland's fiscal problems, like Cincinnati's, derived from several sources. First, the city experienced economic base erosion which was reflected in high levels of structural unemployment as many blacks moved to the city in search of a declining number of industrial jobs. Second, property tax revenues were restricted by a city policy of reducing tax rates whenever possible. Third, on top of these long-term trends came the 1978 statewide property tax restriction, Proposition 13, which caused a severe cutback in expenditures by and services from the city government.

Oakland's response to fiscal stress over the years has varied with the severity of expected deficits. In the early part of the decade, difficult years alternated with periods of revenue growth. During the difficult years the city coped by borrowing from the capital budget, postponing new projects, using state funds for maintenance (freeing up maintenance funds for other operating expenses), and drawing down some of its reserves. In 1973, there was an increase in a variety of local taxes, including the utility users' tax and the property tax, which, when combined with federal revenue sharing funds made the 1974 fiscal year a relatively easy period.

By 1975 the city had to cut back on expenditures and raise revenues again. To facilitate cutbacks, the city reorganized the budget office to make it more responsive to the city manager. Budget instructions to departments that year suggested across-the-board cuts of 10 percent. But the FY 1975 cuts were not across-the-board—in fact, there was about a 7 percent difference between the departments with the least amount cut and those with the greatest amount cut. That the manager began with instructions for equal cuts and ended with such wide variations suggests the emergence of specific criteria for targeted cutbacks. In the first year of cuts, the Department of Parks and Recreation received practically no cuts at all, a surprising result given the presumed high priority of public safety. The budgets for the library, museum, and general government were cut moderately. In contrast, the council cut the Fire Department by 36 positions, but the fire fighters later reversed those cuts in binding arbitration.

For the 1976 fiscal year the city manager's planned cuts proved unnecessary, illustrating the manager's tendency first, to overcut and second, to anticipate problems at least one or two years in advance. The next major change in revenue occurred in 1978 when Proposition 13 increased the level of severity of fiscal stress and thereby required more severe responses. Proposition 13 limited property tax rates to 1 percent of the assessed full value of real property in 1975-1976. It provided for a maximum 2 percent increase per annum in full cash value, and reassessment of property at the actual market value on the sale of the property. The proposition also restricted the passage of new taxes by localities to those approved by two-thirds of the voters. For Oakland, this meant a roll back in assessed valuation to 1976 levels plus an adjustment of 2 percent per year for each of the intervening two years. It also meant a reduction in the tax rate from about the 2.8 percent level to 1 percent. Proposition 13 reduced property tax revenues in Oakland from an actual 1978 level of $35 million to an estimated $13 million in 1979. Oakland calculated its anticipated revenues and found it lost about $21 million as a result of Proposition 13.

While a $21 million loss was a substantial loss of revenue, other jurisdictions through the state were far more dependent on the property tax than Oakland. The state government, in the weeks following the passage of Proposition 13, responded to the state-wide crisis by passing a one-year rescue bill, distributing $4.6 billion of the state's $6 billion surplus among the localities. This legislation brought $9.2 million to Oakland. The following year the state legislature passed a more permanent version of the temporary bail-out measure. The total amount of the bail-out would depend on the size of the state's surplus, and hence, could be reduced or diminished in future years. Oakland expected to receive about 2 percent more from the second bail-out than in the 1978 allocation, but ended up getting less than expected—only $8.7 million.

Thus, in 1978 and 1979 Oakland experienced two consecutive years of moderately deep cuts without new revenues. (The city had been in a position to impose new taxes before Proposition 13 became effective, but chose not to do so because of anticipated opposition from business groups.) In anticipation of deep cuts and no new revenues for several years, the city manager set up a priority scheme whereby departments ranked their programs, which the city staff then re-ranked according to a list of city-wide criteria. Unlike Cincinnati, this list was actually used as the basis for cuts.

Oakland's response to fiscal stress was first, to delay capital projects, to shift capital funds to maintenance, and to try to fill in as much as possible with grants from the federal government; second, to raise local revenues; and third, to cut the departments' expenditures and personnel. There was no apparent attempt to deny the problem or to delay the response. In fact, the manager often anticipated problems in advance and set up systems of decision making to deal with them. There was little, if any, budget manipulation with the possible exception of underfunding pension funds. The city engaged in no external borrowing to cover deficits, although it occa-

sionally drew on its own reserves to balance the budget. In Oakland there was never a stage of across-the-board cuts; instead, there were deep targeted cuts early in the retrenchment process.

SOURCE: Charles Levine, Irene Rubin, and George Woholojian, "Resource Scarcity and the Reform Model: The Management of Retrenchment in Cincinnati and Oakland", *Public Administration Review*, (November–December 1981), pp. 620–21, 623.

NOTES

1. Richard Eribes and John Hall, "Revolt of the Affluent: Fiscal Controls in Three States," *Public Administration Review*, December 1981, pp. 107–21.
2. All material about the Gramm-Rudman-Hollings budget amendment is from Lance LeLoup, *Budgetary Politics*, 3rd ed., (Brunswick, Ohio: Kings Court, 1986), pp. 177–80, and "Doubtful Congress Clears Gramm-Rudman Fix," *Congressional Quarterly*, September 26, 1987, pp. 2309–11.
3. Advisory Commission on Intergovernmental Relations, "States, Localities Continue to Adopt Strategic Policies," *Intergovernmental Perspective 1984*, Winter 1985, p. 19.
4. Ibid., p. 21.
5. Charles Levine, Irene Rubin, and George Wolohojian, *The Politics of Retrenchment* (Beverly Hills, Calif.: Sage, 1981), p. 28.
6. Richard Behn, "Closing a Public Facility," *Public Administration Review*, July–August 1978, pp. 330–36.
7. Thomas Dunn, "The Upside of Jarvis-Gann," *Public Management*, August, 1978, p. 6.
8. Levine, Rubin, and Wolohojian, *The Politics of Retrenchment*, p. 28.
9. Irene Rubin, *Shrinking the Federal Government* (New York: Longman, 1985), pp. 213–14.
10. Charles Levine, "More on Cutback Management: Hard Questions for Hard Times," *Public Administration Review*, March–April 1979, pp. 179–83.
11. John McTighe, "Management Strategies to Deal with Shrinking Resources," *Public Administration Review*, January–February 1979, pp. 86–90. Also see Patricia Ingraham and Charles Barcilleaux, "Motivating Government Managers for Retrenchment: Some Possible Lessons from the Senior Civil Service," *Public Administration Review*, September–October 1983, pp. 383–401.
12. James Coke and Carl Moore, "Coping with a Budgetary Crisis," in Richard Bingham and Martin Aldridge, eds., *Reaching Policy Decisions in Public Administration* (New York: Longman, 1982), pp. 65–72. A formal statement

about how the NGM method is used is found in Andre Delbecq and Andrew Van De Ven, "A Group Process Model for Problem Identification and Program Planning," *The Journal of Applied Behavioral Science*, 4, September 1971, pp. 466–92.

13. Theodore Poister and Robert McGowan, "The Use of Management Tools in Local Government: A National Survey," *Public Administration Review*, May–June 1984, 215–23.

14. Jerry McCaffrey, "Revenue Budgeting: Dade County Tries a Decremental Approach," *Public Administration Review*, December 1981, pp. 179–89.

15. McTighe, "Management Strategies to Deal with Shrinking Resources," pp. 86–90.

16. Most of this section is based on Charles Levine, "More on Cutback Management," pp. 179–83. Other important works include Levine, Rubin, and Wolohojian, *The Politics of Retrenchment*, p. 28.; McTighe, "Management Strategies to Deal with Shrinking Resources," pp. 86–90; McCaffrey, "Revenue Budgeting: Dade County Tries a Decremental Approach," pp. 179–89; Charles Levine, ed. "Symposium on Organizational Decline and Cutback Management," *Public Administration Review*, July–August 1978, pp. 315–57; and Donald Klinger, ed., "Human Resources Administration and Cutback Management—A Symposium," *Review of Public Personnel Review*, Fall 1983, pp. 1–96.

17. Leonard Greenhalgh and Robert McKersie, "Cost Effectiveness of Alternative Strategies for Cutback Management," *Public Administration Review*, November–December 1980, pp. 575–84.

18. Andrew Glassberg, "Organizational Responses to Municipal Budget Decreases," *Public Administration Review*, July–August 1978, p. 328.

19. This section relies heavily upon Levine, "More on Cutback Management," pp. 179–83.

20. John D. Hanrahan, *Government by Contract* (New York: W. W. Norton, 1983), reviewed by Randy Hamilton, *Golden Gate Review of Books* (San Francisco: Golden Gate University, Spring 1984), p. 11.

21. Richard Power, "The Five Way Test," *Public Management*, April 1980, pp. 4–5.

22. Philip Cooper, "Government Contracts in Public Administration: The Role and the Contracting Officer," *Public Administration Review*, September–October 1980, pp. 459–68; and Ira Sharkansky, "Policymaking and Service Delivery on the Margins of Government: The Case of Contractors," *Public Administration Review*, March–April 1980, pp. 116–23.

23. John Marlin, ed., *Contracting Municipal Services* (New York: John Wiley & Sons, 1983).

24. Anne Cowden, ed., "Contracting Out in the Public Sector," papers collected for a conference on contracting out (Sacramento, Calif.: Center for Management and Research, California State University School of Business and Public Administration, October 1981).

25. Most of this section is based on Lloyd Mercer and Douglas Morgan, *City and County User Fees in California: Options, Performance, and Criteria* (Berkeley,

Calif.: University of California, Institute of Government Studies, 1981); and William Coleman, *A Quiet Revolution in Local Government Finance* (Washington, D.C.: National Academy of Public Administration, 1983).

26. Advisory Commission on Intergovernmental Relations, *Changing Public Attitudes on Government and Taxes* (Washington, D.C.: report S–10, 1981), p. 38.
27. Mercer and Morgan, *City and County User Fees in California*, p. 24.
28. Coleman, *A Quiet Revolution in Local Government Finance*, p. 19.

CHAPTER 10

Managers, Their Careers, and Their Beliefs

Everyone has a different point of view about the job of top manager. Some think that anyone can do the job, given the inclination, some hard work, and a smidgen of ability. Others, overwhelmed with the complexity of top jobs, swear that anyone doing such a job must be divinely gifted. Between these extremes is a narrower range of views about the top manager's job.

Some views emphasize the power, visibility, and influence that top management jobs have, while others focus on the stress and pressures felt by the top manager. Some emphasize the size of the job to be done, but others believe that luck plays as great a factor as ability in getting and keeping the top job.

These latter nonmanager views are not far from the mark, only far from each other. They're far apart because each emphasizes one aspect of a complex job. Managers themselves hold divergent views about their jobs, since each manager rates the pains and pleasures of a top position differently. Consequently, even having first-hand top management experience does not assure a universal view about the job.

There are, however, two general ways to understand the jobs and lives of public-sector managers. The first is to concentrate on specific tasks. This is what most books about management do. Hence, the first nine chapters of this book focus on how budgeting is done, what kind of personnel issues beset managers, why budget cutbacks are so difficult, and how managers approach decisions. This first method is accurate, but it doesn't tell much about the reasons that individuals behave as they do. Descriptions of job-related tasks can become so abstract that one forgets that flesh-and-blood men and women are involved.

That's way this chapter is about managers as managers—who they are, how they are motivated, what they believe in, how they become managers, and what kind of careers they have. There isn't much here about maintenance, representation, or planning because those functions are part of the manager's job. This chapter is about managers as individuals and as members of an occupational group. It covers the extent to which managers are representative of the general population, and their values and beliefs in their programs and the virtue of efficiency. There is a section on ethics in public life, which covers more than mere legal accountability. The discussion is tied to the importance of managerial beliefs in the value of public service. Later sections discuss managers' drives for power and how managers move ahead in the organizations. The major reasons for advancement are visiblity, experience, and loyalty. Finally, the chapter provides some perspectives on managers through snapshots of different managers, both as individuals and as members of professional manager groups.

WHO ARE THE MANAGERS?

Demographic Representativeness

Most managers are white, middle class, male, and over 30 years old. They are representative of the dominant social group in America. While this group of managers is changing slowly as more women and non-whites become managers, it will be a long time before managers, as a group, represent the ethnic and gender makeup of the United States. Managers, a group of individuals wielding organizational power, represent the persons in U.S. society accustomed to exercising power.

Managers tend to demographically represent the clients of their agency if clients are predominantly one group. American Indian managers are more often found in the Bureau of Indian Affairs, women in Commissions on the Status of Women, and minority members in Equal Employment Opportunity Commissions. With exceptions, though, most federal bureau chiefs, state department heads, and local city managers and department heads are male, white, and middle class.

If top managers perfectly reflected all major demographic groups in society, scholars would call them passively representative. The phrase major demographic groups cannot be defined to satisfy everyone, but the underrepresentation of minorities and women raises questions. Many argue that until managers are more representative of these groups, socially important views are not heard in agency decision making. In addition, agencies not representative may be considered less legitimate by members of underrepresented groups.

Top managers are far less representative than their organizations as a whole, and their ranks won't be passively representative for years, if ever. However, the public service as a whole tends to be more closely representative. The federal government's work force contains 35 percent females and 24 percent minorities as a whole, although the top managerial class, the Career Executive System, had only 7 percent women and 8 percent minorities in 1984.[1]

The federal totals are similar to state government agency heads. In 1978, state government heads of 27 common agencies were 7 percent female and 8 percent minorities.[2] Low as these figures appear, they represent gains for women and minorities since earlier years. In some states, more minority and female employees hold top positions. California senior executives are 12 percent female and 21 percent minorities, for example.[3] At local levels, about 10 percent of management jobs are held by women. Five percent of all city managers are female.[4]

Another measurement of passive representation is the extent to which top executives mirror the population they serve in terms of social status. At the federal level, for example, they are nonrepresentative. In 1975, half the higher federal executives had fathers who were professionals or business executives, compared to only about 15 percent of the general population.[5] Interestingly, the few women who advanced to top federal positions were even less representative of the general public than male counterparts.[6]

There are other important nondemographic groups in society, such as occupational groups. Some are represented in top management, some are not. To the extent that agencies deal with functional areas related to occupations, such as health care, major occupational groups such as doctors and nurses are adequately represented, although it is hard to be exact. Lawyers are also well-represented, but hairdressers, woodcutters, and professional surfers are not.

Ethnicity and gender are important, and so is social status. That's why we measure them. Gender and ethnicity tend to represent the extent to which discriminated-against groups have risen to top positions, in this case, government management. If more members of these groups enter managerial ranks, the legitimacy of government in the eyes of these groups might improve.

Social status is important for the same reasons—no one wants top management positions isolated as the private domain for the children of high-income and socially prominent people.

Active Representation

Active representation is a better measure of representation than passive representation. Active representation is the extent to which group members in organizations press for group interests. If, as Chapter 5 suggests, agencies are pitted against agencies in the administrative struggle, active representation then becomes crucial. It is crucial that underrepresented groups be represented in managerial and top political ranks so that they can press for group interests, if those interests coincide with agency interests.

Unfortunately, it isn't that simple. Direct conflicts over ethnic or sexual preference rarely consume agencies. When they do, blatant group posturing is counterproductive. More significantly, long-term interests of most managers, regardless of their race or sex, rest with the agency. Agency norms, furthermore, have been internalized by all members—black police officers may be harsher toward black offenders than white officers.[7]

Potential group representation among managers is also weakened by the fact that most managers, regardless of agency or background, are ideologically representative of most citizens. Although there have been claims from the right and left that managers are too liberal or conservative, these charges do not hold up. Table 10–1 suggests that federal executives have views about "the rules of the game" similar to the general electorate. Table 10–2 covers all federal employees rather than managers, and it suggests that their views are similar to the general public.

Heclo notes that 20 percent of 1970 federal executives were right of center compared to 21 percent of political appointees.[8] A 1982 study found that SES members were more liberal than most Americans but by no means members of an "adversarial culture." For example, 36 percent voted for Reagan in 1980, compared to 51 percent of the entire electorate.[9]

Managers may not be ethnically, sexually, and socially representative, but they are ideologically close to the general public, and they are slowly becoming more diverse demographically.

TABLE 10–1   Selected Political Views of Federal Executives

	Percentage Agreeing		
Statement	1957–58 General Electorate	1957–58 Political Influentials	1969–70 Federal Managers
There are times when it almost seems better for the people to take the law into their own hands rather than wait for the machinery of government to act.	27%	13%	32%
When the country is in great danger, we may have to force people to testify against themselves even if it violates their rights.	29	36	25

SOURCE: Herbert McCloskey, "Consensus and Ideology in American Politics," *American Political Science Review,* June 1940, pp. 36–83: and Robert Wynia, "Federal Bureaucrat's Attitudes Toward a Democratic Ideology," *Public Administration Review,* March–April 1974, pp. 156–62.

TABLE 10–2 Opinions and Issue Positions of Federal Employees and the
General Public

Issue	Public Employees Favor	General Public Favors
Vote for Nixon	61%	65%
Republican identification	32	35
Withdraw from Vietnam	48	44
Trade with Communists	83	64
Increase taxes on high incomes	60	53
Legalize marijuana	32	24
Protect rights of accused	51	44
Government should help minorities	51	44

SOURCE: Adapted from Kenneth Meier, "Representative Bureaucracy: An Empirical Analysis," *American Political Science Review*, June 1975, p. 541.

MANAGERIAL BELIEFS AND VALUES

It is important to know what managers believe in as well as to know who they are. Knowing that managers believe in the same political values as most citizens doesn't tell us what other beliefs they have.

Program Values

Perhaps the most important belief of public managers is in the value of the program they manage. To them, police protection for city Y and child protection services from agency Y are critical to the public health. This value is the driving force in their commitment to public service.

Assistant Chief Thayer of the U.S. Forest Service commented to the House Appropriations Committee:

Mr. Chairman, you would not think that it would be proper for me to be in charge of this work and not be enthusiastic about it and not think that I ought to have a lot more money, would you? I have been in it for thirty years, and I believe in it.[10]

Like Chief Thayer, top managers believe that the U.S. Forest Service, the Tallahassee police department, and the Colorado state Agriculture Department provide crucial services to the public. More money and resources for an agency improves the quality of life for clients, if not for the entire public. Individual managers benefit from growth of their agencies, but most managers believe that their agency's services are crucial to the client. As chapter 7 pointed out, the ritual budgetary struggles of managers have real meaning. Their programs are at stake, another way of saying that the meaning of their work life is at stake.

Efficiency

A second major belief of public managers is in efficiency. This is the paramount expressed belief of almost any public official. Efficiency is usually stated in terms of providing services in a cost-effective way—with the highest ratio of outputs to inputs (services to costs). Efficiency, ever since Frederick Taylor's Scientific Management movement early in this century, has been a primary value in management.[11] In many cases, efficiency has become an end in itself rather than a means to a broader goal.

Efficiency is complex. Managers may profess their undying commitment to it: "I feel a serious obligation to keep city operations at an efficient level,"[12] or "I try to promote an economical government, to provide the highest amount of services for the lowest cost."[13] However, efficiency is often a slogan covering other values. At times, efficiency means economy, which provides services at the lowest possible cost regardless of technical efficiency. At other times, it means effectiveness, which provides the proper type and mix of services without necessarily considering economy or efficiency. Efficiency has become a symbolic word used to evoke the proper response from legislative committees or taxpayer groups. Managers who praise efficiency believe what they say, but the word has different meanings to each person. Furthermore, most managers put maintenance of their agency services above efficiency, although they publicly assert that programs should be delivered at the highest level of efficiency.

No serious challenges to the value of efficiency have arisen, although some short-lived fads, like the New Public Administration, do occur. The New Public Administration movement of the early 1970s, an outgrowth of the Great Society attempt to redirect and expand public programs to the underprivileged, flourished in some academic circles. It made an intellectual challenge to efficiency, favoring: (1) social equity, or a strong emphasis on redirecting organizational resources toward the poorer clients of an agency, and (2) an activist administrator who would take chances to aggressively advance the interests of agency clients, particularly the disadvantaged.[14] Unfortunately, the New Public Administration had little impact on practitioners, most of whom were already committed to clients on the organization's terms. Social equity runs a poor second to efficiency in most manager's values.

A third belief held by most top managers is value in serving the public generally. Such a belief is complex, for while managers believe in the importance of public service, the statement is often justification for effort put into one's own agency efforts. Thus, a statement such as this from a senior California executive: "I'm a dedicated public servant,"[15] may reflect true altruism or willingness to further the agency's welfare. It usually involves a complex combination of both reasons.

Basically, most managers have specific commitments to programs, more abstract values to the ideal of efficiency, but weaker or ambiguous beliefs about the importance of public services in general. This set of values may be fine for routine management, but the public clamors for more specific evidence of ethical behavior in the public service.

Ethical Behavior in the Public Service

Events since 1974, most prominently the Watergate and Iran scandals, have focused attention on the ethical values and behavior of government officials. Most misdeeds are committed by political appointees. In any case, ethical behavior by public officials at all levels is not taken for granted by the public. Managers must ensure that individual activities directed toward narrower program interests are legal and free from excessive partisan or program zeal. The excesses of the Watergate burglary attempt and the Irangate diversion of funds were not motivated primarily by lust for personal gain. Rather, they involved contempt for law and desire for ideological gains. When such cases arise, mere concern with eliminating potential personal gains is not good enough. There must also be some assurance that the good of the whole public service and the whole government motivates executive actions.

Ethical behavior in the public service is tied to some notion of the public interest. The public interest is more than the sum of partial interests, which is often a compromise after administrative or political battles between groups. Even though the public interest may not be a "brooding omnipresence in the sky,"[16] which is incapable of being operationalized, it still represents a lofty ideal that public executives articulate whenever they explain a higher justification than personal gain or program interest. Vague and imprecise, the public interest still describes the highest values to which public executives aspire.

It is important to link the value accorded to the public interest to some concept of the importance of public service. Over an extended time, ethical behavior in public careers is maintained only if all employees, particularly top executives who set the organizational tone, show pride in public service. Pride in public service is the key to assuring deep commitment to both individual and public programs. This commitment guarantees, as much as any value can, that public services will operate in a manner conforming to the highest ethical standards.

This means that the public executive will be committed to the public service as a whole, not only to her own agency or program. This does not mean that aggressively advancing one's program is improper or dysfunctional—after all, a clash of interests is the primary way that our system seeks the public interest. A commitment to the public service means that public managers need to have pride in their calling as public servants, that they value services that the government provides, and that they expect colleagues to feel similarly about their agency and the public service. This is reflected in section two of the American Society for Public Administration's Code of Ethics (Exhibit 10–1), which asserts that "service to the public is beyond service to one's self," and section eight, which refers to promoting the public interest.

EXHIBIT 10–1   The American Society for Public Administration: Code of Ethics and Implementation Guidelines

- *Demonstrate the highest standards of personal integrity, truthfulness, honesty and fortitude in all our public activities in order to inspire public confidence and trust in public institutions.*

  Perceptions of others are critical to the reputation of an individual or a public agency. Nothing is more important to public administrators than the public's opinion about their honesty, truthfulness, and personal integrity. It overshadows competence as the premier value sought by citizens in their public officials and employees. Any individual or collective compromise with respect to these character traits can damage the ability of an agency to perform its tasks or accomplish its mission. The reputation of the administrator may be tarnished. Effectiveness may be impaired. A career or careers may be destroyed. The best insurance against loss of public confidence is adherence to the highest standards of honesty, truthfulness and fortitude.

  Public administrators are obliged to develop civic virtues because of the public responsibilities they have sought and obtained. Respect for the truth, for fairly dealing with others, for sensitivity to rights and responsibilities of citizens, and for the public good must be generated and carefully nurtured and matured.

  If you are responsible for the performance of others, share with them the reasons for the importance of integrity. Hold them to high ethical standards and teach them the moral as well as the financial responsibility for public funds under their care.

  If you are responsible only for your own performance, do not compromise your honesty and integrity for advancement, honors, or personal gain. Be discreet, respectful of proper authority and your appointed or elected superiors, sensitive to the expectations and the values of the public you serve. Practice the golden rule: doing to and for others what you would have done to and for you in similar circumstances. Be modest about your talents, letting your work speak for you. Be generous in your praise of the good work of your fellow workers. Guard the public purse as if it were your own.

EXHIBIT 10–1 (*continued*)

Whether you are an official or an employee, by your own example give testimony to your regard for the rights of others. Acknowledge their legitimate responsibilities, and don't trespass upon them. Concede gracefully, quickly, and publicly when you have erred. Be fair and sensitive to those who have not fared well in their dealings with your agency and its applications of the law, regulations, or administrative procedures.

- *Serve in such a way that we do not realize undue personal gain from the performance of our official duties.*

The only gains you should seek from public employment are salaries, fringe benefits, respect, and recognition for your work. Your personal gains may also include the pleasure of doing a good job, helping the public, and achieving your career goals. No elected or appointed public servant should borrow or accept gifts from staff of any corporation which buys services from, or sells to, or is regulated by, his or her governmental agency. If your work brings you in frequent contact with contractors supplying the government, be sure you pay for your own expenses. Public property, funds and power should never be directed toward personal or political gain. Make it clear by your own actions that you will not tolerate any use of public funds to benefit yourself, your family, or your friends.

- *Avoid any interest or activity which is in conflict with the conduct of our official duties.*

Public employees should not undertake any task which is in conflict or could be viewed as in conflict with job responsibilities.

This general statement addresses a fundamental principle that public employees are trustees for all the people. This means that the people have a right to expect public employees to act as surrogates for the entire people with fairness toward all the people and not a few or a limited group.

Actions or inactions which conflict with, injure, or destroy this foundation of trust between the people and their surrogates must be avoided.

Ironically, experience indicates that conflict of interest and corruption often arise not from an external affront, but as a result of interaction between persons who know each other very well. To strengthen resistance to conflict of interest, public employees should avoid frequent social contact with persons who come under their regulation or persons who wish to sell products or services to their agency or institution.

Agencies with inspectional or investigative responsibilities have a special obligation to reduce vulnerability to conflict of interest. Periodic staff rotation may be helpful to these agencies.

Individuals holding a position recognized by law or regulation as an unclassified or political appointment (e.g. Cabinet level and Governor's appointment positions) have a special obligation to behave in ways which do not suggest that official acts are driven primarily or only by partisan political concerns.

EXHIBIT 10–1 (*continued*)

Public employees should remember that despite whatever preventive steps they might take, situations which hold the possibility for conflict of interest will always emerge. Consequently, the awareness of the potentiality of conflict of interest is important. Public employees, particularly professors in Public Administration, have a serious obligation to periodically stimulate discussion on conflicts of interest within organizations, schools, and professional associations.

- *Support, implement, and promote merit employment and programs of affirmative action to assure equal employment opportunity by our recruitment, selection, and advancement of qualified persons from all elements of society.*

Oppose any discrimination because of race, color, religion, sex, national origin, political affiliation, physical handicaps, age, or marital status, in all aspects of personnel policy. Likewise, a person's lifestyle should not be the occasion for discrimination if it bears no reasonable relation to his or her ability to perform required tasks.

Review employment and personnel operations and statistics to identify the impact of organizational practices on "protected groups". Performance standards should apply equally to all workers. In the event of cutbacks of staff, managers should employ fair criteria for selection of employees for separation, and humane strategies for administering the program.

Any kind of sexual, racial, or religious harassment should not be allowed. Appropriate channels should be provided for harassed persons to state their problems to objective officials. In the event of a proven offense, appropriate action should be taken.

- *Eliminate all forms of illegal discrimination, fraud, and mismanagement of public funds, and support colleagues if they are in difficulty because of responsible efforts to correct such discrimination, fraud, mismanagement or abuse.*

If you are a supervisor, you should not only be alert that no illegal action issues from or is sponsored by your immediate office, you should inform your subordinates at regular intervals that you will tolerate no illegalities in their offices and discuss the reasons for the position with them. Public employees who have good reason to suspect illegal action in any public agency should seek assistance in how to channel information regarding the matter to appropriate authorities.

All public servants should support authorized investigative agencies, the General Accounting Office in the federal government, auditors in the state or large local governments, C.P.A. firms or federal or state auditors in many other cases. We should support the concept of independent auditors reporting to committees independent of management. Good fiscal and management controls and inspections are important protections for supervisors, staff, and the public interest.

In both government and business, inadequate equipment, software, procedures, supervision, and poor security controls make possible both inten-

EXHIBIT 10–1 (*continued*)

tional and unintentional misconduct. Managers have an ethical obligation to seek adequate equipment, software, procedures and controls to reduce the agency's vulnerability to misconduct. When an agency dispenses exemptions from regulations, or abatement of taxes or fees, managers should assure periodic investigatory checks.

The "whistle blower" who appears to his/her immediate superiors to be disloyal, may actually be loyal to the higher interests of the public. If so, the whistle blower deserves support. Local, state, and federal governments should establish effective dissent channels to which whistle blowers may report their concerns without fear of identification.

Supervisors should inform their staff that constructive criticism may be brought to them without reprisal, or may be carried to an ombudsman or other designated official. As a last resort, public employees have a right to make public their criticism but it is the personal and professional responsibility of the critic to advance only well founded criticism.

• *Serve the public with respect, concern, courtesy, and responsiveness, recognizing that service to the public is beyond service to oneself.*

Be sure your answers to questions on public policy are complete, understandable and true. Try to develop in your staff a goal of courteous conduct with citizens. Devise a simple system to ensure that your staff gives helpful and pleasant service to the public. Wherever possible, show citizens how to avoid mistakes in their relations with government.

Each citizen's questions should be answered as thoughtfully and as fully as possible. If you or your staff do not know the answer to a question, an effort should be made to get an answer or to help the citizen make direct contact with the appropriate office.

Part of servicing the public responsively is to encourage citizen cooperation and to involve civic groups. Administrators have an ethical responsibility to bring citizens into work with the government as far as practical, both to secure citizen support of government, and for the economies or increased effectiveness which will result. Respect the right of the public (through the media) to know what is going on in your agency even though you know queries may be raised for partisan or other non-public purposes.

• *Strive for personal professional excellence and encourage the professional development of our associates and those seeking to enter the field of public administration.*

Staff members, throughout their careers, should be encouraged to participate in professional activities and associations such as ASPA. They should also be reminded of the importance of doing a good job and their responsibility to improve the public service.

Administrators should make time to meet with students periodically and to provide a bridge between classroom studies and the realities of public jobs. Administrators should also lend their support to well planned internship programs.

EXHIBIT 10–1 *(continued)*

- *Approach our organization and operational duties with a positive attitude and constructively support open communication, creativity, dedication and compassion.*

Americans expect government to be compassionate, well organized, and operating within the law. Public employees should understand the purpose of their agency and the role they play in achieving that purpose. Dedication and creativity of staff members will flow from a sense of purpose.

ASPA members should strive to create a work environment which supports positive and constructive attitudes among workers at all levels. This open environment should permit employees to comment on work activities without fear of reprisal. In addition, managers can strengthen this open environment by establishing procedures ensuring thoughtful and objective review of employee concerns.

- *Respect and protect the privileged information to which we have access in the course of official duties.*

Much information in public offices is privileged for reasons of national security, or because of laws or ordinances. If you talk with colleagues about privileged matters, be sure they need the information and you enjoin them to secrecy. If the work is important enough to be classified, learn and follow the rules set by the security agency. Special care must be taken to secure access to confidential information stored on computers. Sometimes information needs to be withheld from the individual citizen or general public to prevent disturbances of the peace. It should be withheld only if there is a possibility of dangerous or illegal or unprofessional consequences of releasing information.

Where other governmental agencies have a legitimate public service need for information possessed by an agency, do all you can to cooperate, within the limits of statute law, administrative regulations, and promises made to those who furnish the information.

- *Exercise whatever discretionary authority we have under law to promote the public interest.*

If your work involves discretionary decisions you should first secure policy guidelines from your supervisor. You should then make sure that all staff who "need to know" are informed of these policies and have an opportunity to discuss the means of putting them into effect.

There are occasions when a law is unenforceable or has become obsolete; in such cases you should recommend to your superior or to the legislative body that the law be modernized. If an obsolete law remains in effect, the manager or highest official should determine if the law is or is not to be enforced, after consultation with the agency's legal advisor.

EXHIBIT 10–1 *(concluded)*

There are occasions where a lower level employee must be given considerable discretion. Try to see that such employees are adequately trained for their difficult tasks.

Tell yourself and your staff quite frequently that every decision creates a precedent, so the first decisions on a point should be ethically sound; this is the best protection for staff as well as for the public.

* *Accept as a personal duty the responsibility to keep up to date on emerging issues and to administer the public's business with professional competence, fairness, impartiality, efficiency and effectiveness.*

Administrators should attend professional meetings, read books and periodicals related to their field, and talk with specialists. The goal is to keep informed about the present and future issues and problems in their professional field and organization in order to take advantage of opportunities and avoid problems.

Serious mistakes in public administration have been made by people who did their jobs conscientiously but failed to look ahead for emerging problems and issues. A long list of washed out dams, fatal mine accidents, fires in poorly inspected buildings, inadequate computer systems, or economic disasters are results of not looking ahead. ASPA members should be catalysts to stimulate discussion and reflection about improving efficiency and effectiveness of public services.

* *Respect, support, study, and when necessary, work to improve federal and state constitutions and other laws which define the relationships among public agencies, employees, clients and all citizens.*

Familiarize yourself with principles of American constitutional government. As a citizen work for legislation which is in the public interest.

Teach constitutional principles of equality and fairness.

Strive for clear division of functions between different levels of government, between different bureaus or departments, and between government and its citizens. Cooperate as fully as possible with all agencies of government, especially those with overlapping responsibilities. Do not let parochial agency or institutional loyalty drown out considerations of wider public policy.

Adopted by
ASPA National Council
March 27, 1985

SOURCE: *Code of Ethics & Implementation Guidelines*, The American Society for Public Administration.

The public interest is a vague concept with little content for specific guidance. Its utility lies in its use as a widely accepted call for behavior of the highest integrity, behavior that emphasizes a set of values beyond the individual. No specific list of don'ts could establish the same set of values. Injunctions such as "GSA [the Federal General Service Administration] personnel shall not lend money for profit to other GSA personnel or lend money for profit to any other person on Government premises . . ."[17] concern petty rule infractions but do not deal with broader issues. The GSA prohibition does nothing, for example, to deal with important public policies demanding active hiring of minority contractors. Narrowly focused codes of ethics may make it easier to finger petty offenses, but they do nothing to assure positive efforts to advance the public interest. The problem is not to prevent small, narrow, or corrupt behavior but to encourage a larger concept of outstanding behavior. This is why a focus on the value of the public service and the importance of the public interest is important.

Accountability

Another way to view ethical issues is to consider how public managers are accountable for their actions. What institutional means do we use to assure appropriate behavior by public servants? Accountability is the flip-side of ethical behavior. By emphasizing ethical canons, we hope to appeal to the best in employee nature. By emphasizing accountability, we focus attention on how effective performance is enforced.

Administrative Controls. There are three general ways that we try to assure accountability.[18] First, through a set of administrative structural controls. These include: (1) a hierarchy to review decisions at succeedingly higher levels, (2) a chain of command with each subordinate reporting to a specific supervisor, assuring close and immediate review of individual behavior, (3) internal disciplinary controls ranging from oral reprimands to actual terminations, (4) audits, either from the agency or from outside, which review both the legality and the wisdom of expenditures and actions, and (5) by constant inducements and incentives designed to reward loyalty to the organization (one example is limiting promotions to agency insiders). These administrative actions and controls reward predictability, agency faithfulness, efficiency, and precision. These are important administrative values but they are not moral values that transcend narrower concerns for agency or the public.

Another way we attempt to ensure ethical behavior is by representativeness. Representativeness assumes that a broadly based administrative agency, made from all elements of society, is more likely to exhibit the values that all Americans espouse—or at least will gain support for administrative actions by showing all groups that the public service is open to all.

Political Controls.   Political controls from outside the agency attempt to enforce accountability. Administrative officials must defend budget requests in detail and receive considerable grilling over the agency's performance, about the use of funds, and so forth. Legislative oversight is similar to budget hearings, but it fluctuates each year. Hearings focus attention on administrative and agency performance. Legislators also often control top administrator's tenure, from direct control over a city manager to indirect influence over other managers. Passing open meeting laws for administrative meetings is another way that legislators shine the glare of publicity into agency proceedings—on the assumption that this makes shady or unwise actions less likely.

A final legislative control is encouraging officials to reveal potential or actual administrative misdeeds in public, preferably to a legislator. Presently, whistleblowing is dangerous; it ruins administrative careers, although there are more protections for the whistleblower now than in the past. Whistleblowing is a bit controversial. It works against administrative attempts to cultivate loyalty and it can hurt the morale of other organization members. Whistleblowing has, however, exposed many unethical acts in the executive branch.

Judicial Controls.   A third type of control is imposed by the courts. Sometimes checks on administrative actions through lawsuits have proven effective. The possibility of lawsuits for administrative negligence of other criminal acts recently has become more likely. The courts now hold managers liable for abusing authority, criminal negligence, and other crimes. Losing a lawsuit makes accountability a meaningful concept.

There is a higher value, however, than fear of legal liability. One appeal to a higher value, according to Rohr, occurs when courts interpret the constitution. A type of education in public values occurs when the Constitution is applied to administrative actions. (Some examples of this were given in Chapter 5.) These constitutional provisions have been labeled *regime values*,[19] because the Constitution, as interpreted by the courts, established the basic system of rights, duties, and rules of the game for citizens, no matter how popular the action taken by an administrator is. The rules of the game include actions such as not revoking welfare benefits without a hearing, giving the person advance notice of the proposed recission, and giving that person opportunity to respond. Another example is a limitation on the ability to make administrative judgments about citizens based on their social or ethnic group as justification for assuming alien status.[20]

Reliance on the Constitution and the courts is an internal and external check. It is internal since constitutional values such as procedural due process and an appreciation for diversity among citizens must be internalized to be effective. It is external because administrators are held liable for civil suits if they are negligent. In this litigious society, it is common for administrative officials to stand before a judge.

Assuring Accountability. In summary, there are three primary institutional ways of enforcing accountability: through the administrative structure, the legislature or the courts. The other way to enforce accountability and advance ethical behavior is by internal checks that the manager uses as a guide whenever some action is taken. What is the effect of these checks?

Everyone should know the power of courts and legislatures to enforce their ideas of accountability. Few administrative officials come away from legislative review unscathed, and legal liability is an unpleasant fact of life for many managers. However, most managers won't be challenged for their behavior by legislatures or courts. Most administrative actions are legitimate and unlikely to be challenged. The few administrative violations tend to be gross abuses of discretion, so aberrant that they provide little guidance for combating other significant violations of trust.

These other serious breaches of public trust are judgment failures, such as yielding too quickly to vocal but nonrepresentative interest groups or devoting agency resources to insiders rather than clients. The cumulative effect is more serious than a one-time violation, yet there is no law against narrow self interest or excessive dependence on unrepresentative publics. These violations rarely make headlines or court and legislative hearings.

Administrative controls are more likely to result in behavioral change in managers than court or legislative controls. The effect of hierarchical pressures to conform, the demands of one's peers not to display disloyalty by going public, the fear of disciplinary transfers from Washington, D.C. to a distant city, or the threat of a withheld promotion, are real to most managers and have chilling effects on independent action. This control promotes behavior that advances bureacratic interests, but such interests are narrow—not always aligned with the public interest.

If legislative and legal controls fluctuate, while administrative controls may suppress public accountability as often as they advance it, what means assure ethical behavior? We are forced to rely on internal manager values, supplemented by agency, court, and legislative controls.

What are these internal values? They are a belief in regime values (internalized constitutional values of due process and individual rights), a sense of fair play, beliefs in the value of public service, strong professional standards, and a belief in something more than narrow self interest–a vision of the public interest.

According to many critics, these are thin reeds upon which to rest concerns for ethical behavior. Making managers, primarily responsible to themselves ignores outside checks that compel accountability—and most resist allowing everyone to police one's self. On the other hand, punitive controls prevent dishonesty but do little to encourage high performance. Internalized public servant commitments to important values cannot be mandated by outside forces.

These arguments were first raised 50 years ago in a famous exchange between Carl Friedrich and Herman Finer, and since then have not been stated more clearly. Friedrich argued for internal checks largely without outside formal controls, claiming that if officials maintain technical competence and allegiance to popular sentiment, they will remain responsible to the public interest.[21] Finer denounced such ideas, saying that responsibility degenerated to a *sense* of responsibility to professional norms and codes of ethics rather than to some institutional set of punitive controls. He argued that there would be abuses of power if external checks did not exist.[22]

Friedrich foresaw the complexity of public affairs, the development of technology in ways that outside controls could not foresee, and the ultimate infeasibility of a system of controls that could punish malfeasance but not compel rectitude. Finer saw that abuses of power would increase without punitive controls such as the threat of dismissal and, presently, the threat of legal liability.

Our present system relies on internal and external checks. Externally, the threat of administrative controls of discipline combines with legislative and court controls to keep officials aware of legal and political liability. Internally, most professional organizations have codes of ethics (similar to Exhibit 10–2, the International City Management Code of Ethics) and exhort their members to keep the public interest foremost. Backed by the socialization process Americans undergo as they move into maturity, most officials have a sense of responsibility and a belief in the rules of the game.

Internal checks have more impact upon official behavior than external controls because external controls cannot alone do more than prohibit minor violations or punish flagrant excesses. Therefore, how can officials who possess these internal checks be identified and placed in leadership positions?

Years ago, Stephen Bailey provided a short list of attitudes and moral qualities needed by officials in high places. The first attitude is an understanding of the moral ambiguity inherent in public decision making. This is defined as an awareness that public decisions are an endless shade of gray, rather than clear black and whites. The second attitude is an awareness of the context in which public events occur (the nature of public life and its limits and opportunities). The final attitude is an

EXHIBIT 10–2 The International City Management Code of Ethics

The purpose of the International City Management Association is to increase the proficiency of city managers, county managers, and other municipal administrators and to strengthen the quality of urban government through professional management. To further these objectives, certain ethical principles shall govern the conduct of every member of the International City Management Association, who shall:

1. Be dedicated to the concepts of effective and democratic local government by responsible elected officials and believe that professional general management is essential to the achievement of this objective.

2. Affirm the dignity and worth of the services rendered by government and maintain a constructive, creative, and practical attitude toward urban affairs and a deep sense of social responsibility as a trusted public servant.

3. Be dedicated to the highest ideals of honor and integrity in all public and personal relationships in order that the member may merit the respect and confidence of the elected officials, of other officials and employees, and of the public.

4. Recognize that the chief function of local government at all times is to serve the best interests of all of the people.

5. Submit policy proposals to elected officials, provide them with facts and advice on matters of policy as a basis for making decisions and setting community goals, and uphold and implement municipal policies adopted by elected officials.

6. Recognize that elected representatives of the people are entitled to the credit for the establishment of municipal policies; responsibility for policy execution rests with the members.

7. Refrain from participation in the election of the members of the employing legislative body, and from all partisan political activities which would impair performance as a professional administrator.

8. Make it a duty continually to improve the member's professional ability and to develop the competence of associates in the use of management techniques.

9. Keep the community informed on municipal affairs; encourage communication between the citizens and all municipal officers; emphasize friendly and courteous service to the public; and to seek to improve the quality and image of public service.

10. Resist any encroachment on professional responsibilities, believing the member should be free to carry out official policies without interference, and handle each problem without discrimination on the basis of principle and justice.

11. Handle all matters of personnel on the basis of merit so that fairness and impartiality govern a member's decisions, pertaining to appointments, pay adjustments, promotions, and discipline.

EXHIBIT 10–1 (*concluded*)

12. Seek no favor; believe that personal aggrandizement or profit secured by confidential information or by misuse of public time is dishonest.

This Code was originally adopted in 1924 by the members of the international City Management Association and has since been amended in 1938, 1952, 1969, 1972, and 1976.

SOURCE: International City Management Association, Washington, D.C. Used with permission.

awareness of the paradox of procedures. This paradox is the need for rational and clear procedures for making public decisions and operating public agencies, which is counterbalanced by the fact that these procedures often become red tape that strangles public responsiveness.

The moral qualities include optimism, courage, and charity. Optimism is the belief that the administrative struggle is important to our system of government and involves a willingness to take risks within the struggle. Courage is the ability to resist pressure, to be counted on the side of truth, and to make unpopular decisions. Charity is placing principle above personal preference so that equitable decisions can be made.[23]

Much of what Bailey wrote can be summarized in a letter from Thomas Jefferson over 200 years ago: "Whenever you are to do a thing, though it can never be known but to yourself, ask yourself how you would act were all the world looking at you, and act accordingly."[24]

There is substantial overlap between Bailey's qualities and attitudes and the crucial leadership qualities mentioned in Chapter 2. The necessity to operate in ambiguous situations, to appreciate the complexity of public decision making, and to possess the strength and courage to make controversial decisions are qualities seen in effective public leaders who display high ethical standards. Perhaps this is not surprising, for career executives who demonstrate leadership also demonstrate high ethical standards. Many acts of administrative leadership involve acts of moral leadership.

Holding the high moral ground is not enough, however. Moral leadership is a powerful force, but it must exist hand-in-hand with a drive for power and achievement to effectively manage an organization. Stalin once asked how many regiments the Pope had, a cynical question but perhaps pertinent in war-time situations.

Power and Achievement

Power. Employees who don't care about the organization and about its policies don't become top managers. Employees who care greatly but lack strong personalities don't become top managers. Caring deeply about the organization is not sufficient for becoming a top manager. Caring about the organization and its programs and wanting to have impact on the organization or program are the features that mark most managers; top managers, or persons destined to be top managers, want power.[25]

Emphasizing power seeking in managers oversimplifies one of the two basic drives of top managers. It is not always a popular way to describe these managers because the United States is ambivalent about power. Our culture criticizes people who seek power, yet it is enchanted with the application of power for approved purposes.

A drive for power, a wish to succeed, the use of influence, a dream for the organization—people have to use power to achieve organizational goals. It's no surprise that power is one of the basic drives in managers. Without power, managers would have to rely on reason—depending only on the good intentions of others. Managers with power often rely on reason and the good intentions of others, but power provides a club behind the desk if other means fail.

Managerial power is the ability to influence or decide organizational events. These events include matters such as how organizations should allocate funds, which employees will be promoted, and in which direction the organization should move. While subordinates make some of these decisions, the views of top managers are more significant than others, and they are decisive in many cases. The opportunity to make these decisions leads individuals to seek top positions. One California state official, asked to cite the advantages of his top-level position, responded as follows:

> Advantages are 1) more money, prestige and authority, 2) great ego satisfaction, 3) fulfilling a desire to increase your ability to influence what happens.[26]

Describing it in a slightly different manner, another California state official noted:

> There's an advantage that my position is Career Executive Assignment (in the group of very senior state officials) because it gives me more independence and more respect. What I say can't be said just out of defiance or anger because I can be canned any moment.[27]

Interest in wielding power doesn't mean that managers are consumed in seeking power. It means that the ability to influence or control events requires that managers have some power. Thus, persons who dislike seeking or holding power, regardless of other abilities, are unlikely to head organizations.

Power, by itself, may help an executive gain the top position, but it won't necessarily help one become effective in the position. Successful managers have strong needs for power, but this drive is balanced by equally strong drives for achievement. A desire to achieve organizational goals is the glue binding organizational members to the manager. Effective managers don't flaunt their power but use it to achieve organizational goals and to help lower-level managers achieve individual goals consistent with organizational goals.[28] They use power in positive ways, making subordinates feel effective and increasing support from lower management. Lower-level managers are less interested in how much power top managers wield than in how well goals are achieved.

Successful managers find meaning in their work, and they try to give meaning to the work of subordinates. High-achieving managers are sensitive and open to their employees, bringing out the best in them. They are both task and person-oriented, for both the job and the person performing it are important to them.[29] While focusing their energies upon achieving organizational goals, they don't forget responsibilities for maintaining employee organizational commitment. Goal attainment and maintaining organizational commitment complement each other. They can be achieved only by managers comfortable with using power.

GETTING AHEAD IN ORGANIZATIONS

It may be lonely at the top, but there's plenty of company on the way up with many managers jockeying for positions.[30] There are many supervisors and middle managers in large agencies, but only a few survive the winnowing process to become top-level managers. Why do the select few rise to organizational heights?

For one, competence is an important factor in choosing between aspirants to a top management job. This will be clarified later for several reasons, but for now it means that most individuals competing for top jobs are able. Allen Campbell, a Carter administration official and vice president of ARA services said:

> The quality of top managers I knew in the federal government . . . is every bit as high as we have at ARA; and on the whole, the people at ARA are paid from one and a half to three times more than their public sector counterparts.[31]

Loyalty

There are three general characteristics of managers who achieve the highest organizational levels. They have loyalty, experience, and are highly visible. Loyalty is the most crucial factor. No one rises to a top leadership position if there are questions about her loyalty. Organizational members, who have career commitments to the agency, won't support anyone who doesn't believe in the agency. In this sense, loyalty is not the servility of a lap dog, but demonstrated commitment to organizational values. Thus, the top manager will not take the organization or its supporting interests lightly.

Loyalty is an absolute requirement for certain positions such as staff to political appointees or elected politicians. For most other positions, loyalty is important but not crucial.

Loyalty is demonstrated in many ways. Professional loyalty may suffice. Engineer R, new to the state highway commission, may ascend the organization quickly, perhaps claiming the top position. He must, of course, be sound, which means showing loyalty over time to the civil engineering profession and to the commission. This is demonstrated by serving as a member of the profession outside the specific organization, as a consulting engineer, for example, or working for other commissions. Other professions exhibit the same process. Loyalty means being committed to the values of others in the profession. Long experience in the specific organization, is not always required if the person appears to hold proper professional values.

Certain other executives, such as city managers, also demonstrate loyalty to the employer, in this case, a city or other local government, by demonstrating commitment to professional norms. In this case, loyalty means belief in a system of local government rather than a specific city. Anyone becoming a manager pledges to this ideal. The incumbent may job-hop to larger cities, but this is a minor infraction of the loyalty norm. The manager is still committed to local government.

There are many exceptions to the rule of demonstrating loyalty. Often, nonprofessionals are appointed to management posts. In general, such individuals experience more difficulties in heading the organization and are often at odds with the dominant professional group in the organization.

Experience

Experience is required for top-level positions. Meeting this criterion means some seasoning in top-level posts, although not necessarily in a given organization. Some positions demand long experience within the organization. Examples include the police chief of a large city department or the head of a forestry department. Both involve a promote-from-within strategy. Conversely, university presidents often come from outside the organization, while city managers usually come from other cities. In these cases, however, appointed persons have substantial experience in similar organizations.

Experience is not expertise, for experience does not guarantee the candidate is highly skilled. It means that he has coped with many situations. Experience is a knowledge of the organization's business, its peculiar problems and particular ways of dealing with them.

Visibility

Visibility is being in a prominent place at the proper moment. In theory, all individuals of equal ability and experience should have an equal chance for top management positions. This isn't what happens, however. Some individuals are more noticeable and more likely to be chosen. Sometimes the reason for visibility is a strong personality. Sometimes it is linkages to top management. A high-ranking manager in the California Social Services Department noted "Another reason (I was selected) is I have known the Chief Deputy and the Deputy Director for a number of years."[32]

In every case, the "paramount factor is personal knowledge of the manager (or potential manager) by the decisionmaker."[33] Top engineers are more visible in highway departments than transportation planners or finance managers largely because top management rarely looks beyond the engineering ranks. Assistant city managers, sometimes with little experience, often are promoted to city manager positions over department heads because they are more visible in an administrative position. Managers in large agencies with several divisions are well-advised to head the most prominent divisions if they crave top promotions.

Visibility is enhanced in a number of methods. For example, mentoring, a means of transmitting organizational lore and wisdom from older managers to younger ones, is also a primary means of assuring visibility. Mentors provide strategic career advising and suggestions for individual career development, as well as monitoring and feedback for upwardly mobile subordinates. This informal system is used in many federal agencies such as the Internal Revenue Service and the Agriculture Department.[34] One reason that managers who have mentors seem to progress more rapidly than persons without mentors is probably because a mentor assures visibility at top levels.

Organizations frequently limit searches for promotional candidates to their own employees. In 1973, a federal executive program was designed to identify and train managers on a government-wide basis. By 1976, it had been scrapped because bureaus resisted it. They would not choose candidates other than from their agency.[35] An official responsible for the program described the experience as follows:

> We haven't accomplished much. A number of those selected in the first two years felt they were taken out of the stream for promotions in their old bureaus. And the bureaus resisted because they knew the whole idea of the program was to arrange things so that a good guy didn't necessarily return to spend his entire life in one bureau. I guess I shouldn't have been so surprised at how unwilling and parochial the agencies would be.[36]

This phenomena is not limited to federal agencies. Most agencies attempt to promote available employees before looking outside. This is natural and lets employees know that faithful service is rewarded. Promotion from within represents organizational preference for loyalty, experience, and visibility.

Other Characteristics of Upwardly Mobile Managers

Proven loyalty, experience, and visibility are the major reasons managers rise in organizations. However, successful managers exhibit other significant qualities as well, the most important of which are hard work, decisiveness, energy, expertise, and a good educational background.

Speaking of these qualities, Comptroller General Elmer Staats, after many years in politically appointed positions, said,

> I have worked with business people who have been in the government
> . . . And I have yet to find a single one of those business executives after
> their experience here who doesn't go out and have nothing but praise for
> the caliber and the hard work of the people in the government.[37]

Hard work means, as one pundit noted, "showing up for work every day." Of course, it means more, but the heart of the matter is interest in and commitment to the organization proven by "showing up." Top management expects hard work and long hours from managers-to-be. Representative Rooney of New York once commented favorably on the Census Bureau, noting he had called there late at night and found its employees ". . . on the job far later than usual closing hours."[38]

Energy and decisiveness are two characteristics of most top executives. Energy is the ability to focus one's abilities on a task and pursue it to the conclusion.

Decisiveness is a trait admired by many because of its presumed relationship to leadership abilities. A decisive leader inspires confidence among subordinates by a willingness to act quickly when action is required. Decisiveness is crucial because decisions in many organizations are often delayed or avoided unnecessarily. Someone who quickly makes a difficult decision and takes the heat is an admired person. This admiration may lead to overrating one who easily makes decisions, even if he lacks other characteristics. It explains the value put on decisiveness. Top managers always look for subordinates who can weigh evidence, gather as much information as time permits, then quickly act even if the course of action is not clear.

Another characteristic, often more influential than it should be for top positions, is expertise. Expertise is a powerful factor, particularly in professional organizations that value mastery of the agency's subject matter. The best traffic engineer, or the welfare worker who knows the eligibility rules best, will be promoted. Expertise is more important for early promotions in a person's career than for top-level jobs. This is because supervisory and middle-level jobs require more job-related information. The higher in the organization a person rises, the less pure expertise is weighted. If organizations overweight technical expertise for top jobs, other factors such as breadth of experience may be overlooked. Even so, individuals who are not experts in their fields will not get early promotions and qualify for higher positions.

Education, while usually a secondary factor, is crucial in some cases. In many organizations, certain levels of education or degrees are necessary for serious advancement considerations. Examples of this might be a Master of Social Work degree in a welfare office, a degree in psychiatry in some mental health agencies, and a certified public accountant certificate in a large accounting firm (although the latter is not technically an advanced degree). Possession of the degree demonstrates expertise.

In other organizations, education is a way of distinguishing one person from another without a degree. Obtaining a degree demonstrates self discipline, perseverance, and ambition, qualities which are more important than the information the diploma represents. Degrees such as a Master of Public Administration (MPA) or Master of Business Administration (MBA) are screening devices. Persons with advanced education often move ahead of others even when they have similar levels of experience or ability.

TOP MANAGER SELECTION

This discussion of top manager characteristics doesn't constitute a blueprint for success. It notes what characteristics mark top managers and explains why they move upward. The actual selection process is subjective and judgmental. At lower levels, civil service examinations, seniority credits, oral examinations, assessment centers, and formal credit for certain experiences are common. This is not so for higher-level positions.

Idiosyncrasy

The selection process for top jobs is idiosyncratic. There are good reasons for this. First, since top jobs are not always well-defined, more than one leadership style is effective. A multitude of management styles and behavior patterns will fit any job. Selection revolves around how well potential candidates fit the incumbent's role, or how well the person's skills will create a new role. Estimating how well different candidates will perform in a position, when each has different experiences, values, and styles, is not a precise science.

Making a choice is further complicated because it is often made by individuals unfamiliar with the organization or unconcerned with bureaucratic needs. Two factors are often present in selection. First, the appointing authority, who is often an elected or appointed politician, may not know what good agency management is. Second, assuming the interviewer has some knowledge of good executive qualities, lack of experience in making these choices means that the appointing authority may be unable to choose among applicants based on those qualities. Thus, selection is often random.

Choices are made for vague policy reasons. There may be a desire to find a tough manager or a desire to turn around the organization toward different policies. Conversely, the appointing authority may want to maintain the agency's policies; in that case, the heir apparent, usually a deputy director, may be elevated. Political leaders may want to reduce costs; in that case, a person with financial management credentials may be chosen—even from outside the agency.

There may be a wish to eliminate any traces of the previous administration. In California, a new gubernatorial appointee may remove civil servants holding Career Executive Assignment (CEA) positions, sending incumbents back to their previous civil service rank. In one case, a new superintendent of corrections shifted all incumbents among existing CEA positions, assuring herself that all held posts by her choice. This strategy minimized the potential loss of expertise and maximized the superintendent's control over the organization.

The reasons for selection of top-level public executives vary. While politicians make idiosyncratic choices, so do careerists. Most appointing authorities want to make the best choice, but there are legitimate differences over what type of candidate the organization needs and who best fills that need.

Interviews are usually conducted, even if the appointing authority knows each candidate. Often these interviews are irrelevant, sometimes held because civil service procedures require them. One California CEA reported that his oral interview "didn't consist of much except friendly conversation. The outcome was already decided [in his favor]."[39] When the appointing authority is unfamiliar with candidates, interviews become important, sometimes more important than an evaluation of the candidate's previous experience. This occurs when, for example, a city council appoints a city manager.

At its worst, the selection process degenerates into a form of "bogsat," an acronym for "a bunch of guys sitting around a table" brainstorming potential candidates. At top management levels, bogsat refers to an unstructured, random exchange between top officials that results in selection of someone who has not undergone a review.

UPWARD MOBILITY—
SOME ORGANIZATIONAL ISSUES

The broadest organizational questions, in terms of the behaviors and perspectives of top executives, involve the type of manager who ascends to the top of organizations, the way she looks at problems, and the breadth of experiences she brings to the top position. These latter issues involve the issues of mobility and overspecialization.

Inside Promotions

Many large organizations tend to look first to their employees for promotions. The result is that managers who approach the top of the organization have few experiences in other organizations. Their views, perspectives, and decisions are shaped by early experiences (or lack thereof).

This limited upward movement within the same agency is not suprising since many agencies are specialized and perform only a single function heavily tied to certain education and training. Agencies such as the U.S. Forest Service, Army Corps of Engineers, state highway departments, geological surveys, and state agricultural departments hire foresters, engineers, geologists, and agriculturists for entry-level positions. Managers trained in this way have few experiences outside the agency or bureau because there are few other agencies dealing with forests or geological surveys. Engineers and foresters are specialists by education and by long service in agencies that deal with specialized functions. In these agencies, it is unusual for any nonspecialist to receive a top position.

Mobility

Managers trained in less specialized areas assume positions in staff functions such as personnel, budgeting, finance, and procurement, or they become expert in areas requiring less specialized education. They move up from staff job to staff job, exhibiting more mobility because staff positions are available in many agencies. Many generalists enter public service as administrative assistants or budget analysts, although there is enormous competition for few jobs. Most federal entry-level jobs are specialized, such as forester, defense procurement agent, or internal revenue agent. This intensifies the tendency of federal executives to spend their entire career in one agency. In addition, managers trained in specialized areas such as accounting or finance may exhibit mobility because they also hold finance or staff positions available in several agencies. However, the majority of staff managers do not show high mobility. They tend to spend their careers in one agency. This most often occurs in large state and federal agencies. Two 1970s studies concluded that only about 5 percent of all senior federal officials had worked in more than one agency. Ten years later, only about 8 percent of all appointments to the Senior Executive Service came from outside the agency.[40] Managers identify with an agency. A winner of a distinguished federal performance award said:

> I've never thought of myself as a career civil servant. . . . ask a civil servant who he is and you'll probably find he'll say he is an economist who works for the Treasury Department, a manager for the Housing Department, and so on. What he's not likely to say first is that he's a civil servant.[41]

Powerful forces in the agency, from formal training to informal socialization patterns, strengthen this tendency. A Transportation official noted pointedly:

> We train our own people so they have to serve in every section of the department. You can say this substitutes departmental for bureau parochialism . . . but I'm not training people to go to Health, Education and Welfare or any other place. What interests me is this department.[42]

This parochialism is not limited to the federal government. California departments, despite a statewide list of senior executives, have only within the past five years begun to select managers from outside.

Not all top positions are held by insiders. Nationally, about one third of state agency heads came from outside the public sector, often with no government service. Nearly a fifth came from another state agency and only a third came up from the ranks. This latter group averaged 11 years with the agency before its members were elevated to the top position.[43] It's not clear how many of these directors are careerists and how many are political appointees, but such lateral movement is unheard of at the federal level.

Most academic observers and many practitioners believe that top manager effectiveness is reduced by the lack of mobility. Individuals with experience in one organization allegedly have less flexibility, are less responsive to political direction, are less familiar with the operation of different agencies, and are more committed to specific interests associated with their agencies.[44] Perhaps some of these weaknesses could be reduced if managers were more easily shifted to various posts when they near the top of their organizations, but this is often impossible. Arrangements like the federal SES and the California CEA, where managers are easily shifted or nonpunitively removed, are uncommon. Thus, many large organizations may suffer on both counts—their top executives have few organizational experiences, and it is difficult to shift them as needed to different jobs.

This is harsh criticism, much of it opinion, since there is little evidence about any damage done by lack of mobility. It's hard to conceive of complex organizations directed by nonexperts. Engineers will always control highway departments and foresters will always staff key forest service positions. And, since these agencies are large, it's hard to assert that there aren't a range of jobs to provide various experiences for potential managers. Most agencies want to reward loyalty, which is why they select insiders for promotions. This improves morale. Given these reasons, it's not hard to see why agencies shun the benefits of mobility in favor of promoting insiders.

CAREERS, JOBS, AND PEOPLE

Some examples of public service careers and incumbents will put this discussion in focus. The first example is a visible and prestigious group, city managers.

The City Manager-Generalist Par Excellence

City managers are classic public management generalists. Most cities over 2,500 in population have a manager responsible to the council who prepares the budget, appoints department heads, and manages day-to-day city affairs. The average 1984 manager was a 43-year-old white male with a Master's degree. Married, he is a member of the Democratic party with five years in his current job, his second city manager position. Only about 5 percent of managers were female, although the number is increasing. Another 5 percent of managers were minority group members, mostly Hispanics from cities in the South and West.[45]

There is a popular view that managers are a mobile group of experts who serve tenuous positions at the whim of city councils. This image is strengthened by in-group jokes:

Manager One:

Why did you leave City X?

Manager Two:

Illness and fatigue.

One:

Oh.

Two:

Yeah, the council got sick and tired of me.

Stories like this help perpetuate the stereotype, which is only partially true. The average length of service for 1984 managers was 5.4 years in a current city, similar to the 5.2 year average in 1974.[46] A 1977 study indicated that most Pacific Northwest region managers left the profession for salary and council disagreement reasons.[47]

An average tenure of 5.4 years per city is not as brief as conventional wisdom suggests, and it disguises substantial variations from less than one year to 43 years. Twenty-six percent of all managers serve seven or more years in their current city. Tenure is longer in large cities. Managers in cities of populations over a million serve an average of 10.2 years in their current post, as compared to colleagues in cities under 2,500 persons, who only average 4.3 years.[48] Managers, originally engineers because of the public works emphasis of cities earlier in the century, now come from the ranks of assistant managers. In 1984, 48 percent of managers had been assistant or deputy managers in the same city prior to becoming manager. Assistant managers are the group whose makeup foreshadows the city management profession in the future.[49]

The average assistant manager in 1983 was 37 years old, with 10 years of experience in two local government units, receiving slightly over $34,000. Demographically, 5 percent of all assistants are Black, three percent are Hispanic, and about 2 percent are Asians or American Indians. Women comprise 28 percent of all assistants.[50]

There are wide ranges of views by assistants about their career objectives. These views are not always consistent with the belief that assistants are an upwardly mobile, overambitious group of managers-to-be waiting in the wings. One ambitious assistant commented:

> I want to get sufficient experience now to obtain a position with local government that would allow me the latitude to implement social change. The time is ripe for creative management. A job as city manager would, presumably, be the best position to make use of innovation and have a positive impact on a community.[51]

This is what an upwardly mobile assistant might be expected to say. However, not every assistant holds these views, some opting for less mobility and more stability.

> My perceptions and observations of being an "assistant" have changed drastically since entering local government over six year ago. At this point in time, I see nothing at all unprofessional about being a career assistant-which is quite a reversal of thought for me. Nor do I feel that I lack ambition because of this. I do aspire to become a city manager, but it is not the all-encompassing or ultimate goal that it once was.
> . . . In fact, I enjoy my work more now than ever. I would not be at all disappointed at spending my career in my city, at least at this point in time.[52]

Finally, some take a jaundiced view of a city manager career:

> While I enjoy working as an assistant, I do not believe I will strive for employment as a city manager for several reasons, these being: commitment to job interferes with personal life; and lack of job security; and lack of compensation as compared to the private sector.
>
> I feel my experience qualifies me to fill a position in the private sector which more closely parallels my personal and professional goals.[53]

Some years ago, it was assumed that every assistant sought a city manager post. Perhaps the profession has matured so that more realistic aspirations are legitimate. Yet, it is ironic that in the past 10 years, manager's jobs have stabilized but assistants are more aware of security issues.

Other Careers

There are other generalist manager jobs, although they are not as prominent as city manager. State budget officers are an example of generalist managers. Most start their career immediately after college. A third now have master's degrees. They are increasingly recruited from public administration and economics majors rather than from business-related majors.[54]

Another occupation, the public school superintendent, often achieves the community visibility of a city manager. Since these individuals are usually trained in educational administration and have spent most of their lives in school districts moving through the ranks of school teachers, they are trained in a specialty. The average superintendent is a 48-year-old male who became a classroom teacher at age 24, a school principal at age 30, and a superintendent at 36. The typical superintendent is a Republican, Protestant, married, and a small town or rural resident.[55] There were approximately 35,000 superintendents and assistant superintendents in the United States in 1974, compared to 3,500 managers and deputy managers. Many superintendents manage districts so small that the superintendent position is called top-level only for courtesy's sake.

University presidents occupy a similar role to managers and superintendents in the community, although their organizational lineage is often more complex. The typical president is a college professor who moved into administration. She probably became, in order, a department chair, a dean, a vice president, and president, although there is no specific line of progression. Presidents have more prestige outside than inside the University, since most talented professors regard administrative work with disdain—preferring to teach and do research.

In some cases, prominent individuals from outside the university become president. Dwight Eisenhower was president of Columbia University, exgovernor Daniel Evans of Washington state became president of Evergreen college, and exgovernor Terry Sanford of North Carolina served as president of Duke University. Conversely, many universities pride themselves on appointing only their alumni, almost always from their faculty, to the presidency. Universities are strange cases, partially because presidents are often not hired to manage the university (although that is their ostensible job). They perform primarily representation and strategic planning functions. Sometimes the president restores order to a fractious faculty, or redirects the academic program, but for most private universities, she must raise money. The president's role of *not* managing the institution is underscored by a Supreme Court ruling that the faculty constitute management.[56]

Most managers do not become city managers, school superintendents, or college professors. Their jobs are neither as visible nor as clearly defined in the public mind. To indicate some of the jobs and career patterns that managers hold, here are four examples of middle to top-level managers in the state of California:[57]

G. R. was chief, division of facilities construction (major nonhighway construction), California Department of Transportation, where he has spent his entire career:

1950–61   Engineer—Design, Construction, and Survey Section

1961–64   Executive Assistant to Los Angeles County District Engineer

1964–67   Traffic Engineer, Los Angeles District Office

1967–69   State Traffic Engineer

1969–73   Legislative Representative (department lobbyist)

1973–77   Systems Operation (maintenance, traffic engineering, equipment)

1977–80   Chief, Maintenance Division

1980–81   Deputy Director, Project Development and Construction

1981–83   Chief of Transportation Laboratory (returned to this lower level in protest over director decisions)

1983–85   Chief, Division of Facilities Construction (moved upward under new director)

G. W. was deputy director for planning and research, Department of Corrections, where he has spent his entire career (dates unavailable):

Deputy Correction Officer

Sergeant

Lieutenant

Prison Training Officer

Central Officer—field representative for counties in jail planning

Departmental Training Officer (four years)

Associate Director of Soledad Prison

Deputy Director for Job Training and Placement

Deputy Director for Planning and Research

J. J., in 1982, was chief of the management services division of the Department of Water Resources. His early career included service in several organizations, although he stayed in water resources after reaching a top management position:

1950	Trainee with the State Personnel Board
1952	Assistant Personnel Manager for Department of Mental Health
1954	Business and Personnel Manager for Stockton State Hospital
1956	Personnel Director for the Department of Water Resources
1965–82	Personnel Director job expanded to include management services

D. D. was Deputy Director for physical planning and construction of the Department of Corrections. This is the highly sensitive and potentially controversial prison construction program.

1961–64	State Compensation Insurance Fund Adjuster
1964–66	Break in service, received MA in psychology
1966–67	Division of Vocational Rehabilitation—Counselor
1967–72	Department of Rehabilitation
1972–74	Department of Mental Hygiene
1974–77	Health Department—Chief, License Section for Quality Services
1977–78	Housing Department Program Manager (unhappy with previous position, resigned to take a lower level position)
1978–79	Health Department—Chief, Hospital Operations Support System, (promoted to senior-level job)
1979–83	Department of Developmental Disabilities—Assistant Deputy Director, Hospital Operations

1983–85 Department of Corrections—Deputy Director, Prisons Construction

Of these four individuals, D. D. had the most visible position in state government since he headed the highly charged prison construction program. But, all were key positions achieved by long service in one or more departments. Notice that all careers are not continuously up-ward—D. D. and G. R. both returned from high level to low-level positions because of policy disputes or because they would not work with their supervisors.

Gordon Chase is a career public official who held positions at all levels of government, beginning with the federal government:[58]

1954 U.S. Marine Corps; Foreign Service Official, tours of Pakistan and England; Staff member, National Security Council

1967 Staff Director, U.S. Equal Employment Opportunity Commission

1969 Deputy Director, New York City Human Resources Administration

1970 Administrator, New York City Health Services Administration

1974 Harvard University professor

1978 Massachusetts Secretary of Human Services

1979 (until death) Brandeis University professor

Chase was famous for his administrative ability and personal vitality and few can match his career. It was mixed, meaning he served at several levels and in several agencies. Many observers believe that serving in different organizations provides better perspectives for top managers than years of experience within a single agency.

Careers in the Future

The public sector is undergoing drastic changes. The upward spiral of spending for state and local government programs ended some years ago, partly because federal aid ran out. Tax limitations and taxpayer resistance have also ended further expansion of local tax sources for some time. These changes will significantly affect managerial careers.

Management jobs in the public sector will be more stressful, difficult, and shorter in tenure than in the past, although city manager tenure has remained constant since 1974. On the other hand, about 40 percent of all members of the Federal SES have retired or resigned in the past six years. Levine reports that this represents the visible part of an erosion of the skills, morale, and commitment of the federal work force, brought about by the reduction in missions of domestic agencies and the increasing politicization of the higher civil service.[59]

Several studies have shown that public executives at all levels have less favorable attitudes toward their organizations than private executives. They have less commitment to the organization and find less challenge in their work.[60] This could result in less time spent in each position or in public service as managers burnout. Burnout is related to stress, but stress is only one of two things that may reduce job tenure in the future. The other is the change in societal values in the United States described in Chapter 8. An increase in unwillingness to tolerate a distasteful job or working situation, greater interest in personal fulfillment, and a greater concern for off-the-job activities is predicted for workers. This will increase the pressure on managers and make their job more difficult, but societal pressures also affect managers. Managers will not only face stress caused by a less interested work force, but they may exhibit less interest in their career, job, or organization.

Managerial, job, and career changes may become more common. Individual managers may change jobs or careers much more readily than in the past. In addition, career paths from public to private agencies or back will be common. After all, technical skills such as computer programing, accounting, opinion polling, personnel management, and collective bargaining are similar in both sectors. So are broader tasks such as strategic planning, which effective public managers are increasingly familiar with. Many career changes will come from more contracts with the private sector for provision of services previously provided by public work forces. San Francisco, for example, even contracts out the city budget work to its previously employed staff, who are now private contractors. In addition, more careers in a working lifetime are now possible. A city manager can move to a private position as executive manager of the local chamber of commerce, and then move to academic life (an increasing number of executives have doctorates), and back to public life managing a state agency. A federal executive may be "topped out" in salary and status at an early age and forced to take a political appointment or choose a new career. One federal careerist outlined this dilemma:

> I was reluctant to take it (a political appointment) because it means I'll go when the administration goes and I can't imaging anything in private business as interesting as government work. But when Goerge Schultz offered me this job I look at myself and at the people around here who had stayed on for a long time. At my age I was at the top of my career. I had no place else to go.[61]

Future careers will evidence more diversity. More city managers and top-level state and federal officials will be women and minorities, although the pace of change will be slow.

Presently, the working environment of many public managers is unsatisfactory. Not only is there less public support for public services, as witnessed by federal cutbacks in the Reagan administration, but there is a negative view of many public employees. It's significant that President Carter justified the 1978 Civil Service Reform Act as a means to control bureaucrats rather than improving the civil service system.

It's easy to be pessimistic. The fact that management jobs will be more difficult in the future does not mean that there won't be a number of candidates willing to fill them. As Chapter 8 indicated, there will be more people looking for management jobs than positions available. In fact, although the federal SES recently had enormous turnover, the slots were filled immediately from within. The question is whether the ablest people will be attracted to management. The jobs, becoming more stressful and complex, will still require the three basic functions of organizational maintenance, representation, and planning. The future success of public agencies, as in the past, depends on how well managers perform these functions.

SUMMARY

This chapter changed directions, from management tasks such as budgeting and decision making to a general look at the values, beliefs, and careers of managers. Managers are not demographically representative of the whole U.S. population, but they share the values of most citizens. They are able, upwardly mobile individuals who thrive in organizational life and can handle stress and pressure. Most of them progress through a single agency or profession such as forest ranger or accountant, although they shed these narrower job perspectives when they near top management positions. Despite differences in jobs, level of government, and occupation, managers share many things in common: a belief in efficiency, a commitment to the agency, and a future even more complex and challenging than the past. Most of today's successful managers have also taken the high moral ground, demonstrating moral leadership in managing public affairs. The future of public agencies demands top management skills in maintaining, representing, and planning for organizations. I think public managers will rise to this task.

NOTES

1. John Rehfuss, "A Representative Bureaucracy? Women and Minority Senior Bureaucrats in California State Government," *Public Administration Review*, September–October 1986, pp. 390–94.
2. Ted Hebert and Deil Wright, "State Administrators: How Representative? How Professional?" *State Government*, 55, no. 1 (1982), pp. 22–27.
3. Rehfuss, "A Representative Bureaucracy?" pp. 390–94.
4. Mary Shellenger, "Local Government Managers: Profile of the Maturing Profession," *1985 Year Book* (Washington, D.C.: International City Manage-

ment Association, 1985), pp. 181–89. See also Ruth Ann Burns, "Women in City Management," *Urban Data Service*, 12, no. 2 (Washington, D.C.: International City Management Association, February 1980).

5. Hugh Heclo, *A Government of Strangers* (Washington, D.C.: Brookings Institution, 1977), p. 115.

6. Kenneth Meier, "Representative Bureaucracy: An Empirical Analysis," *American Political Science Review*, June 1975, as quoted in Heclo, *A Government of Strangers*, p. 114.

7. Frank Thompson, "Types of Representative Bureaucracy and Their Linkages," in Robert Golembiewski et al., eds., *Public Administration* (Skokie, Ill.: Rand McNally, 1976).

8. Heclo, *A Government of Strangers*, p. 183.

9. Stanley Rothman and Robert Lichter, "How Liberal are Bureaucrats?" *Hearings on the Senior Executive Service*, Subcommittee on Civil Service of the Committee on Post Office and Civil Service, 98th Congress, Serial 98–12, November 7, 1983; February 28, April 12–13, 1984, pp. 358–64.

10. Quoted in Aaron Wildavsky, *The Politics of the Budgetary Process*, 3rd ed., (Boston: Little, Brown, 1979), p. 19.

11. Federick Taylor, *Scientific Management* (New York: Harper & Row, 1923). See also Herbert Simon, Donald Smithburg, and Victor Thompson, *Public Administration* (New York: Knopf, 1950), for a textbook concerned with efficiency.

12. Ronald Loveridge, *City Managers in Legislative Politics* (Indianapolis, Ind.: Bobbs-Merrill, 1971), p. 74.

13. Ibid., p. 74.

14. Frank Marini, ed., *Toward a New Public Administration* (San Francisco: Chandler, 1972). Also see Andres Richter, "The Existential Executive," *Public Administration Review*, July–August 1970, pp. 415–22.

15. Rehfuss, "A Representative Bureaucracy?," pp. 390–94.

16. This phrase is from Supreme Court Justice Oliver Wendell Holmes.

17. See the General Services Department code of ethics in David Rosenbloom, *Public Administration* (New York: Random House, 1986), pp. 470–71.

18. Ibid., pp. 468–79.

19. John Rohr, *Ethics for Bureaucrats* (New York: Marcel Dekker, 1978).

20. *U.S. v. Brignoni-Ponce*, 422 U.S. 873 (1975). Rosenbloom, *Public Administration*, pp. 423–55, has a useful outline of constitutional of "regime values," along with numerous examples.

21. Carl Friedrich, "Public Policy and the Nature of Administrative Responsibility," *Public Policy*, 1, (1940), pp. 4–23.

22. Herman Finer, "Administrative Responsibility and Democratic Government," *Public Administration Review*, 1 (Summer 1940), pp. 337–49.

23. Stephen Bailey, "Ethics and the Public Service," in Roscoe Martin, ed., *Public Administration and Democracy* (Syracuse, N.Y.: Syracuse University Press, 1965), pp. 283–98.

24. Thomas Jefferson, letter to Peter Carr, August 19, 1785, quoted in Frederick Mosher et al., "Watergate: Implications for Responsible Government," in Jay Shafritz and Alfred Hyde, *Classics of Public Administration*, 2nd ed., (Chicago: Dorsey Press, 1987), pp. 489–95.

25. This chapter relies on the work of William Eddy, *Public Organization Behavior and Development* (Winthrop, 1981), chapter 6. The concepts of power and achievement are taken from David McClelland and David Burnham, "Power is the Great Motivator," *Harvard Business Review*, March–April 1976), pp. 100–110. McClelland and Burnham also emphasize affiliation or the desire of managers to be liked by associates. At the risk of oversimplification, affiliation is not discussed since it is not closely related to the behavior of effective managers.
26. John Rehfuss, unpublished research on the California Career Executive Assignment (CEA) system, 1981.
27. Ibid.
28. McClelland and Burnham, "Power is the Great Motivator," pp. 100–110.
29. This is typical of the high-performing manager described by Robert Blake and Jane Mouton, *The Managerial Grid* (Houston Tex.: Gulf Publishing, 1964). Also see Jay Hall, "To Achieve or Not: The Manager's Choice," *California Management Review*, July 1976, pp. 5–18.
30. This section is not a review of research in the field, but it summarizes some general reasons why some managers achieve high-level positions and others do not. Certain basic abilities, such as intelligence, minimal interpersonal skills, and so forth, are assumed and not mentioned because they don't distinguish between managers who achieve the highest positions and those who don't. Emphasizing loyalty, experience, and visibility means that candidates not possessing these attributes do not ascend to high levels. Simple good fortune is a factor—many managers selected for top positions are luckier than others. Other studies show that success in achieving high-level positions is related to general broad skills rather than specific abilities. McCall and Lombardo quote a corporate observer of corporate executives as saying that only two issues separate successful and unsuccessful individuals. The first issue is integrity, involving honesty and predictability. The second is the ability to understand other perspectives. Morgan McCall and Michael Lombardo, "What Makes a Top Executive?" *Psychology Today*, February 1983, pp. 26–31.
31. Alan Campbell, in a symposium, "The Public Service as Institution," *Public Administration Review*, July–August 1982, p. 315.
32. Rehfuss, CEA Research.
33. David Stanley, "Selecting Managers: A Tedious Task," *Public Administration Times*, January 1, 1981, p. 5.
34. Rudi Klauss, "Formalized Mentor Relationships for Management and Executive Development Programs in the Federal Government," *Public Administration Review*, July–August 1981, p. 496.
35. Heclo, *A Government of Strangers*, p. 31.
36. Ibid., p. 31.
37. Elmer Staats, interview, *The McNeil Lehrer Report*, March 6, 1981.
38. Wildavsky, *The Politics of the Budgetary Process*, p. 75.
39. Rehfuss, CEA research.
40. Rehfuss, "Mobility among California State Senior Managers" (Sacramento, Calif.: California State University School of Business and Public Administration, Working Paper 103–86, 1986), Tables 1, 3.

41. Heclo, *A Government of Strangers*, p. 116.

42. Ibid., p. 130.

43. Deil Wright, Mary Wagner, and Richard McAnaw, "State Administrators: Their Changing Characteristics," *State Government*, Summer 1977, pp. 152–59.

44. Eugene McGregor, Jr., "Politics and Career Mobility of Bureaucrats," *American Political Science Review*, March 1974, pp. 18–26. See also Michael Cohen, "The Generalist and Organizational Mobility," *Public Administration Review*, March–April 1970, pp. 544–52, for documentation of different career paths for line and staff federal executives. For further evidence about limited federal executive mobility, see "Documentation—Characteristics of the Federal Executive," *Public Administration Review*, March–April 1969, pp. 169–80. This document indicates that most executives had only worked in one federal agency during their career.

45. Shellenger, "Local Government Managers," pp. 181–89. For perspective on the stresses facing managers, see Charles Henry, "Trends in City Management Careers, 1970–1980: A Profession Under Stress," *Urban Data Service Reports*, 14, no. 3 (Washington, D.C.: International City Management Association, March 1982).

46. Ibid.

47. Fremont Lyden and Ernest Miller, "Why City Managers Leave the Profession: A Longitudinal Study in the Pacific Northwest," *Public Administration Review*, March–April 1976, pp. 175–80.

48. Shellenger, "Local Government Managers," pp. 181–89.

49. Ibid., pp. 181–89.

50. "Local Government Assistants—1983," *Baseline Data Reports*, 16, no. 4 (Washington, D.C.: International City Management Association, April 1984).

51. Ibid., p. 5.

52. Ibid., pp. 6–7.

53. Ibid., p. 7.

54. Robert Lee and Raymond Staffelt, "Educational Characteristics of State Budget Officers," *Public Administration Review*, July–August 1976, pp. 424–28.

55. Edith Mosher, "Educational Administration: An Ambiguous Profession," *Public Administration Review*, November–December 1977, pp. 651–58.

56. *National Labor Relations Board* v. *Yeshiva University*, U.S. 444, 672 (1980).

57. Rehfuss, unpublished CEA research.

58. Information about Gordon Chase from Gordon Chase and Elizabeth Reveal, *How to Manage in the Public Sector* (Reading, Mass.: Addison-Wesley Publishing, 1982), p. 180.

59. Charles Levine, "The Federal Government in the Year 2000: Administrative Legacies of the Reagan Years," *Public Administration Review*, May–June 1986, p. 197.

60. Bruce Buchanan, "Governmental Managers, Business Executives, and Organizational Commitment," *Public Administration Review*, July–August 1974, pp. 36–43.

61. Heclo, *A Government of Strangers*, p. 131.

Index

About the Author

John Rehfuss is currently Professor of Public Management at California State University in Sacramento. He taught at two other universities after receiving his Doctorate in Public Administration from the University of Southern California. He is active in the American Society for Public Administration, having served as Chicago Chapter President and on the National Council. Dr. Rehfuss is the author of *Public Administration as Political Process*, *Urban Politics in the Suburban Era*, and *Contracting Out in Government*, as well as over 40 professional articles. Early in his career, he served in local government culminating in a brief period as City Manager of Palm Springs, California. His hobby is freelance writing.

A Note on the Type

The text of this book was set 10/12 Palatino using a film version of the face designed by Hermann Zapf that was first released in 1950 by Germany's Stempel Foundry. The face is named after Giovanni Battista Palatino, a famous penman of the sixteenth century. In its calligraphic quality, Palatino is reminiscent of the Italian Renaissance type designs, yet with its wide, open letters and unique proportions it still retains a modern feel. Palatino is considered one of the most important faces from one of Europe's most influential type designers.

Composed by TCSystems

Printed and bound by Arcata Graphics/Kingsport